The Golden Heart

This book has been authored by and published under the supervision of the Living ECK Master, Sri Harold Klemp. It is the Word of ECK.

The Golden Heart

Harold Klemp

Mahanta Transcripts
Book 4

ECKANKAR
Minneapolis, MN

The Golden Heart
Mahanta Transcripts, Book 4

Copyright © 1990 ECKANKAR

Printed in U.S.A.
Library of Congress Catalog Card Number: 89-82637

Compiled by Joan Klemp and Anne Pezdirc
Edited by Mary Carroll and Anthony Moore
Cover design by Lois Stanfield
Cover illustration by Steve Salek
Text illustrations by Fraser MacDonald
Text photo (page *x*) by Luanne Lawton
Back cover photo by John Jenkins

Second Printing–1991

Contents

Fcb

the Mantle of Heaven • The Goal Every Person Seeks • Recognizing the Jewel of God

Is Love? • Accepting the Gift of Love • Living ECK Every Day
• The Give and Take of Love

JUNE

JULY

Foreword

The Way of the Eternal, *The Shariyat-Ki-Sugmad,* Book One, states: "The knowledge that the true, living Master gives is direct and immediate, coming from actual Soul experiences apart from the physical senses and human consciousness. His words are charged with the ECK currents surging within him. They sink into the inner self of the listener, leaving little doubt about the existence of Soul experiences."

Sri Harold Klemp, the Mahanta, the Living ECK Master travels throughout the world to give out the sacred teachings of ECK. Many of his public talks have been released on audiocassette, but others have never before been available beyond the particular seminar at which he spoke.

As a special service to the students of ECK and truth seekers everywhere, all of Sri Harold's public talks are being transcribed and edited under his direction. Now these transcripts can be study aids for one's greater spiritual understanding.

The Golden Heart, Mahanta Transcripts, Book 4, contains his talks from 1984–85. May they serve to uplift Soul to greater areas of consciousness.

Sri Harold Klemp, the Mahanta, the Living ECK Master in a meeting with future ECK leaders at the 1984 Worldwide Seminar.

1

The ECK Is Trying to Tell Me Something

Paul Twitchell often said that his most difficult task was to take the wisdom and knowledge of ECK, which seems to hover in an unformed cloud in the invisible spaces of the inner worlds, and put it into words.

When the Holy Spirit, or ECK, is trying to tell us something, It can use means other than the ECKANKAR books and discourses or the dream state. It will work with us every day and try to show us, by gentle nudges, that there is something we can do for our own good. But our level of consciousness, or our circle of initiation, expands out only so far.

Circles of Awareness

If the circle of our awareness could expand just another ring, or another initiation, we would have more of the information we need to make a good decision. We would have a greater ability to figure out how to benefit from this information the ECK brings to us. The only reason we are not able to do this is because of the limitation of our own spiritual consciousness.

There's a very readable book called *The Richest Man in Babylon*. The story, which takes place in ancient Babylon, is about a wealthy man who began life just as poor as many of his schoolmates. He didn't seem to be outstanding in any way, except that one day he looked at himself and wondered why he was poor while others were rich.

Why me, Lord? is the age-old question we ask God. It is a form of prayer; it covers up our ignorance of the laws of life. Problems with life occur when we don't understand the laws of ECK—the laws of Spirit.

Certain poorer friends of the richest man in Babylon later said that he was in no way different from them when they were young. What made him so special? Why was he a success and they weren't? As they rattled the few meager coins in their leather pouches, they had a real problem with it.

In this book, the richest man in Babylon lays out a program consisting of seven simple principles based on common sense. The idea is that the gathering of wealth is and has been accomplished in the same way ever since man came to earth. The sun that rises and sets today is the same one that did back then, so why shouldn't the same principles work today?

If the spiritual program could be made as easy as listing seven steps, I would give it to you tonight. But your spiritual initiations—your capacity for truth—have to be earned.

The ECK speaks to us in secret ways. This is why ECKANKAR is sometimes known as the secret way or the secret path. It isn't that truth is hidden; it's that man is often blind and deaf to the words of ECK. He goes to church and prays, and because his prayers are strong, they are answered for a while. Then all of a sudden, it's like an economic cycle gone bad—the charts don't work anymore.

If God is credited with bringing the blessings in the first place, then man can't blame God for the turnaround. So who does he blame? Certainly not himself. It's easier to blame the devil, his neighbor, or anybody else who's handy.

The point is that prayer works with an unstable psychic force. This isn't bad in itself; it's one of the levels of consciousness that we come to as we walk the path to God. But one who is in ECK can enter this field of psychic knowledge and walk through it the way you would walk through a forest.

On the other hand, some people go into the forest and get lost. They wander around endlessly in the nettle, plagued by deerflies and horseflies and grass snakes, never understanding why life is so rough. Well, it's not. It's only rough in the forest. The ECKist learns to get out of the forest.

A Tolerance for All Life

A book called *The Golden Kingdom* demonstrates the karmic ties that occur between races, explaining why the people of certain races don't get along even today.

The book expands on the history of mankind as told in *The Shariyat-Ki-Sugmad*. First came the Polarians, the tillers of the soil, who later reincarnated as the Hyperboreans, the second root race of man. The Hyperboreans began to build cities with walls. Eventually they developed weapons and became the first warriors. In time, the people elected the Varkas kings to rule over their empire of Melnibora, and these kings ruled through the use of the psychic powers.

Until this period in history, man had never known the awful power of the dark forces. The Varkas kings started out as priests, later became priest-kings, and then kings.

3

But in their transition to kingship, they began to lose their inner powers.

The leaders used mass hypnosis on the crowds in the same way that governments today use propaganda, which is a watered-down version of the black arts, to stay in power. An example is when the government issues optimistic statements proclaiming that the economy has never been better, even after a rash of bank failures.

The misuse of power and information through the psychic arts began way back during the time of the Golden Kingdom, as described by the author of this book. Its importance is in the way it points out how many of us lived in another era when there was conflict between the blacks and the whites. As Soul, we incarnated as a black, then a white, as both man and woman, back and forth, until we got a rich assortment of experiences.

The Hyperborean empire lasted for several thousand years. This gave us a good opportunity to get in on both sides of the fight, so that today many of us are tired of the old prejudices that are still part of the human race.

Behind all prejudice is the fear of something different. This is an indication of Soul operating in a state of unknowing. Soul in the lower bodies is in a state of ignorance and blindness, afraid of anything that is different from Itself; and so It proceeds to attack anything that seems strange.

As one rises in consciousness, he finds an increase in his tolerance for life and all living creatures. And as his consciousness unfolds further, he begins to see the Light of God shining within others, regardless of their color or caste. This individual has now come very near to the state of a saint. He sees the same spark of God, the shining Light of the Holy Spirit, in his fellowman that he recognizes in himself, even in the ego consciousness. And once he recognizes the God-state in himself and others as being an identical factor, an identical element of the nature of God, how can he hate any other living thing?

The Golden Kingdom gives an example of how the lessons of the past are carried over to the present day. We are here to become involved in life. We don't dwell on the past, but by learning from it, we can enjoy a richer life today. As we grow in consciousness today, we are building our tomorrow.

If you live the life of ECK correctly, you should have the abundance of life. That doesn't necessarily mean a million dollars for everybody; it means having enough. Some people don't want a million dollars. They know that having a lot of money can be a nuisance. They just want whatever it takes to live this life with happiness. This is what we want to reach in ECK.

You'd be surprised how many people are unhappy. Some were unhappy with their life before ECK, and that's why they're here. Others were unhappy with what passed as wisdom and truth, and that's why they're here.

We are here because of the Light and Sound of God. Those are not just words. The Light and Sound are the purifying elements of the Holy Spirit that come in to uplift you in consciousness.

The Illumination of God

The whole basis of ECKANKAR is the Light and Sound of Spirit, and how to bring It into your life so that you can have the illumination of God. Not all at once, of course. Too much illumination at one time can unbalance an individual to the point where he may feel he has been called by the Lord to perform a special mission. This feeling is misleading.

5

God Consciousness comes in small degrees. This may even include some of the states of imbalance that certain people go through. But in some lifetime—maybe not this one—you come out of it a stronger person.

Either in this lifetime or in a past life, most of you have gone through states of emotional and spiritual imbalance in your steps toward the purification of the mind, which leads to the freedom of Soul. It is easier to feel compassion for others who are unbalanced in their emotions when you realize they are simply passing through the ripples and rough currents of life. They too will come out of it, either in this lifetime or in another.

Most people who step onto a path to God find a beginning point that suits them. The early stages of preparation for God-Realization occur in traditional churches, metaphysical groups, and places like this. Then, in some lifetime, the person graduates and goes a step further.

Explaining the Light and Sound to Others

An ECKist couple were planning to start a dream class, and they approached the minister of an Episcopalian church that had a room suitable for this purpose. In this class, they explained, the students can begin to make contact with the inner self and with the Light and Sound of the Holy Spirit through their dreams.

The minister was quite liberal in his thinking. "Sure, go ahead," he said. "I don't see anything wrong with that."

But some of the church members heard about the couple's plans. Soon rumors and gossip were raging throughout the congregation. The board of trustees of the church was brought into the matter. "Why are you giving our church hall over to these people who are not even Christians?" they asked the minister. "What exactly are they teaching?"

The minister wasn't really sure, so he went back to the ECK couple. "Would you be willing to come before the board of trustees and explain to them what ECKANKAR and the dream class are all about?" he asked.

So the meeting was set up. The husband and wife were allotted ten minutes each. The husband's approach covered some of the basic principles of ECK. The wife went through the Bible and made a study of passages where the ECK, or the Holy Spirit, was spoken of as Light and Sound.

When the couple finished their presentation of ECK, the minister turned to the board members. "You can see that everything they have said here makes sense." And it did, because the couple had chosen a wise approach. The people on the board weren't ready to hear anything too different from the Episcopal doctrine. But they could understand the principles of fairness and justice, and this is what the ECKists spoke to them about.

The husband concluded by saying, "We don't want to impose upon you. If it will cause any kind of a stumbling block for you to have us here, then we would rather not stay." They had no desire to push themselves on the church people.

As the ECKists spoke, a woman on the board of trustees of this Episcopalian church seemed to be having an inner experience. Her face took on a glow. It's possible the whole presentation that day was given for that one woman. One day in the future, she may want to approach them to find out a little more about ECK.

The ECKists are moving out into society. You go where your talents lead you. You draw on experiences that have made you what you are today. But talk only to people who want to hear, and to a degree they can understand. Otherwise, you might as well be talking to yourself. You don't have to force ECK on others—there isn't any reason for it. Until a person is ready, he can't hear the words of ECK anyway.

Work quietly, in your own way, in situations where you feel comfortable. This is the way of ECK. Pushing and imposing the teachings on others is not.

The Writing of Paul Twitchell

Paul Twitchell wrote a lot of books since he started in the early 1940s. He attempted to sell everything he wrote, but if a manuscript got too many rejection slips, he would sit down and revise it, laboriously retyping the whole thing. At any given time, he had perhaps four or five unsold manuscripts in the rewrite stage.

Paul wrote to sell. This was the way he earned his living. He sold several articles to *Collier's* and other national magazines. In the early days he had time to do a lot of the editing and rewrites on his books, but when he became the Mahanta, the Living ECK Master, his schedule speeded up.

By 1970, his schedule was so hectic that he wrote the discourses cold, putting on paper the ECK wisdom as it came through. The unformed had to be arranged into the petty, awkward words of the human language. He did what he could to find the proper words and metaphors that would strike an image in the reader's mind. Sometimes he used a word that wasn't quite right; at other times he would leave in an extra word or two that appeared to cause a contradiction.

For example, when Paul wrote about the trance method of leaving the body, he went into great detail about how to make postulates to get out of the body. He told how to make a mind impression of where you want to go, when you want to go, and how long you'll stay. It wasn't until the last paragraph that he added, almost as a postscript, that you have to make a postulate to get back in the body. You can imagine the eager chela going through the steps to get out of the body, even before reading to the last paragraph, and then wondering how he was going to get back in.

In our image of the inspired writers of the Old Testament, we envision them putting down the words exactly as God spoke them. We sometimes like to believe Paul operated like this.

But it's foolishness to think that the words come out golden the first time; they don't. The human language, at best, is only a poor reflection of the truth that comes from a higher level. What is known as truth on each plane is but a poor reflection of the truth on the next higher plane. This is life. It takes sweat, hard work, ability, talent, and training to be able to express the ECK in a certain way. There is no magical way to do this.

Paul was a remarkable writer. You respect him more and more as you grasp the extent of what he had to accomplish and the way he was able to use the English language. Paul wrote discourses when he was too busy, too tired, or too sick to write them. Why? Because the monthly mailings were scheduled to go out on a certain date, and Paul did what he had to. With his background as a newspaperman, he knew about the importance of deadlines. When you have a deadline, you meet it.

When you make plans, whether for ECK activities or other goals, you've got to have a deadline. Life needs more than just a plan; it needs a time frame in which to accomplish the plan. But be kind to yourself: Start with an easy goal, and set deadlines you can reach.

First Steps to God-Realization

How badly do you want God-Realization? Since you have never had God-Realization, what must you do to get it if you don't yet know the rules?

There's a young cat in our neighborhood. His name is Mittens, but we call him Mitty for short. He's a friendly little thing, but from what I can tell, he has never been a cat before. Mitty is a bit like the ECKist who has never been God-Realized.

Mitty was an orphan, so he didn't have a mother to set an example for him. Nor had he ever studied himself in the mirror to see that he was a cat: he had two pointed, fuzzy ears, a button nose, and tiger-striped fur.

Because he didn't know he was a cat, Mitty thought he was a human being. The little boy who took care of him was short, and he was a good ballplayer, so Mitty probably thought he'd grow up to be one too. He was relating to what was nearest to him.

One day Mitty must have decided that being a boy wasn't really his destiny. He spotted a big black tomcat walking around claiming his territory, and Mitty began to study him. The little tiger-striped kitten followed the big black cat everywhere he could, watching how he walked and trying to figure out what the tomcat was thinking about. But whenever Mitty got too close, the tomcat would turn around and attack him as a warning.

The first time it happened, the kitten ran away and hid in the bushes. But as soon as the big black cat moved away, Mitty began to stalk him again. I watched him one day. "You fool, Mitty," I said. "Don't you know what's going to happen? That cat is going to attack you again." But Mitty was learning how to be a cat, and you can't learn something like this at a distance. By getting close, he found out that cats have sharp claws, they growl, and they make a ferocious spitting sound.

Pretty soon Mitty graduated—he learned to leave the black cat alone. Next he found a white cat, bigger yet. This cat was friendly to humans, but he didn't like kittens following him around. Maybe because the new cat wasn't black, Mitty didn't associate this species with danger, so he began to follow him around. Again, he got his ears boxed and his little head pounded in the dirt. Mitty was learning some valuable lessons, and like it or not, he was growing up to be a cat.

One afternoon, while walking along the back fence, he saw a beautiful Siamese cat. Mitty just couldn't help himself—he had to get a closer look. She attacked him, too. He took off along the top of the fence, tore through the hanging branches, and lost some of his fur in passing.

But Mitty was patient; he was learning. He crept back along the fence and hid behind the branches, still watching and studying. I was watching Mitty while petting the Siamese cat, Angel. She's a very jealous cat: If I was petting her, that meant I belonged to her, and she certainly wasn't about to share the attention with Mitty.

Mitty is starting to grow up now. He's beginning to feel his strength and claim bigger parts of the territory for himself. He no longer limits himself to the little plot of grass in front of his house; more often than not, he roams other people's backyards and creeps along their fences. It's just a matter of time before he'll be strong enough to prove himself to the rest of the cats. He'll probably even take back some of the fur he lost.

As ECKists who want God-Realization, this is how we are, too. Because we've never been God-Realized before, at first we don't know how to go about it. One way is to observe someone you feel has a golden light flowing from within. It may or may not be a Higher Initiate, it may or may not be an ECKist. Start by observing someone who lives the kind of life that you want to live.

If you want to look inward to find an ideal, "The Easy Way" technique given in the book *In My Soul I Am Free* tells you to look to whomever you trust and feel is your spiritual guide. The spiritual principle behind this technique is that the Holy Spirit, the Divine ECK, comes into the form of the master you image on the inner screen in the Spiritual Eye. A Christian, for instance, will probably see Christ. If your state of consciousness goes to another master, that is who you might see. The master that forms on the inner screen is one who will fit your state of consciousness.

The way to do this is to close your eyes, look into the Third Eye, and chant HU—a name for God. You can also chant *God* or another holy word. Try this for fifteen or twenty minutes a day. It generally won't happen overnight, but when the time is right, you will begin to see lights, usually blue or white. You will then be led to the next step within your own worlds.

When you are ready, you will find the peace, comfort, and joy that come from the illumination of God. This connection with the Light and Sound of the Holy Spirit is all that I can give you in ECK.

World Wide of ECK, Washington, D.C., Friday, October 26, 1984

Fourteen years later, as the gentleman was leaving a bookstore, Paul Twitchell walked up to him in the physical body, took him by the arm, and asked him the very same question: "Are you ready?"

2

Paul Twitchell—The Man

Paul Twitchell was the unique individual who brought out the teachings of ECKANKAR in 1965. The more I study his life and writings, the more I respect him.

I regard Paul as the great compiler. Some people like to believe that every time he put pen to paper the words flowed out in impeccable English, every punctuation mark in place, as befits a great message from the Godman of the twentieth century. It didn't happen quite like that.

Spiritual Traveler

Paul Twitchell was a spiritual traveler, and he did have spiritual power. He was seen on the inner planes by people years before he finally began his mission in 1965, while he was still training to become the Mahanta, the Living ECK Master.

One gentleman met Paul in the dream state fourteen years before meeting him in the physical. In the dream state, a man came up to the dreamer and said, "Are you ready?" The dreamer was puzzled. He feared this was the angel of death, and he knew he wasn't ready for that kind of invitation. "No thanks," he said. Then one day fourteen years later as he was leaving a bookstore, Paul Twitchell walked up to him in the physical body, took him by the arm, and asked him the very same question: "Are you ready?" The veil from the past snapped up like a window shade, and he recognized Paul as the man from his dream.

The spiritual power was working in Paul Twitchell even then. Instances of this kind have been related about all of the ECK Masters. Even while they go through the many years of training required before they take the Rod of ECK Power, they are already High Initiates in the secret teachings of ECK.

A Difficult Mission

Soul, through Its many incarnations in all the lower worlds, is a unique entity. We are each one of a kind. Each Living ECK Master comes to the position with a specific mission. In order to carry out his mission, the ECK Masters of the Order of the Vairagi help him develop specific talents and abilities unique to himself.

Paul was a man given a most difficult mission. As evidenced by the fact that a disturbed person attempted to kill him with poison in September 1970 and the resulting illness he experienced in the final year of his life, Paul had little to gain materially from this mission. Yet right to the end, he continued to gather together and put out the teachings of truth.

Paul planned very carefully. Whenever he started a book, he would write the book's title at the top of the page and then list the numbers one through twelve underneath it. These represented the twelve chapters of the book, and he would fill in the chapter titles as they came to him. At the time of his translation in 1971, he had several of these sheets started, including some that didn't have all the chapter headings filled in.

Eve of Translation

When Paul was to give a talk, he would write out an outline that started with only a title. He had a series of talks prepared for the seminar in Cincinnati, Ohio, the weekend he translated. You may wonder: Does a man like Paul know ahead of time the moment he is going to translate?

At the Fifth Initiation there is a point where some of the initiates know when they will leave. But in a higher sense, you come to the point where it doesn't matter. You are willing to let the ECK use you as a vehicle until there isn't anything more to give.

On the evening of Paul's translation, he joined a number of people in the hotel restaurant. He ordered a tunafish sandwich on white bread, but since he wasn't feeling well, he excused himself and took his sandwich up to his room. A little while later, according to the physician's report, Paul translated from a heart attack.

Some of the ECKists at the seminar knew that something had happened to Paul. They gathered in front of the elevator in the lobby and went into a contemplation. Soon the elevator door opened, and several people emerged carrying the stretcher with Paul's body. One of the ECKists watched the stretcher as it went past. He just could not believe that a human body could have gotten so worn out.

These remembrances of the ECKists who knew Paul represent the history of ECKANKAR. This is important for its survival in the future. One of the initiates who sat there observing him at the checkout counter on the eve of his translation recalls it this way: There stood the Godman, in

17

rumpled blue clothing, carefully counting out his pennies and nickels and dimes.

Just before he left, the initiate said to him, "See you tomorrow, Paul." Paul looked at him in a very peculiar way. "Yes, you will," he said. Shortly after that, Paul left the physical body. But later during the seminar he appeared to this initiate—because he said he would.

Not everyone will see the Spiritual Master after his translation, but one of the marks of a true Master is the power to reappear to those who were his close disciples.

Ultimate Service to God

Rarely does anyone serve so close to the total capacity of his human body as did Paul Twitchell. Even after he was poisoned in Spain, he carried on with his mission and his duties as the Mahanta. The ECK worked through the physical form which we knew as Paul Twitchell until it simply wouldn't run anymore. He continued to write the ECK discourses, and today the editors recognize by his writing the times he was too sick to write. But he did it anyway because there was a deadline.

This is the ultimate service to the SUGMAD as a Co-worker with God. Paul served Spirit to the most extreme measure he was capable of. Without the full consciousness of the highly evolved spiritual beings, one's idea of serving God is more limited. We might think, Sure, I'll serve God—when I get off work at 5:00 p.m.

Service to God doesn't mean you have to work yourself into a state of exhaustion. Sometimes that happens, but usually life works in cycles. There are high periods of activity, and there are rest points in eternity. If we know this principle, we can work with it and use it to maintain our health.

You learn that you can drive yourself only so far; you can eat junk foods only so long. Some people's bodies are stronger than others, and they can do it longer. You have to know when you're strong and when you can do the things that tax your body. You also have to know when your physical energy is down and you need to be gentle and easy with yourself.

The same principle applies when presenting the message of ECK. You talk about ECK when there's someone who wants to listen. If no one wants to listen, don't tell them what they don't want to hear. You learn to go with the Spirit of life. This is a greater law than even the ECK-Vidya, whereby one can foresee the future in order to sidestep the troubles that would come.

When you rise in consciousness, you know that it doesn't matter where you serve the SUGMAD. It doesn't matter if it's in the physical body or in one of the other bodies which are not seen by the physical eyes. Life in the inner words is as real as it is right here; the same things that you are doing here are probably what you will be doing there. The scope is going to be different since you will have a different state of consciousness: you'll experience more contentment and greater happiness, and yet there will still be something that drives you on to look for more of the truth.

Public-Relations Person

What was behind Paul Twitchell? We know he planned, we know he had spiritual power. But what kind of training did he go through?

Paul was truly a character. An employer reviewing his résumé might have pegged him as a drifter because Paul had so many jobs that never lasted more than a year or two.

Paul had accumulated a wide range of experiences in public relations which he used creatively all his life. He was an assistant public-relations person at the United States Chamber of Commerce. He also worked for an association for the handicapped; he even wrote and produced two scripts for television on behalf of the handicapped, one including participation by well-known senators.

Writing was Paul's life and love. A Western story written by Paul appeared in *Collier's*, a magazine that was very popular in the 1950s; it was published under one of his several pen names. He had plenty of them. If he wrote along philosophical lines, he frequently signed his name as Paul Twitchell. But when he wrote Westerns or detective stories for the pulp market, he used pen names. Writers do this so their reputation in one market doesn't taint their credibility in another.

Paul's Seal of Approval

While working for a newspaper, Paul arranged with the staff artists to create stickers bearing either his personal seal of approval or his sour-grapes award. The one labeled "Recommended by Paul Twitchell" had a cartoon drawing of him wearing a sports cap. Underneath that was the OK sign—a hand with the thumb and forefinger formed into a circle.

Paul sent these seals of approval to many notable people: Eleanor Roosevelt (he included a nice little letter saying how much he liked a column she had written); Milton Caniff, the creator of the *Steve Canyon* comic strip (Paul complimented him on his upbeat story themes); and the manager of a Shakey's Pizza Parlor, in praise of the food and the atmosphere.

Paul was using these stickers to promote himself. As the reactions and questions came back to him from various recipients, he would incorporate them into newspaper articles—under still another pen name—about Paul Twitchell, that interesting fellow from Paducah, Kentucky.

Paul spent a large part of his life developing the ability to promote himself and his writings. At times Paul admitted that everything he did in his early years had turned out badly; he didn't have money or happiness. On the other hand, when he had on his public-relations hat, he gave the impression that everything was great. He once responded to a newspaper reporter's inquiry by saying although he had nothing against earning enough money to pay his own way, he would not work just for the sake of having luxuries.

Each day Paul read at least one book and twelve or more newspapers. At one point, an ad for a sausage company began to catch his attention. They had been using a series of slogans to promote their meats and sausages, and Paul invariably tried to improve upon the poetry. He not only sent them his seal of approval, he submitted his own suggestion for a slogan: "Our sausage is made with a curse; that's why our best is our wurst."

Paul was always experimenting with different promotional methods. One time a salesman in a men's clothing store agreed to conduct a little test for him. If a customer was having a problem selecting a tie, the salesman would randomly point to one and say, "This tie is recommended by Paul Twitchell." And Paul, ever the scientist of marketing studies, said the salesman reported that the tie often sold on this recommendation. The customers rarely even bothered to ask who Paul Twitchell was.

Paul also knew how to get under a person's skin. A customer of a credit-card company responded to a billing by writing a cute little verse. The company's publicity people decided to use it in an ad campaign. The reply was in the form of a poem from the general manager, which was supposed to show that the company had heart.

When Paul saw this poem, he fired off a long letter to the general manager. He called the poem the most infantile approach he'd ever seen in his twenty years of public-relations work. By the time he finished, you were left with the feeling that the general manager would have been totally devastated by Paul's letter.

About two weeks later, Paul had a change of heart. I don't know what prompted it, but this time he wrote a nice letter to the same general manager. He may have been a little harsh in his recent criticism of the man's poetry, he said, when it probably was just some adman's gimmick. But whatever the case, Paul wanted the general manager to know he used their credit card all the time because it served his every need as he traveled around the world. He then went on to suggest that the company might find a use for his personal seal of approval, and invited them to contact his agent. I don't know how this turned out, but I suspect Paul's letter ended up in the general manager's garbage can.

Early Training

Part of Paul's training was to learn how to carry himself, his work, and his thoughts out into the world. But many people still like to think of Paul as an ascetic, a man who spent his early years in training with Rebazar Tarzs in the vastness of the Himalayan mountains. They believe he must have suddenly stepped from this ascetic life right

22

into the twentieth century, probably surrounded by a shining light.

Paul came into this lifetime as an advanced Soul, but he had a difficult life. He was going through the fine-tuning needed to become the carrier of the message of ECKANKAR. He was training to be the spiritual leader who would bring word of the Light and Sound of ECK to the modern-day world.

Paul joined the navy in 1942, about the time World War II was heating up. As he usually did whenever he made a move, Paul wrote up a press release on himself and sent it to the editor of the newspaper in Paducah, Kentucky. He wanted to assure the folks back home that although he could have waited to be accepted into officers' training, the enemy made him so angry that he signed up as an enlisted man. But far from an assignment in the combat zone, Paul's first two years in the navy were spent at the public-relations office in Pawtucket, Rhode Island. He was later assigned to ship duty, which brought him to Okinawa and the Philippines.

Discharged from the navy in 1945, by 1946 Paul had moved back to Washington, D.C., with his wife Camille, whom he had married in 1942. He took a position as correspondent for *Our Navy,* the old navy magazine which had been in existence since about 1892, and left a year later with a nice letter of commendation from the editor.

In Washington, D.C., Paul came in contact with Scientology. This was to haunt him later: some of the people in the movement were persistent and continued to pester him for a long time. Over the next several years, he also joined various Eastern groups. This was a wide-open period of searching in his life which culminated in the experience recorded in *The Tiger's Fang.* This experience in the God Worlds took place around 1957.

The Cliff-Hanger Period

By this time Paul's marriage was on the rocks. (He and Camille would later divorce in about 1961.) Paul then left Washington for England, saying he had grown tired of the whole artificial scene and especially the social consciousness which was prevalent at that time. Paul as the Cliff Hanger was now coming forth. He began to reassert himself as the rugged individual who had suffered a lot, simply because he wouldn't take life the way society dished it out.

When he had been in England for about six months, news came to Paul that his sister, Kay-Dee, was dying. He went back to Paducah, Kentucky, and remained there for the final two months of her life. Paul loved his sister very much, and her death left a great vacuum in his life.

He returned to Washington, D.C., long enough to sell off some things he had left in storage and then headed for San Francisco. At a stop in Des Moines, Iowa, he met a young lady named Edith who convinced him to come with her to Seattle, Washington, instead. And so Paul, a flesh-and-blood man, not a god who suddenly appeared from the mountain highlands, went to Seattle.

The ECK will draw us along in the way that is needed, many times through the power of Its love as It manifests through another human being. It will take us here and there, and if we are willing to go, It will always take us higher.

In Seattle, through his contacts in the newspaper business, Paul got a job with the Seattle *Post-Intelligencer.* One year was about all he could stand. But he had a way out. According to his correspondence, two of his books, including one written back in 1945 entitled *To Walk Alone,* sold to a major Hollywood studio.

All of a sudden his personal letters began to reflect life on easy street. He was now able to quit his job and travel. And travel he did. First he went down to Acapulco, back up through San Francisco, then on to Canada to visit a few Scientology friends who were staying at a ranch, followed by a swing across the southern part of the United States. After stops in Houston and Dallas, he went back to Washington, D.C., and even made a return trip to England.

Paul was the original rebel. He had money for a while, but after spending it or lending it, he didn't have it for long. But he was very confident in his ability—if he did it once, he could do it again.

The first indications of his future position as a spiritual leader came in 1961. A young lady, aware of his vast knowledge of Eastern religions, wrote him a letter expressing her desire to know more. Paul responded in November of that year by sending her his manuscript of *The Tiger's Fang*. He cautioned her not to read it too fast, but apparently this lady got quite caught up, either with his writings or Paul himself.

She began to make a nuisance of herself, often banging on his door while he was busy writing, entertaining guests, or in contemplation. Paul handled it by writing her a letter. He explained that her unexpected pounding on his door was very disruptive. When he was in a deep trance or in contemplation, he said it hurt his body to be forced back so abruptly. To soften the blow of his blunt request for privacy, he sent her a bottle of champagne.

Ever the diplomat, Paul was very kind to people who deserved it. But at times he also displayed a sharp tongue and a readiness to defend himself against those who attacked him.

25

Ancient Science of Soul Travel

By May of 1965, Paul was conducting Soul Travel workshops at the California Parapsychology Foundation in San Diego. In trying to find a way to express the movement of consciousness—Soul's movement from the human state to a spiritual state or one of the psychic states in between—the best word he could come up with at the time was *bilocation*.

He later discontinued use of the word: people were confusing it with the phenomenon of appearing in two different places at the same time, which, incidentally, Paul was also known to do. But this didn't reflect what he was teaching. His instruction was in the Ancient Science of Soul Travel, the movement—or liberation—of Soul to walk freely in the heavens while still in the human body. This was the gift he was giving to us.

As interest in these workshops grew by word of mouth, Paul was asked to put the teachings down in writing. This marked the beginning of the ECK discourses.

The ECK discourses were a reflection of what Paul was doing at any given time. If he was teaching Soul Travel, he expressed it in those terms. You can see the evolution in his writings from the very early days. As time went on, as people grew in understanding of what the Mahanta Consciousness meant, he was able to give out more of the truth.

The Future of ECK

On the advice of Paul's attorneys, in 1969 ECKANKAR was established as a nonprofit organization. This would provide financial stability, continuity of the ECK teachings, and insure the future of ECKANKAR.

We can dream and hope all we want that God gives truth to us simply because we ask, with no effort required on our part. This is a fallacy. The ECK exists here on earth as the teachings of ECKANKAR, but it doesn't just happen. To manifest and distribute these teachings takes a lot of planning and a lot of hard work—by you and by me.

When the influence of the ECK comes into us, It says: You cannot live at peace with yourself unless you give out my blessings to the world. As this wisdom or knowledge comes to you, in some small way you have to serve the ECK, to carry forth Its message.

ECK is love. There isn't any truth unless we know that ECK is love. And if ECK is love, there is a way for us to put our forces together, individually and collectively, to bring forth the message of ECK to the people of the world who are ready to hear it.

World Wide of ECK, Washington, D.C.,
Saturday, October 27, 1984

It finally occurred to her that the ECK had been trying to give her the message to turn off her car lights—and used a yellow tow truck to do it.

3

The Jewel of God

The four precepts of ECK, as they are presented in *The Shariyat-Ki-Sugmad,* represent the heart of the teachings of ECK on earth. Reading them may serve as an occasional reminder of the spiritual foundation upon which to build. Without this foundation you will never find love; and without love there is no foundation, because love is the foundation of life.

Four Precepts of ECK

According to *The Shariyat,* these four principles must be imprinted in the heart and mind of the ECK chela: "(1) There is but one God and ITS reality is the SUGMAD. (2) The Mahanta, the Living ECK Master is the messenger of the SUGMAD in all the worlds be they material, psychic, or spiritual. (3) The faithful, those who follow the works of ECK, shall have all the blessings and riches of the heavenly kingdom given unto them. (4) The Shariyat-Ki-Sugmad is the holy book of those who follow ECKANKAR, and there shall be no other above it."

These four precepts embody the entire ECK teachings. Within them you will find love, protection, and guidance;

the precepts themselves are the ideal from which spring these other aspects. The trick is to become aware of them every day.

The simplest way I've found to hint at their importance is through stories that illustrate or give an example of what to look for in your own life. They can help you see whether or not you are being a child of the ECK. For instance, even unintentionally we often invade the space of others.

Respecting Another's Space

An elderly man was visiting with his two-year-old grandson, Jeddie. The little boy sat on the floor eating a candy bar, which was smeared all over his face and dripping from his mouth. His dog, Sam, sat next to him. The two-year-old couldn't yet say *Sam,* so he called the dog *Tham.* Occasionally Sam came over to lick the chocolate from Jeddie's face, but Jeddie didn't mind sharing. After all, what are friends for?

Grandpa was half watching them, and he didn't like what he saw. At one point Jeddie gave the dog a bite of the candy bar and then took another bite for himself. That was enough for his grandfather.

Grandpa is a large, heavyset man, about six feet four inches tall. He likes to joke that he's bald because he has so much brains they pushed his hair right out of his head. But he wasn't in a joking mood now. Grandpa rose out of his chair, walked over to Sam, and smacked the dog clear across the room.

The little two-year-old was stunned. His grandfather never treated his own dog that way. He looked up at the older man. "Grandpa?" he said.

"Yes, Jeddie."

"Rags your dog?" Jeddie asked.

Grandpa didn't quite know what Jeddie was getting at. "Yes," he answered. "Rags is my dog."

"Do you hit Rags?" Jeddie asked.

"No, I don't hit Rags," said Grandpa.

"Tham is *my* dog," said Jeddie. "Don't hit Tham!" Then the child walked up to Grandpa and kicked him in the shin as hard as he could. That, for Jeddie, settled the matter.

Ways of Protection

The ECK also works in ways of protection. It can come so quietly that we often overlook the message It carries: how to protect ourselves and avoid unnecessary problems. We overlook the message because our state of consciousness hasn't quite expanded into the next circle of awareness. But when it does, we then get a bigger picture of life and a better idea of how the ECK is talking to us. When your inner feeling says, How about going left here a couple of steps, then right, then two more to the left, it's the ECK or the Mahanta trying to guide you through life. And because you are being guided by the spiritual power, you will be led in a better direction than the highest degree of reasoning could ever hope to steer you.

Recently in California we had a series of rainstorms. It rained so heavily, in fact, that you couldn't even drive in the daytime without the headlights tured on. On one of these rainy days, an ECKist went to visit a friend. Unfortunately, she didn't have one of the cars that beeps or talks to you when you leave your lights on.

As she pulled into the driveway of her friend's apartment building, she noticed a yellow tow truck parked out on the street. The driver sat there, looking around strangely. She thought there might be something wrong with him.

After she parked her car, the image of the tow truck stayed with her. It was such a strong feeling that she walked back out to the street to see if the tow truck was still there. It was.

She forgot about the tow truck as she visited with her friend for several hours. But when she got in her car and tried to drive home, the engine wouldn't turn over at all—the battery was dead. She had forgotten to turn off the car lights. She then had to go through the inconvenience of finding someone to jump-start her car. It wasn't until the next day that it occurred to her the ECK had been trying to give her a message.

Rainstorms present an unusual condition for Californians. The ECKist had to drive with the lights on in the daytime, and she wasn't used to it, which means she also wasn't used to shutting the lights off.

Because the ECK works in every area of life, It tried to find a way to tell her to shut off the lights. In this case, It brought a truck—a yellow tow truck. This is part of the waking dream, which is another form of the Golden-tongued Wisdom. It's actually a form of the ECK-Vidya working in your daily life.

You start with a certain degree of consciousness. It then begins to expand in concentric circles around you. As it reaches out farther and farther, you encompass more of the knowledge that you need to make better decisions so that your life runs better. Every time you're on the wrong track, the ECK will try to tell you that something is amiss.

Message from the ECK

When we come to a seminar, we generally secure two or three rental cars to transport the ECK staff, pick up supplies, or run errands. And with two or three cars, you may not always get the same one.

To use a car, you simply present a slip of paper to the person in charge of the hotel parking garage, and from the deep recesses of the hotel, here comes a car.

Usually you have no reason to question what they bring you; you just get in and go. So when my wife Marge and her friend had to use a car on Wednesday, they went down to the lobby, handed their slip of paper to somebody, and the parking lot attendant brought out a car.

One thing you become used to when you're working with ECK is that things aren't always laid out perfectly for you. But there are always clues.

The ECK staff generally requests that the rental companies deliver clean cars, but this car had full ashtrays and a strong odor of cigarette smoke. And there was something else that puzzled them: Unless we need a station wagon to haul a lot of people, we usually rent smaller, inexpensive cars. This car was big and expensive.

Instead of questioning it, the two women simply got in and took off. But all day long, everything kept going wrong. Each time they tried to get someplace, they got lost. They were given this same car again on Friday.

When I got back up to the room around noon that day, there was a big official-looking note taped to the inside of my door: "Please call Security at once!"

It seems the security people were worried about this car. A couple who were checking out that morning had given their parking receipt to claim their deluxe Oldsmobile. A few minutes later the parking attendant had presented them with a little economy model. So security launched a major search mission, with people running all over the place looking for the Oldsmobile. Marge and her friend were out driving in it, but I wasn't sure where. The hotel staff were greatly distressed. They had visions of the car being damaged in an accident, and because the hotel would be held responsible, that could mean a lawsuit.

Someone finally located the two women and suggested that they get the car back to the hotel. They were greeted by the parking lot attendant, who apparently was afraid of losing his job. He immediately placed the full blame on them: "Why did you take that car?" Marge's friend, who is too feisty to let him get away with that, said, "Why did you *give* us that car?"

The couple who owned the big car had arrived in town earlier in the week. After taking it out a couple of times, they found parking to be a problem in that area, so they decided it would be easier to just leave the car at the hotel and take cabs. They had been using cabs since Wednesday. Until they tried to check out on Friday, they had never missed their car. And all the while, the ECK had been trying to find ways to warn Marge and her friend that it was not their car!

A Bridge of Love

Another way the ECK works is to build a bridge for us when we go from one area of life to another. When Paul Twitchell's sister died, he felt such an emptiness inside that he didn't know where to go next or what to do with himself. And so the ECK brought a woman into his life, and through the element of love, It took him from one area of unfoldment into the next. This is how the ECK works, and It works everywhere.

A young kitten named Mitty was the third in a series of little bundles of love that the ECK had sent to my daughter when she needed it. A few years earlier, when she was about seven, we lived in an apartment. One night we heard a loud meowing in the garage beneath our apartment. We finally coaxed a huge orange cat from underneath our car, and we called him Sunny. He adopted us just when my daughter was having a hard time at school and was very lonely. This cat became her special friend.

Sunny was huge. Sometimes he would jump up on the window ledge, where he barely had enough room to perch, and scratch on the window to let us know he was there. Then one day, after my daughter's crisis had passed, Sunny disappeared. She was afraid he may have been hit by a car, and she carried this sorrow for quite a while. I tried to tell her that she had to let go.

Eventually we moved to another home in the same town. One of our new neighbors had a young orange cat named Zack, with whom my daughter formed a very strong bond. Zack helped her make it through another difficult period of adjustment in her life.

When the couple who owned Zack told us they were moving, my daughter realized there were powers on earth greater than the bond between a cat and a little girl in grade school, and these powers would be pulling them apart. She knew she had to get used to not having Zack around. So for two weeks before his family moved, she kept away from him as much as possible. That's when our next-door neighbor brought home Mitty, the little tiger kitten. When Zack left, Mitty walked in.

The new kitten meowed constantly. He had been taken from his mother, and he hadn't known any other cats. For a while he made quite a racket. My daughter and a neighbor boy tried to figure out ways to make this little cat happy, hugging and holding him so he would feel loved.

By trying to make the cat feel loved, she was able to give her love; and by giving her love, she was able to get love back—not only from the cat but also from the neighbor boy. Up to that point, he and his buddies had picked on her so much that she was almost afraid to go outside. Little boys may like little girls, but not when their buddies are around.

Because of their mutual interest in the little cat, the neighbor boy could now accept her. One day he even invited her to play soccer with him and some of his friends; and because she could kick the ball past them, they began to think of her as one of the guys. He even went so far as to invite her to join his soccer team. So the mutual interest in Mitty built another bridge for my daughter with a new friend.

Samadhi and Nirvikalpa

There are a few other things I'd like to touch on. Two of the states of contemplation are known as Samadhi and Nirvikalpa. Samadhi is a lighter form of contemplation. Nirvikalpa is a deeper form, closer to the ECKshar state. Nirvikalpa can reach into the higher states, even to God Consciousness.

When you do the Spiritual Exercises of ECK, you chant a word and look into the Spiritual Eye. What generally happens in the First, Second, and sometimes the Third and Fourth initiations is that you go into the lighter form of contemplation, which is Samadhi.

Samadhi is more than the contemplation itself; it is a form of enlightenment. People who reach the cosmic consciousness are following the Samadhi road: this is where they are in their spiritual unfoldment.

Samadhi means becoming one with the Kal, and this isn't necessarily bad: It means coming into an understanding of all the forces that occur in the lower worlds. You eventually become a Pinda Master, which means a master of the Physical Plane.

What the Initiations Are About

You have to master each plane, first the Physical, then the Astral, Causal, Mental, and Etheric. This is what the initiations are about. When you get the Second Initiation, it means you are at the entrance to the Astral Plane; you are now ready to master the Second Plane. But it also means you have mastered the Physical Plane, the one below the Astral. Whether you are aware of it or not depends on you.

At the fifth plane, the Soul Plane, you enter into the initial state of Nirvikalpa, the deeper form of contemplation. This is a state of consciousness higher than the Christ Consciousness, or cosmic consciousness. It will lead you to the state where you become the ECKshar.

You then go further, and eventually come to the eighth plane, the Hukikat Lok. Here you come to the highest state that Soul can generally reach. It is known as total awareness. Nirvikalpa can take you beyond, into the Ninth Plane, where you will be invited to join the Order of the Vairagi Adepts; into the Tenth Plane, where you come to the divine wisdom pool; and into the Eleventh Plane, where you become the Kevalshar. Here the full realization of God occurs.

The Realization of God

The realization of God begins as Soul makes the transition between the Eighth and Ninth initiations, increases through the Ninth and Tenth, and reaches fulfillment in the Eleventh. But trying to explain God-Realization to someone who has never had it is not easy. It's like trying to tell a kitten like Mitty, who has never been a cat before, what it's like to be a cat.

Beyond God-Realization is the Akshar state. It is often believed that there is nothing higher than God-Realization—but there is always one more step.

As you travel into the other worlds, you go through the lower heavens of Christianity which are found on the Mental Plane. The higher you go into the spiritual planes, the greater becomes your capacity for love; compassion; and the attributes of wisdom, freedom, and charity.

Those who are in the Order of the Mahantas, who have served the SUGMAD for the longest time, are also in a hierarchy. The longer they have served, the greater is their compassion and love for all creatures and beings of God.

A World of Golden Light

Occasionally we go to a far world which has a beauty beyond words. There is no true way to describe what is seen. The closest is to say it's a world illuminated by two golden suns, and everything is seen through a golden veil. When Soul comes here and begins walking into the land of gold, It wants never to return; It wants to go on forever. And I found myself in the same position.

I walked with the ECK Master Fubbi Quantz in this world of golden light. Two golden planets were in the sky. Since there is no time and no space, it's interesting how things are perceived in the spiritual worlds.

I'm trying to describe a unified world. But since we are now in a world of duality, I can only express it by dimensions. The planets were moving very fast but they weren't going anywhere; and yet they were able to move across the entire expanse of this golden world, which wasn't round.

We went further into this God World of golden light, but we didn't walk at all. Yet there was a yearning to go even farther, farther than ever before, because the love of the SUGMAD always draws you on.

At one point Fubbi Quantz turned to me and said, "You have to go back now, my son." It was spoken with a great deal of kindness, compassion, and love, borne of the understanding that comes only to one who has walked into the golden worlds himself. At one time, he too wished to go on forever, to never come back; but someone had said to him, "You must go back now, my son."

Returning Home

And so when you go home from a seminar, you, too, have to return from a world of golden light. Whether you are aware of it or not, you have attained an expanded consciousness, and somehow you now have to carry the light of this golden consciousness back with you.

It glows very strongly for a number of days. Gradually you come back completely into the physical consciousness, and then there may be an awful emptiness inside. It says: I wish to go further into the heart of God.

But our responsibilities bring us back. And the only way we can ever go further into the heart of God is to face our responsibilities to serve the SUGMAD. This is the paradox that both allows us to grow and gives us the yearning to want to grow.

In closing, I would like to read a poem by Mairi McDonald, one of our initiates in Australia. It's called "The Jewel of God."

I walked in fear and darkness, and then he came
And lifted up my face to Light,

And I knew not his name.
A jewel he had for me like a million stars.
I did not know its worth;
I thought it glass.
'Twas many aeons again before he came,
And only then I knew his holy name.

He offered me this jewel one more time,
Its heavenly Light could once again be mine,
To cherish or to cast away,
Perhaps forever, who can say?

The jewel of God is truth. It has been offered to us many times before. We have taken the truth and stepped on it, abused it, thrown it away, until in this life, the jewel of God is brought before us again. And again we are faced with the same choice: Will it be the Mahanta or the Ahanta? Will it be the greater consciousness or the consciousness of the ego?

The tests and the challenges go with us every day, but are always presented in ways we can handle. They uplift and uphold the spirit in ways that are good for us as the children of ECK.

I want you to know that the love of the Mahanta is always with you. Baraka Bashad.

World Wide of ECK, Washington, D.C.,
Sunday, October 28, 1984

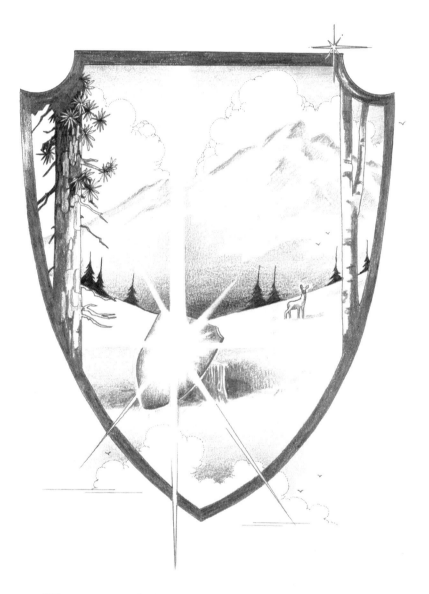

When you reach the clearing in the middle of the forest, you will find the Shield of Silver Light, which is the shield of love.

4

The Shield of Silver Light

The Shield of Silver Light is actually the shield of love, which is the ECK, and this is what we look to find as we come into ECKANKAR.

The path of ECK deals entirely with the Light and Sound of God. This is what it can offer you. The way to reach the Light and Sound is by Soul Travel, which simply means the movement of consciousness.

Methods of Soul Travel

Soul Travel can be done in two ways. One method is by the movement of Soul as a unit out of the physical body to another state, to another place. In the second method, as the contemplator sits in silence, the Soul awareness simply expands outward in concentric rings, going to the far ends of the universe or to the place where consciousness wishes to be. This expansion of consciousness may not always be recognized as actual movement, but you will come in contact with the Light or the Sound of God.

The different ways in which this happens are explained in the ECK books. In *The Tiger's Fang,* for example, Paul Twitchell describes his journey to the inner planes. He traveled through the heavens as he was used to seeing them. In your own contemplations, you may not see worlds and heavens that fit the descriptions Paul gave. Your experience on the journey to God is going to be along your own path.

An individual who comes from a traditional Hindu background, for instance, is more likely to see people in robes and long beards, similar to those described in the Biblical stories, or a walled city of diamonds and streets of precious gems. But a person whose background is along more modern lines is likely to see people dressed in twentieth-century attire in worlds similar to those of the physical plane, but broader and more spacious.

Broader Views of Heaven

The inner planes are filled with many different heavens, and we each are attracted to the heaven where we feel most comfortable. It's that simple.

Heaven is much broader than the concepts or stories reported to us by those who have had Soul Travel experiences in the inner planes. Putting the inexpressible into words can tend to limit the experiences to the images evoked by those words. Therefore, the account of a saint— someone who went to the inner planes and saw one of the great beings who lives there—becomes the ideal the followers strive to reach.

Most of the Western orthodox religions are based upon an account of a saint or founder who came in contact with Sat Nam. This is the manifestation of God on the Fifth Plane—the Soul Plane. Very seldom do any of the followers of the orthodox religions come in contact with Sat Nam themselves, but the experiences of the founders or saints are generally claimed to be a meeting with the lord of the highest heaven. The best any of the followers can do, then, is to make every effort to attain the height of their leader.

When the founder dies, his teachings eventually become crystallized into a formal doctrine, protected from change, and promulgated to the world by followers who haven't had an inner experience of any kind. In time, the doctrine formed from the original Soul Travel experience of the founder becomes a dead religion based on dogma alone, and its acceptance is based on the factor of belief.

In ECK, belief is only the beginning. The true basis of ECKANKAR, the Ancient Science of Soul Travel, is experience. At some point, if you don't have the experience of the Sound and Light, or Soul Travel, or meeting with one of the Masters on the inner planes who will take you to a world beyond, then you really ought to find a religious teaching that is more in tune with your development up to this point.

The Importance of Flexibility

When something out of the ordinary comes up, we generally resent the intrusion. We often have definite ideas about how our plans should work out. As events change, if we are too rigid to change our ideas, we become angry, upset, and unhappy—with our co-workers, our spouse, and everybody else.

The fact is, if we refuse to be flexible, life will pass us by at great speed, and we'll be left to sit in the dust at the side of the road. When we ask, Why isn't this working our way? maybe it is because it's not supposed to work our way. Perhaps our way is old, slow, and backward. Maybe the ECK is trying to bring us a hint to speed up, catch up, or change our direction.

45

Even if we are moving in the right direction, we may be going too fast or too slow. The ECK wants us to adjust our pace, but sometimes we won't listen. You often notice this when you travel by car.

In an effort to get somewhere by a certain time, you'll sometimes run into one delay after another. It doesn't matter whether you left home five minutes late or right on time, you may run into one red traffic light after another. And as you impatiently sit through the red lights, you probably won't recognize that maybe Spirit is trying to put you into the proper synchronization for the meeting that is going to take place when you reach your destination. Instead, you become angry because you're in a hurry. Sometimes you race to beat the red light, and though you may get through the light, something else happens down the road—perhaps a near accident. This happens because you're pushing.

Whenever you're pushing, you're not listening to Divine Spirit. You can't hear the message the ECK is giving you—the silent guidance of what to do, how fast to go, and what direction to take in order to do it right. And so we come to grief in big and little ways, and our unhappiness is always someone else's fault.

Seasoning with Love

My daughter came home from school one day and told me this story. There was a family that loved all the cooking and baking the mother did. Year after year, any meals prepared by the mother were special. She had a mysterious spice jar, and just before she served the food, she would sprinkle some of this spice over it. The family never knew what the spice was, but they did know that meals were always a happy, congenial time.

As the years went by, the father passed away and then the mother. Soon after her death, the children got together to sort through her belongings. In the kitchen they eventually came across her special spice jar. One of the daughters said, "I wonder what kind of spice she used that always made the food taste so good." If they found out, they could prepare the same kind of tasty meals for their own families.

They opened the spice jar, and inside was a little slip of paper with a few handwritten words: "I made this meal with all my love." And there wasn't anything else in the jar.

When you prepare food or do anything else with the love of the SUGMAD, with the love of God, it turns out better. You can impatiently throw a meal together in a hurry, or you can take your time and carefully select the ingredients you're going to put into it. If you prepare the meal with care, everyone will notice that there is something special about it. It's that way with everything you do in ECK.

Being a Co-worker with God

Our purest purpose for learning Soul Travel, or anything else, is to eventually become a Co-worker with God. This may sound like a very dull thing to aspire to. When I first heard about ECKANKAR, all I wanted to do was Soul Travel, and that's what I did. Being a Co-worker meant nothing to me at the time.

Recently someone asked me, if he dedicated himself to serving the ECK, how would he fill time when there weren't any ECK activities going on? Well, you do whatever is needed to take care of yourself financially, maintain your health, work with others, do the things you like to do, and help other people. But however you spend your time, you don't do it for someone else; you do it for the love of God, for the SUGMAD. It will make a big difference.

In the past I have worked in several different camera departments at various companies. When somebody would bring me a job to do, I'd have to take it to the printing camera and decide the quickest way to do this task. After I came into ECKANKAR, I sometimes remembered to say, "I'm doing this in the name of the SUGMAD." And I'd proceed to do the job with every bit of skill and love and attention I could muster.

But a funny thing can happen: You get too many rush jobs, you start getting busy and tired, and you forget about being a Co-worker. Soon you're doing the job as a favor for another person.

One time someone appealed to me to rush a job through. Because I was anxious to help him, I got right on it. All of a sudden the camera stopped working. I put the negative into the developer, but for some reason the exposure was wrong. So I took it out and checked it under the light.

The whole procedure should have taken three or four minutes. But since I had to do it twice, it took a little longer. It didn't work the second time either. So I tried it again.

Ten or fifteen minutes later, after the third miss, it suddenly occurred to me that the camera didn't work because I was trying to do this particular job for a certain person. I wasn't doing it in the name of the SUGMAD. As soon as I caught on to this, I said to myself, Since all this hurrying wasted fifteen minutes with nothing to show for it but aggravation, why don't you just stop, think, do it in the name of God, and do it right. It made all the difference. I think you'll find this, too.

Giving Others Space

When people work together to set something up, it's necessary to have a good chain of command. If five different people have five different ideas of how to do everything, you won't get the job done efficiently. In order to get it done well, someone has to be in charge. But we still have to learn how to give others their space.

If we really love another person, we are willing to give them this personal space. But there are many ways we unknowingly invade it. For example, someone tells you all about something that is really precious to him, but you always add something on top of what he says: "Not only that, but also..."

This not only contradicts what he said in a subtle way, it also puts a little wall around the other person's thoughts. In effect, you're saying, Your thought is OK, but I have a better one. We may not intend to get in the person's space, but we often do it anyway.

This is not meant to imply that if you just watch your words, your spiritual life is sure to go right. That would be working with the letter of the law rather than the spirit of the law. When you really care about another person as much as you do yourself, you are more apt to listen to what he says. You are less apt to interrupt with your own bright ideas about what he really means.

Many times we may show a lack of regard for another person's state of consciousness, but not because of any ill will and not necessarily through our own doing. Sometimes it's caused by other people. For instance, you're at home talking with your spouse, and one of the children interrupts with a totally different topic. You wonder if you should be patient and polite to the child, or if you should tell him, Hey! Mom and I are talking. Is it so important that you can't wait until we're finished?

It sometimes works the other way around. You may be talking with the child when your spouse comes over and interrupts. To compound the dilemma, she interrupts with a topic that you'd really enjoy getting into: "What do you think about the latest political elections?" Your child, on the other hand, was talking to you about Little Red Riding-Hood, a subject that is very important to him or her. Now you have a choice to make about the degree of love and respect you are going to demonstrate toward another person.

Seeing through Illusion

I know an individual who performs an excellent coin trick. He'll hold up a coin and say, "Here's the quarter in my left hand. Now I'll put some whiffle powder on it." He sprinkles the imaginary powder with his other hand, claps his hands together, and the coin is gone. Then he reaches into his pocket or behind your ear and feigns surprise: "Oh, here it is. How did it get there?" And just like magic, the coin is in his hand again.

This individual likes to do it for fun. It keeps his mind limber. Most people enjoy this trick, but the day he performed it for a couple who were members of one of the fundamentalist churches, he got an unexpected reaction. At the time they were tenants in an apartment building he owned. The woman was a very gullible sort, and to make sure there was no misunderstanding, he explained that it was only a trick. Then he did his routine, and the coin disappeared.

The woman's eyes grew as big as the coin. "Demonology!" she shouted. "The work of the devil!"

The magician was shocked. "It's just a trick," he said, "but I can't tell you how it's done because magicians don't reveal these things."

The woman and her husband seemed to calm down. "We know it's only a trick," they said. But apparently they were quite disturbed. Two weeks later, they moved out.

It's quite a simple trick, really; I saw how it was done. It's more fun not knowing. But when the ECK wants you to see, you see.

You don't always know what you're dealing with in another person's state of consciousness, even when you're talking about ECK. You can explain Soul Travel in the most straightforward way—as one of the best means to begin the journey home to God—but some people will still manage to take it all wrong. They will interpret your words to mean all kinds of fantastic things, such as astral travel, mind travel, or even the works of the devil. These ideas and concepts are established in their minds, either from this lifetime or another, and there is no hope of getting through to them.

The only way to protect yourself from people of that level of consciousness is to steer clear of them. They resist truth. They wouldn't accept truth if it came walking up to them like a camel in the desert, offering them the only way out. Instead, they would view it as something dangerous that might spit at or bite them. They would rather chase it away—and die there in the desert.

A person may be thirsting for truth, but if he doesn't recognize it when he sees it, he'll throw a stone at it. And so he loses salvation—the liberation of Soul. This is what we do so often before coming onto the path of ECK. Even after coming into ECK, some people say, "It's not what I want. I don't believe any of this is true."

The Spirit of Love

The real problem that people have with the Spiritual Exercises of ECK and their inability to see the Light or hear the Sound of God is a lack of self-discipline. They simply do not have the self-discipline to do the spiritual exercises every day, with love. This is where we find the Shield of Silver Light, which is the principle of love.

The spiritual exercises work best when done with goodwill, a feeling of happiness in your heart, and with joy in the expectation of seeing the Mahanta. On the inner planes, the Mahanta is the representation of the SUGMAD, which is often seen in the form of the Living ECK Master. If you can fill yourself with love, you have a very good chance of being successful in Soul Travel.

How do you evoke the spirit of love? You can do it in any number of ways. For instance, when you go into contemplation, you can put your thoughts and mind upon a past experience where you were filled with love. This will set the tone for your state of consciousness. Then begin chanting one of the secret names for God or your personal word.

You are the one who must set the tone of love and let it fill your heart. Your whole being has to be filled with love, not from the head but from the heart. And then, as you make your preparations to go inwardly, you say to the Inner Master: "Mahanta, please take me to the place that is right and fitting for me at this time. I put myself into thy hands."

This is sometimes difficult to do, especially when you're new to the path of ECK. I don't expect you to be able to do it right away. If you are new to ECK and you still have feelings for and reliance on a past master—Christ or anyone else—then look to that master; ask him to help you.

In time, as you progress in your spiritual unfoldment, you will come into an awareness of the true nature of these masters, which is Divine Spirit, or ECK. It uses the images of these masters to come to you in a way you can understand.

When you are ready to graduate from your present level of understanding, a new master will come to you. But as you go further, you begin to realize that it wasn't a new master at all; it was still the Holy Spirit, the Divine ECK. In Its highest form on earth, It is known as the Mahanta. At other levels It is known as the Christ Consciousness, Buddha consciousness, cosmic consciousness, and so on. What you see is still the ECK but at different levels.

You touch the level where you belong at that time. So instead of rejecting the image, accept it and move forward with it. This is the path to God.

Regaining Contact with the Light

I met an individual who said she had experienced the Light of God as a golden light. She had this experience a few years before she came in contact with ECK, and she wanted more. An advertisement in a magazine led her to a certain metaphysical group, so she sent for their monographs. But after studying them for several months, the Light went away.

It was lost to her for a number of years. Then she came to ECK, and gradually the experience of the Light of God is coming back to her. She finds it enlightening and heartening that in ECK she can regain the state of consciousness she had before, but lost.

It is a very sad condition for those who have some experience of God and then lose it, never to find it again in this life. They wander around like the shadow-walkers, haunted by the image of this Light or Sound of God.

Once It touches you, It haunts you; and the only way you can live is to have more of It, because It is love. Once you have tasted love, at whatever level—whether human, emotional love or the more impersonal divine love—you can't live without it. If you can't find it again, your life becomes one of misery.

There are people who, having once touched the garment of God, are never again able to recapture that split second in eternity when they were in the divine presence of the Holy One. They go through churches, metaphysical groups, and occult teachings, always searching for this missing element they can never seem to find.

It's even worse when they come to ECK and then walk on by. What they seek is here, but because they haven't wandered along the narrow, dark streets long enough to recognize the truth of the teachings of ECK, they walk right past. And so it must be.

Recognizing the Master's Voice

If you meet a person like this, let them go; there isn't any way in the world you can convince them. But when the state of consciousness has been prepared by the experiences and hardships of life, Soul will recognize the Master's voice. At that point, nothing can keep them apart.

In the old West the calves ran very close to their mothers on the plains. The smells and sounds of the mother were so strongly imprinted in the calf's mind that even if it got separated from the mother, it would be able to find its way back.

This is what happens to us, too. Through the hard knocks of life, we become imprinted with the ideal of the

Holy Spirit. The education we gain from the hard experiences of life is necessary: Most of us have such hard heads that it's the only way we can wake up when the Master comes calling, either on the inner or the outer planes.

The inner experience through Soul Travel is as definite as if it were engraved in marble. Once you make contact with the Inner Master, he will give you the direction you need for your spiritual unfoldment.

Our Connection with the Holy Spirit

A lady was afflicted with a serious illness. The family health insurance didn't cover many of the additional expenses incurred, and they had been forced to dip into their savings. They wondered if they could afford to travel all the way across the country to attend an upcoming ECK seminar.

Her husband reviewed the finances and felt they shouldn't go. But one night on the inner planes this woman saw a block of marble. Carved on it, in letters emblazoned in gold, were the words: "You both should go to the ECK seminar."

This woman's husband had a favorite expression that he used whenever she came up with an idea. He'd say, "Is it carved in stone?"

When she woke up, she said to her husband, "We should both go to the seminar."

"Is that carved in stone?" he said.

"As a matter of fact," she said, "it's carved in marble—with gold letters!" He simply said, "We'll find the money." They did, and they went to the seminar.

The Holy Spirit, the ECK, had seen that it was important for their spiritual unfoldment to be there. Perhaps they found a new way of healing; perhaps they were shown a way to learn how to accept her condition. Whatever the result, it came through contact between her and Divine Spirit through the workings of the Mahanta, the Inner Master.

This is what we are working for—the connection with our inner reality in a way that we can understand. When the time is right, and if such is your mission, you will be approached on the inner planes by the ECK Masters with the precise instructions and directions needed for you to take the next step in your life.

The Secret Doctrine of Truth

One fellow you may meet on your inner journeys is an old man without a name. He looks like an old codger. He generally stands outside a farm gate, grumbling and mumbling to himself. You may even try to avoid him; after all, you're on a Soul journey and you don't want to be bothered with that sort of stuff. But this individual is an engaging sort of person, and soon he catches you up in conversation.

He tells you that he served as the Living ECK Master for a period of ninety-one years. You notice that his skin isn't even wrinkled; it's baby pink and smooth, like the skin of a youth. And you want to hear more.

He goes on: "When the time is right, I will give you the secrets of health, step-by-step over the weeks, as you need them. This will aid your health and increase your longevity. You will receive these directions sometimes in a conscious way, sometimes in an unconscious way. This secret doctrine will be given to you because you have earned it."

With that, he opens the gate, goes through it, and walks off with the energetic gait of a young man. You realize now that the whole thing was an act just to give you, the Soul Traveler, the opportunity to decide for yourself: Was this man a part of truth or not?

Maybe you would rather not talk with him, but you do. And because you do, because you are willing to give up your concepts of what this man might or might not be, the truth will come to you in its simple, clear way. It always works like this.

Truth is simple. So why doesn't everybody know it? Because it's too simple. Because we have our preconceived notions about what truth is or what it should be.

Loosening the Bonds of Soul

We have our built-in prejudices that are as familiar to us as old friends and as much a part of us as our hair or our fingers. You don't have to think twice when you grab a piece of paper; you just automatically move your fingers. In the same way, the prejudices that are built into us from past and present karmic experiences react as reflex actions that can automatically turn away truth.

But just as some people reject wealth while others accept it, truth is not turned away by everyone. Two people may have similar backgrounds and education, but one will be rich and one will be poor. Why? It always goes back to attitudes and prejudices which have become so firmly entrenched that we aren't even aware of them.

We always come back to the Spiritual Exercises of ECK. As you chant the name of God, with love, for twenty minutes a day, the bindings and bands that constrain Soul will begin to unwind. Not all at once but very slowly, at a rate you can understand and accept. As these bindings are released, Soul rises in spiritual freedom.

As Soul, you are like a balloon that rises above the ground. The higher you go, the farther you can see. And the farther you can see, the better you can plan your life.

This is why the initiations in ECK are referred to as circles of initiation. When you get the First Initiation, the balloon is very close to the ground, your horizon is quite near, and your circle of vision is limited. But the ring of awareness becomes greater with your Second Initiation, even more so with your Third, and so on.

Self-Responsibility

The meaning behind the circles of initiation is simple: As you come to see more of the spiritual horizon of your own life, you find you have a greater capacity to plan and live a happier life. One day you will notice you are no longer asking God to make your life better; you are now taking full responsibility for your own actions. This change comes as you take on more self-responsibility for gaining a higher state of consciousness.

The Living ECK Master does not call upon God or anyone else to help him out of troubles. He does get help from the Divine Being, but he acts as if everything depends on him to work it out himself. Then the Divine ECK steps in and brings help as it is needed.

You do what you can for yourself, and you trust in Spirit. You use your own creative imagination, the faculty that makes you more Godlike. When a problem comes up and you can't find an instant solution, sit down and think: What can I do to solve this problem that I haven't tried before? It may help to talk to a High Initiate. This doesn't always mean that you'll instantly get the answer that's going to work for you. Other people's solutions may not be your own. But by asking, you have reached out and taken the initiative—a first step that will lead you to the next answer. Now you are actively doing something instead of passively sitting around waiting for the Divine Power to shower wisdom and riches down upon you. It doesn't happen that way.

We have to take the responsibility for moving forward in our own spiritual life, and the best method I know is through the Spiritual Exercises of ECK. These are given mostly in the ECK discourses, but there are also some very good introductory spiritual exercises given in the ECK books.

The Shield of Silver Light

In the forest of the SUGMAD is an enormous clearing. It is set in a breathtakingly beautiful landscape, where the sky is baby blue, speckled with fluffy white clouds.

Against the stump of an ancient tree, all by itself in the middle of the clearing, stands a silver shield. It appears as a mighty warrior's shield from medieval times. The Light of God shines down from above, strikes the shield, and comes off in a ray of light so brilliant that it will blind anyone who approaches it with an impure heart. Only the Mahanta can approach this shield, for it is used in his travels on the inner planes.

This Shield of Silver Light stands as a protection for the children of ECK, those who make the commitment to follow the shield of love. No being can approach it except in the spirit of love. And when you can approach the Shield of Silver Light in the spirit of love, you have the protection of the Mahanta with you. Nothing can touch you, nothing can harm you.

When battle must be done to bring protection to Its own, the Inner Master, the Mahanta, will go to the clearing, pick up the shield, and with the sword of the SUGMAD he will take the field in battle for you.

If you know and accept this, then you have the love and protection of the Holy Spirit against every psychic attack, against all harm and all danger. In times of danger, you have the ability to wrap this aura of love so tightly about you that nothing can touch you.

In your contemplation, see yourself walking beside the Mahanta through the meadows to this great forest. When you reach the clearing in the middle of the forest, you will find the Shield of Silver Light, which is the shield of love. Stand within its circle of protection, and know that you are standing in the love and protection of the SUGMAD.

Sydney Regional Seminar, Sydney, Australia,
Saturday, November 10, 1984

When Soul comes out of the initiation, the individual may or may not have a conscious awareness of what transpired on the inner planes.

5

The Rope of Karma

The rope of karma is an interesting thing. We are on earth because of karma, whether it's from this life, the last life, or ones before that. A heavy load of karma makes us feel stuck, and this generally makes us unhappy and frustrated. The good karma is also in the background, but often we forget the happy times and dwell on the bad times.

On the other hand, studies indicate that in times of extreme pain, the mind does a reversal: It forgets the real bad things and remembers only the good. It's as if the mind can deal with only so much negativity. When this reaches a certain peak, the mind either blanks it out or somehow softens the memory of the trauma.

For instance, we like to remember our childhood as a golden age when all we did was run and play. The sun was always shining, and there were always pets around to play with and share our love. But actually, children have their problems and karma to deal with too. Such as a messy bedroom.

Keeping Things Simple

Every time my daughter cleans up, she assures me, "Dad, I'm really going to keep my room clean this time."

But right after she has cleaned her room, I can see the mess start to accumulate.

I'm trying to get a lesson across to her. "Do one thing at a time," I tell her. "If you put something down, clean it up or put it away. This way you stay on top of it, you live moment to moment, you keep things simple.

"When you do one thing at a time, you can do an amazing amount of work because you don't get confused. You have an idea of where you are going. You set one goal, then another, and then another. And if you make them manageable goals, you can get right through them."

A few hours after so brilliant a lecture, I go back to my daughter's room and am amazed at how it has self-destructed. But that's life, and I think most parents cope. The children cope, too.

The expectations and standards of parents and children are different. For the parent the importance is in being clean; for the child it's in being alive. And this causes karma. Mom gets mad and says, "You don't get to eat until you straighten up your room," and the child feels like a victim, unjustly punished.

Effects of Unknowingness

This type of karma goes on every day. One person expects a certain standard and the other person is only willing to deliver something of a lesser standard. And they may not know they've missed the mark. Karma is quite often caused by such an act of unknowingness.

Several of us had a meeting to attend in the hotel. The meeting room was two floors below my room. One of the ways to get there was to walk down the long hallway, turn the corner, take the elevator down two floors, and double back down the long hall to the meeting. But there was a fire exit right outside my door that could take us downstairs and right to the room where the meeting was being held.

"Let's take a shortcut," I said. So we all used the fire door, walked down two floors, and turned the knob to get back in. It was locked. We decided to try the door on the next floor down; but that door was locked, too.

We were down to the ninth floor when somebody suggested we try a room key. Two of us pulled out room keys and tried them in the door. They didn't work.

Our walk grew leisurely as we made our way down to the seventh floor, chatting about the reason this was happening, and secretly blaming each other. We tried the keys again on each of the floors, hoping one of the fire doors would respond. By the sixth floor, we were making jokes about how to slip the lock open with a credit card.

Soul's Journey

Our journey was a little like Soul coming from the high planes of God, working Its way down into the lower worlds. You start trying to figure a way to get back to where you were—the good place where there are rooms and people; not this desolate hollow well with whitewashed walls and solitude.

Anyway, the credit card wouldn't work. So we went even lower, dreaming now of special little wires with hooks that you could just place underneath the latch, give it a nice tug, and the door would pop open. At the fifth floor we realized that even if we got inside, we'd still have to make the long walk down to the end of the corridor, turn left, punch the button, and wait for the elevator. Except now we were seven minutes late for the meeting.

We ended up in the basement, and from there we trooped through the lobby, found the elevator, punched the button, and were delivered to the floor that had been our original destination. When we arrived at the meeting, we were greeted by a room filled with people wondering where we had been.

We had been speculating: Why had the ECK made us take this detour? What's going on in the meeting room upstairs? It was our way of trying to justify why we did such a dumb thing.

It turned out there had been a question which others were better able to answer than I could have done. So we said, "Well, that must be the reason we were ten minutes late—the ECK wanted them to answer the question." Anyway, we needed the walk, so it worked out well for everybody.

You justify your whole trip from the top down to the bottom. But when you finally hit bottom, it's like coming in contact with truth, which then leads to a path that will take you back up to the top.

Like an elevator, ECKANKAR takes you back up. You can go directly up, or you can make an occasional stop at a floor along the way. But even when you stop to rest you know where you're going, and you know the elevator is there to take you to higher levels. So by the time we had worked our way back upstairs to the meeting, we were both smarter and humbler. We went about our business as we had originally intended to do before the detour.

This is the way that Soul, too, once took a detour. In the spiritual worlds, the SUGMAD saw that Soul was just resting, having a good time, serving nothing but Itself. What an easy life It had in the spiritual planes! Now, the SUGMAD had a rope—we'll call it the rope of karma—which was attached to a trapdoor at the floor of the spiritual worlds. This trapdoor emptied out into the lower worlds of time and space. When SUGMAD pulled the rope, suddenly all these individual Souls came tumbling down through the worlds of Light into the worlds of darkness, screaming and crying and carrying on.

The Importance of Each Soul

SUGMAD isn't concerned about the individual's concept of problems. All SUGMAD cares about is that one day Soul will become ITS Co-worker. Soul is a spark of God, and as such, is required by God; for it is through Soul that God sees and realizes ITS own worlds.

This is a paradox. It may even sound like a contradiction. We think of God as being all-powerful, so why would SUGMAD need the individual Souls at all levels of consciousness throughout ITS worlds?

Let me put it another way: We need the ECK, and the ECK needs us. The ECK is all-powerful, but it needs us in order to know Its consciousness, the higher realizations, God-Realization, and ultimately even beyond that. Why? So that this great expression of life can have ever-greater realization.

As It does, we do; and as we do, It does. For this reason, when even one Soul unfolds, there is an upliftment in consciousness realized throughout the worlds of SUGMAD. This is why the initiations in ECK are so important.

Relief from Karma

The initiations given by the masters of other groups are actually little more than baptisms. When people on different paths claimed that Paul was initiated by them, they ran into Paul's rebuttal. He may have had initiations in other groups, but only in the same way that he may have had a baptism by the Christian church in which he grew up. He said the initiations outside of ECK were pretty much the same as baptisms. Baptisms remind me of the way some people wash dishes. They splash water on, but the dirt's not gone.

Baptism cannot save Soul because Soul is not lost. This may come as a shock to the orthodox Christian mind. Soul isn't lost; It is in a well-regulated, established school of karma which takes up the whole lower worlds of time and space. This includes the Physical, Astral, Causal, Mental, and Etheric planes.

Soul may take a detour, It may spend a great number of lifetimes playing with the rope of karma, but Soul is never lost. Its one and only destiny is to become a Co-worker with God.

Baptism is a control factor used by the priestcraft. It gives them something to do while they lead the people who need to be led, giving them nothing in return for it except a life of religious servitude. Baptism cannot relieve Soul of karma. The only thing that can do this is the initiation in ECK.

Initiation in ECK is not given in such a way that the karma burns off all at once. To do this would destroy the body in which Soul is residing.

Much of this karmic burnoff occurs during the First, or Dream, Initiation, which takes place on a subplane of the Astral world. The Second Initiation is given on the Astral Plane, and the karma removed from the individual at this level is taken into a cave and burned.

This is the test of the cave of fire. In this part of the karmic burnoff, the power of the rope of karma is weakened; it now has less ability to hold Soul down.

Soul gains a little more freedom, a little more ability to be spiritually liberated. Like a balloon rising above the

68

horizon, Soul can now go a little bit higher. As It rises, It is able to get a broader view of the circles of activity over which It has influence and which influence It. Our vision of our own life becomes greater, which means our ability to solve our own problems increases; and as a result, we continue to rise into the higher worlds.

Past-Life Patterns

In 1968, Paul gave an ECK-Vidya reading to an individual who was having problems in this lifetime with anger and frustration. Paul studied this individual Soul's entrance into the lower worlds on the physical plane. He first incarnated on another planet, a warlike planet. Then, about fifty thousand years ago, the individual incarnated on earth and took up a body on the continent of Atlantis, where he was a healer in the royal court.

It was a time when black magic was strong. The black magicians had gained control over the king by making him believe that their tricks were the real source of power. But whether they looked at the future or did a healing, it was done through the use of the lower psychic powers.

The queen would have nothing to do with the psychic powers. She recognized this individual's ability to work with the greater power—not the pure spiritual power, but the positive power. He was eventually betrayed and killed by the black magicians. But not understanding why this happened to him, why he was a victim, he died with a great deal of perplexity.

Other lifetimes followed. In ancient Greece the individual ran into a couple of similar situations. Paul showed him a series of lives. Each one, building one upon the other and compounding his problem, led to the karmic ties he was facing in this lifetime.

Each Soul has lived thousands of lives. The ECK-Vidya reader selects those which brought about the strong traits and characteristics of this present life. This can lead to an understanding of why we have certain fears, loves, or other feelings, and how they make our life easier or more difficult.

Paul laid out the entire pattern for this man. At the end he concluded: "Since you've come on the path of ECK, you have taken great strides to break this karma. By the time you finish out this life, much of this will be behind you."

The ECK-Vidya is generally something that the initiate in ECK is better off learning for himself. The Inner Master will give you an insight into the karma of past lives as you need it, as you can handle it, so that you can take the next step in your spiritual unfoldment to greater freedom. The whole purpose of ECKANKAR, the Ancient Science of Soul Travel, is always spiritual liberation

Eternity Road

There's a peculiar road in Australia called "Eternity Road." It's a rough gravel road that runs between two improved stretches of highway. As you enter this rough stretch of road, there is a sign that reads, *Beginning of Eternity*. You drive down this road for what seems like an eternity, and eventually you come to a sign that reads, *End of Eternity*. By then you are only too happy to get back onto the smooth paved road and move along again the way you had wanted to in the first place.

This gives another example of Soul's journey to the lower worlds. It started out in the higher worlds on a paved road, but then It came to the worlds of time and space—the beginning of eternity. In ECK, the concept is that eternity is limited; it has the limitations of time and space. Any-

70

thing that can begin must end. Even some of the sacred writings of the world state that Soul came at the beginning of eternity and will endure to the end of it.

In the spiritual worlds, this concept of limitation does not apply. Therefore, we simply say, Soul is. Soul exists.

Soul, coming onto the road to eternity, experiences gravel for the first time. But it is a condition that lasts for only a certain stretch of road, after which the conditions of eternity no longer exist. Soul then can work in the regions of roads that interconnect in all directions without limit.

ECK in Our Culture

The message of ECK is coming out into the public in a quiet and good way. There was a highly rated American television series called *St. Elsewhere*. It takes place in a busy hospital. One episode had a brief segment in which the Living ECK Master and out-of-body travel were mentioned.

In the scene, a handsome young doctor is being interviewed by the administrator of the hospital, an older doctor wearing little wire-rimmed glasses—just the type you would expect to be running a busy hospital. After the interview, the administrator says, "Well, I have a few more people to talk to, but you seem to have the best qualifications. I'll probably ask you to start work on Thursday morning."

The young doctor, the epitome of mental acuity and winning personality, suddenly looks concerned. "Thursday morning?" he says.

"Yes," says the administrator. "Thursday morning."

"Well, I can't start then. I have an appointment."

The administrator is surprised. "You do?"

"Yes," says the young doctor. "I'm going to have an out-of-body experience."

The administrator is taken aback. "I beg your pardon?"

The young doctor goes on to explain, very clearly and with no hesitation: "I'm going on a trip to the Astral Plane with the Living ECK Master." In this quiet way, the ECK was brought to the public.

Because it came up in a humorous way, some of the ECKists who viewed it felt it displayed a lack of respect for the Living ECK Master and felt we ought to respond to it. But my guess is that there was an ECK writer on the staff.

This is how the ECK is going to move out into the culture. The power of ECK is here, the love of ECK is here; It is moving out into the twentieth century. People are going to sense the freedom that comes with this path.

It's difficult for a teaching such as the Ancient Science of Soul Travel to be tied down with rules and regulations. As an organization, we have only as many as we need in order to operate and exist.

The organization of ECKANKAR provides a necessary vehicle for the Living ECK Master. It is his responsibility to reestablish a golden age in the ECK works. Again and again, he has to breathe life back into the different aspects of the outer teachings of ECKANKAR. This is what gives it vitality; this is what prevents it from becoming like the dead orthodox teachings.

What Happens during Initiation

I would like to mention one more thing about the rope of karma. As we finish our karma, we eventually come in contact with the path of ECK. We study for a few years, and then we get the Second Initiation. A number of people have no awareness of what is happening on the inner planes during the initiation.

The Mahanta, the Living ECK Master connects Soul with the Sound Current, which is the Holy Spirit, the ECK. The whole function of the path of ECK is this linkup of Soul with the Light and Sound of God—the ECK. Once this linkup is made, each initiation beyond the Second Initiation increases the power and the love of ECK in your life.

What happens during the initiation is part of the secret practices of ECK. It is only for the individual who has earned it. But to explain briefly, the Mahanta meets with Soul on the inner planes. He comes to the individual in the Light body, a sparkling body of light which is also called the Nuri Sarup. The connection is made. Often the Master will put his arm around the individual's shoulder, or shake hands, or something of this nature. Generally this meeting takes place alongside a river.

Stranger by the River is actually indicative of what happens between Master and Soul on the inner planes during the initiation. It is the meeting by the river; not the great wave of God, but a river. The Master and the chela sit down together on luxurious grass, and they talk about ECK.

In the higher initiations the talk gives way to a stream of Light that comes down from the higher planes and enters directly into Soul. This generally happens at the Fifth Plane and higher. In the initiations in the lower planes, there is a discussion; in the higher planes, the truth of the Shariyat-Ki-Sugmad, the Way of the Eternal—which is the ECK Bible—comes to Soul directly through the Light and Sound.

The Light Giver

When Soul comes out of the initiation, the individual may or may not have a conscious awareness of what transpired on the inner planes. Nevertheless, the Light and Sound of God has put a greater light to Soul than ever before.

This is why the Mahanta is called the Light Giver. It is not an empty title at all. Soul is given a greater amount of the Light and Sound of the Holy Spirit.

The true initiation is totally unknown to the people who rely on baptisms for their salvation. They have no awareness of anything occurring outside of the physical act of having water splashed on them. They have no knowledge of the Light and Sound of God or the power of upliftment, enlightenment, spaciousness, and happiness that It brings.

Nor do they have any conception of the cleansing that occurs—the purification that burns out and removes karma so that henceforth you are able to live your life with a greater degree of self-control and freedom. It is another step toward self-mastery.

Self-Mastery

Self-mastery simply means that a person has the ability to run his own life according to the laws of Spirit. This presumes, first of all, that you know the laws of Spirit. The understanding of these laws comes through the Light and Sound of God; it is a direct infusion of the Shariyat-Ki-Sugmad into Soul.

On some occasions during the ECK initiation, the Light and Sound comes through so strongly, bringing a feeling of such happiness, that the individual has to just sit and let it balance out for about five minutes. These are the fortunate ones.

Even if you have no awareness of what is occurring on the inner planes, the initiation is still valid. The truth that you need is instilled in your heart. It will now come out as an expression in your daily life.

Occasionally the Sound in a person's ears is so strong as he comes out of the initiation that it takes a few minutes for It to subside. The Sound can be heard in a number of different ways, such as a roaring wind or music. This is the action of the Holy Spirit working on Soul, uplifting and bringing the purification which is needed before there can be the liberation of Soul. This is what we are looking for. When the liberation of Soul comes, we are on the threshold of becoming a Co-worker with God.

When the ECK has something to say, I have found that It will put the words in my mouth. And during my talk, in one way or another, the ECK opens your heart and the truth enters in.

When you go home from a seminar, the inner door stays open for two or three days to a week, during which time you are filled with the lightness and spaciousness of the love of God that you picked up at the seminar. Then the door begins to slowly shut. Within about a week, you are back into the regular flow of living. But the memory lingers, and many of you will notice increased experiences during your spiritual exercises.

If you have a sincere desire to move forward in the worlds of God, continue to do the Spiritual Exercises of ECK, faithfully and with love. Put your attention on the SUGMAD, the ECK, or the Mahanta in whatever way is suitable and comfortable for you. Walk in the Light and

Sound of God; be a vehicle for ECK wherever you go. As you work with It, the Holy Spirit—the ECK—will work with you. May the blessings be.

Sydney Regional Seminar, Sydney, Australia,
Sunday, November 11, 1984

God has established so many different paths and means for us to reach heaven that there is a way for everyone, including the atheist.

6

Before You Say Yes, Is ECK Really for You?

How can a person who has gotten an initiation lose it? And once we get God Consciousness, can it be taken away from us or can it be lost?

In the Biblical writings there is a saying, "Let him that thinketh he standeth take heed lest he fall." In the ECK writings it states that anyone, even the spiritual leader of ECKANKAR, can lose his high spiritual status if he does not keep up with his duties. In life we either go forward or backward; we really never stand still.

Walking the Path to God

We may walk the path to God very slowly for a number of lifetimes. At some point we may take up a particular religion, such as Christianity, and become so comfortable with it that we turn off our spiritual motor. We stop thinking for ourselves. We become self-righteous.

What we have actually done is shut our ears to God or the Holy Spirit, and we are the last to know it. But it really doesn't matter if we go through life spiritually deaf and blind. Because after we die, leave the body, and have a short stay on the Astral Plane, we are right back here again as a newborn babe, all memory of the past erased from our mind. Once again, we go through troubles and hardships, asking, Lord, why have you done this to me? or What is the meaning of life?

For the disasters and the heartbreaks, we find no answers at all. And yet, if anyone dares to threaten the religion into which we were born, we become defensive, antagonistic, and angry.

This is partly because we are afraid of our own God. The God of the Old Testament is an angry and fearful one, and as we make the switch to the New Testament, we find a gentle, loving God. It's not the same being at all. But because we do not have the full picture, we cannot resolve the disparity of the two natures of this God.

The Dangers of Passivity

Since we don't get the answers, fear hangs over us like the sword of Damocles. So we rely on faith and belief for yet another lifetime, afraid to even look into other books that may give us another picture about the meaning of life. Not only would that threaten our beliefs, but our fear of hell is so great that we are petrified into inaction. The next lifetime, then, may be spent as a Hindu practicing meditation.

Meditation is one of the extreme examples of an individual Soul putting Itself into a passive state. This method is simply another way to tie Soul tighter to the human body. Soul is an active, happy being. Meditation slows the spiritual process. In your spiritual evolution, as in the rest of life, you either go forward or backward; you do not stay in one spot.

In Western civilization people are in a more active mode of Spirit. This means we have the opportunity to actively seek our spiritual education. Whether we do it or not, however, is up to us. The jewel of God is all too often picked up, looked at, and then tossed aside into the mud, simply because we do not recognize the precious jewel that is before us.

Learning from a Master

The human condition is pretty bleak. For this reason, it is important that you be willing to become the best that you can be in your religion.

It's much like learning a trade. You start by going through an apprenticeship program. If you want experience, take a job with a company that is staffed with good people to learn from. Then seek your next opportunity. Maybe you can be assigned to work with someone knowledgeable in a specialized field, who can teach you the secrets of the trade by example. Learning through experience is always a better way to learn than through a book; but if a book is all that is available, it will provide a start.

The same principles apply to our spiritual life. Spiritual discipline requires that we find someone who has the experience that we want. The path to Mastership actually requires an ideal. But this ideal is not to be found in the physical presence of the teacher, because at some point or another, the personality will be misleading.

A Relationship with Divine Spirit

What you are looking to achieve is the ultimate experience within your spiritual path. A Christian seeks the Christ Consciousness within, which is the highest state to which a person can aspire in that religion. If you are in ECK, you look for the Mahanta Consciousness, which simply means an individual who most clearly recognizes the relationship between himself and the Holy Spirit.

At the top is SUGMAD, or God. The Voice, or the Word, of God—that which puts life into all creation—is known as the Holy Spirit. We seek to establish a relationship between ourselves and the Holy Spirit so that one day we can have God Consciousness.

This is difficult to talk about because the conditions of consciousness from the Soul Plane on up to the God Planes are far beyond the Mental Plane, where we have to deal with images, symbols, alphabets, and words. Trying to use these tools as a means to explain and identify the qualities that exist far beyond the mind is impossible.

Overcoming the Fear of Death

In ECK, we don't look for explanations; we look for experience and realization. This comes through Soul Travel, which is simply the separation of the spiritual consciousness from the human consciousness. Through the Spiritual Exercises of ECK, when you are ready, this experience may come about in a number of ways. And once you have this experience, death will never have a hold on you again.

Fear of death is one of the reasons we fail in life. It governs a great part of one's life. For example, it is the whole basis for the insurance business. It can even make us afraid to take a chance on a new job. We have a lot invested in the old job. What happens if we give it up and can't replace the income? How will we survive without it?

Fear governs us more than the love of life. The only way we can hope to break through this fear is when we have some type of an experience that shows us that life continues after the demise of the physical body.

Socrates, in the *Phaedo,* said a philosopher's purpose is to achieve the separation of the Soul as much as possible from the human body, so that when death comes, he can meet it with confidence in the life that exists beyond.

A book called *The Glass Ship* brought up an interesting concept. The glass ship is a symbolic way of saying the Soul body. This is the eternal part of you which is invisible to those around you. The glass ship is actually Soul freed from the body, enabling or empowering you to go to the invisible planes.

Through the power of the HU, the word of God, you can gain the ability to bring about the separation of Soul from the physical body and become aware of the place you will go after you leave here in death.

We are looking to achieve the Kingdom of Heaven, which means the state of high awareness or God Consciousness, while in the physical body. The co-workers of God exist and labor in all planes, even on earth.

Just because the saints worked on earth does not mean they were ever separated from the high consciousness. When necessary, they endured torture, poverty, and hardship at the hands of others, and yet they were able to be happy and content.

The question is, Can we have this, too? Some will not, but there are others who have the ability and the potential to learn Soul Travel, to take those first timid steps out of the physical body. They will explore the inner planes, sometimes through the dream state, and come in contact with the two aspects of the Holy Spirit—the Light and Sound.

What Happens after Soul Travel?

A fellow had been in ECKANKAR a number of years ago, but he wasn't any longer. Though he still considered himself a silent follower of ECK, he said he saw absolutely no purpose for the Light and Sound. But he wanted to do Soul Travel.

After you have learned Soul Travel, there comes a time when you give it up. Soul Travel is merely one part of your evolution.

Those in ECK who make any degree of progress will, at some point, reach the Soul Plane, which is a realm beyond the areas of time and space. And without time and space, there can be no movement of anything, including Soul.

Therefore, when you get above the Mental Plane to the Soul Plane, you no longer Soul Travel. At this point you are often in the condition of seeing, knowing, and being, simply finding yourself on another plane of spiritual consciousness, in another heaven. You are simply there. But until then, to bridge the gap from the physical body to the Soul Plane, we have Soul Travel.

Some of the experiences with Soul Travel are quite phenomenal, but the whole point of the Inner Master taking you on a Soul Travel journey is to give you experience that is vitally needed for you to become a mature Soul. Without this experience, you run the course of karma and reincarnation lifetime after lifetime. A person may not agree with this, but it really doesn't matter how you feel about it. The laws of Spirit prevail.

The Laws of Spirit

It makes absolutely no difference whether or not we, in our petty human state of consciousness, agree with how it is all set up. We can resist the laws of Spirit all we want, but like a child trying to stop a tornado, it's pretty ineffective.

The laws of Spirit command all the worlds. Yet man in his self-conceit, supported by book knowledge and mental education, sometimes feels he stands above these laws. He thinks that he can take shortcuts.

There are many routes we can take to heaven. God has established so many different paths and means for us that there is a way for everyone, including the atheist. This sounds almost like a humorous paradox, but it's true. An atheist can be closer to God than a Bible-carrying, born-again Christian, simply because the atheist may have a better understanding of the Law of Love.

If Divine Spirit wants you for Itself, to serve Its cause in any way, It will take you, shake you, and mold you through the harshest treatment you can imagine until the tempering of the Soul body is exactly correct. Only then are you a purified channel fit to be put into the world to become Its Co-worker, to walk silently among the sons of man and give the nourishment of the Holy Spirit by your presence and sometimes by your actions.

The First Step

The first step is to learn Soul Travel. This is done through the Spiritual Exercises of ECK, which involve active contemplation rather than passive meditation. In meditation you sit down, become still, go within, and just wait; whereas in contemplation you sit down, become still, go within, and use the creative imagination to do something. These creative techniques are described in the ECK discourses. The book *ECKANKAR—The Key To Secret Worlds* has several spiritual exercises, and *In My Soul I Am Free* has a very good one called "The Easy Way" technique.

If you are ready for the path of ECK, you will be given some kind of an indication through the inner channels that it is time to take another step. If you are not ready, then take the step to the religious teaching where you feel most comfortable.

The Best You Can Be

To become a conscious vehicle for God requires that you become the very best that you can possibly be in whatever you choose to do. If you are more comfortable in a church, then become the best church member you can be in whatever way you believe is required. Becoming a master of any sort means you are going to be one of the chosen ones, one of the people at the top of the spiritual ladder.

A Soul Travel Technique

If you are interested in Soul Travel, you can try out a technique tonight in the dream state. Close your eyes, and place your attention very gently on the Spiritual Eye. Then chant HU, and fill yourself with love. This feeling of love is needed to give you the confidence to go forward into an unknown, unexplored area. One way to fill yourself with love is by calling up the warm memory of a past occasion that filled you with pure love.

Then look inwardly for the individual who is your ideal at this time—whether it is Christ or one of the ECK Masters. In a very gentle way, say: "I give you permission to take me to the place that I have earned, for my greatest spiritual unfoldment." And then silently or out loud, continue to chant HU, or God, or a holy word. Try to visualize yourself walking into the inner worlds, and know that the individual who comes to meet you is a dear friend.

If it doesn't work the first time, do it again and again. The spiritual exercises are like physical exercises: Before your muscles grow strong, you have to exercise them a number of times; it doesn't always happen in one try. It's quite likely that if you take up an exercise routine for thirty days, you're going to be stronger than you were at the beginning.

It's the same way with the spiritual exercises. The purpose of the Spiritual Exercises of ECK is simply to open a conduit or a channel between yourself and the Holy Spirit, which we know as the Audible Life Stream—the wave that comes from the heart of God. From the moment you begin chanting and looking for truth in this particular way, whether you are conscious of it or not, changes are being made in you.

The changes may be so small at first that you won't even notice them, but others will. You're not going to walk around looking like a deified being; it may seem to go the other way for a while. As Spirit brings about purification, the dross that is part of all of us rises to the surface and spills over.

Now you will have to be more aware of the words you speak and the thoughts you think. Because if you let negativity go out and pollute the world, it will come back to you in the form of karma. But whatever happens, as long as you learn from it, you have gained in your spiritual unfoldment.

Changes in Consciousness

When you start to do the Spiritual Exercises of ECK, the Light and Sound of the Holy Spirit begin to enter you through an invisible communication line, and changes come about in your personality. You become a more independent, thoughtful, self-motivated individual because you are taking the first steps toward self-mastery. And self-mastery means that you are in charge of yourself.

This is not to say you start ignoring the laws and the expectations of people around you; but you become well-versed in how to guide your life to avoid unnecessary hardships and problems, and to get the most out of everything that you do, both physically and spiritually.

In the process of your spiritual evolution, the changes in consciousness are going to produce changes in health. At first they may not necessarily be for the better. Karmic conditions that are imbedded in you may now come to the surface as health problems. But at the same time, you have now gained the ability to find the elixir needed to soothe each particular problem.

When you open yourself to divine truth, the mere fact that you can identify a problem means that you have the solution within you. What you are attempting to achieve through the Spiritual Exercises of ECK is the expansion of consciousness whereby you can better see the solution to your problem. This doesn't mean you're going to get an immediate cure or that your purse is going to be filled instantly just because you asked for it. This isn't how life works.

The purpose of life is to give Soul—and that means you—an education so that It can become a Co-worker with God. Whether you like it or not, no matter how you resist, your destiny is to someday be one of the exalted ones, a Master in your own right. Some of you have already done your kicking and screaming in other lifetimes. All you need to do this time is pick up where you left off before, and your path will be very quick and smooth.

The Role of Doubt

And yet there is room in ECK for the doubter, because as you express and exercise your doubts, you gain in strength. If you need to have something proven to you, it will be proven to you. It won't necessarily happen in a smooth and easy way, but it will come in such a way that you will know the truth of the matter.

Others may offer you their philosophies and theories about it, but at this point you will know what is right and true for you, whether it concerns your diet, how to make a good living for yourself, or the spiritual exercise needed to take your next step on the path to God. As you go along, you become more independent of thought. And this is what we hope to achieve—strong individuals, not sheep.

A Matter of Attitude

A young boy often wondered if he were adopted. Finally he got up the courage to ask his mother about it.

"No, of course you're not adopted," she said. He didn't believe her. The family album had baby pictures of his older brother, but there were none of him. It must be because he had once belonged to other parents. "No," his mother said again, "you always belonged to us."

He stared up at her with big round eyes. "Then why aren't there any pictures of me?"

His mother looked very uncomfortable. Finally she said, "You were such an ugly baby, we were ashamed of you." She hesitated for a moment, then reluctantly continued. "When you were a little baby, you were so ugly. All anyone saw in your crib were two big eyes staring back at them. Whenever visitors asked to see the baby, I'd tell them you were upstairs taking a nap, and I didn't want to disturb you." When she took him outside in the baby carriage, she said, she would put a blanket over his head.

The boy still couldn't figure out why his mother had thought he was so ugly. It wasn't until he grew up that she finally showed him a photograph of himself as a baby. "Sure enough," he agreed, "I was an ugly baby. Nothing but these two huge eyes staring back." Today the man still has big eyes, but his head, face, and hair have filled out around them.

As an adult he told his wife this story. She said, "If you still have the picture, I'd really like to see it."

He showed her the photograph. "Oh, what a beautiful baby!" she said. "It looks just like me when I was a baby." It was the first time anyone had ever found something nice to say about his baby picture.

Truth comes to us like a baby with two big eyes, not looking at all the way we expected. We like to pride ourselves in the thought that if truth came, we would instantly recognize it and embrace it. But because of our prejudices and the narrowness of the human consciousness, we could as easily call it an ugly baby and throw a blanket over its head.

This attitude explains why we have problems and why life seems to run us when we should be running our life. And most people don't have the slightest idea how to turn this around.

The best way I know is through the Spiritual Exercises of ECK. But the mere fact that you begin to do the spiritual exercises doesn't mean that you will instantly be on the straight path to God. Each of you will approach it differently.

Some of you will be more persistent than others. The individual Soul is a unique being with Its own pattern of karmic behavior. Two people who do the same spiritual exercises are not going to progress at the same rate.

No matter who you are, no matter how good or bad you think you are, you are a unique individual. Soul, both in Its being and in Its relationship with God, is unique. If you are ready, the Spiritual Exercises of ECK will help you to find your own custom-made approach to the Kingdom of God.

Going On Trust

The story of Jonah in the Old Testament gives a good example of trust in Spirit, trust in truth. Jonah was given the assignment by God to go to the city of Nineveh. He was to tell the people they were doing it all wrong, and if they didn't repent, God was going to destroy the city.

Jonah was a prophet for the Israelites. He had no use for the gentiles. "I don't want to go," he said.

"Go anyway," said God.

But instead of going to Nineveh, Jonah got on a ship headed for Tarshish, which was in the opposite direction.

A fearsome storm blew in. The sailors, being a superstitious bunch, cast lots to see who was responsible for upsetting the gods of the sea. And guess who the lot pointed to?

Jonah then told them all about his God and how he had tried to flee from His presence.

As the storm continued to rage, the mariners decided they had no choice but to cast Jonah into the sea. No sooner had he splashed into the water than a big fish gobbled him up. Jonah's account says it was a great fish, but in the New Testament, Jesus calls it a whale. Whatever it was, it didn't chew him at all, it just swallowed him whole.

The fish eventually spit Jonah out on dry land. "I've seen the light," he said. "Now I'll go to Nineveh and give the message to the people."

You can't just walk into a city and expect a great big welcome from people when you're telling them to clean up their act. No one likes to hear that, especially from a guy in ragged clothes who's been living three days in the belly of a fish. But he managed to convince them to change their ways. They accepted everything he said.

When you declare yourself a channel for God, you are going to be given directions. Occasionally you will be nudged to meet someone you would rather not meet, under conditions you would rather not be in. But you always have a choice: Either go and act as a pure channel for the Holy Spirit, or not. Of course, when Jonah chose not to, he ended up in a fish's belly.

The Angel of Love

When you ask to see the face of the Angel of Love, you must be pure of heart. If you aren't pure of heart, the angel will destroy you.

If you are sincere in your search for truth, then go ahead and make the statement at bedtime: "Lord, show me thy truth, show me thy path, show me thy way." Repeat this each night. Soon you may begin to become more aware of your dreams, or you may be taken out of the body by an ECK Master or one of the other masters. In some way, something will occur to give you absolute knowledge that there is existence beyond the physical body, that there is life after death.

A Test of Faith

Like it or not, each of us is one day going to have to cross that threshold. Nowadays death is pretty much hidden, especially from children. In the Western world a person often dies in a hospital, not at home, and it's all handled very antiseptically. We are isolated from the inevitable thing which we would rather not think about. But someday, whether we are ready or not, it comes.

There was a man who was very strong in his Christian faith. He had trusted and followed the Holy Spirit throughout his whole life. One day an inner voice told him to sell his business, move to another state, and start a peach farm.

His friends told him he was an utter fool to do something like this, but he did it anyway—and became a highly successful peach farmer. He worked at it for a number of years, enjoying not only the money but the benefits of being outside in the the fresh air and sunshine.

One day the voice came to him again. This time it said: "In the years you have been here, you have learned enough to go into the construction business." He gave it a try, but he didn't do very well; there were already too many contractors and not enough business to go around.

He wondered what to do. The voice said, "Build churches." He listened, and it turned out to be a very profitable venture. None of the other contractors liked to work with church building committees because it was a slow, ponderous process. It took forever for them to make a decision—and then they would reverse it. But this man was very easygoing, patient, and mentally sharp, and he liked people. He got into a field nobody else wanted, and within a few years he became a millionaire.

But there is always a shadow. It was discovered this man had a terminal illness. For ten years he went through one kind of medical treatment after another, until finally the years caught up with him. He had always kept an unloaded gun by his bedside, but in the last week of his life he started to keep it loaded. He was afraid to die alone, and he formed a crazy notion that his wife should go with him.

Even though all his life this man had been very strong in his church, he never lost the fear of death. A person is afraid to die when he doesn't understand, or have knowledge of, the continuity of life.

A Look at the Worlds Beyond

The purpose of the ECK teachings is to make you aware of yourself as Soul. You begin to realize your ability to move beyond the physical body even while you are still alive in the body. When Saint Paul said, "I die daily," he referred to this process. It is similar to death in that in the Soul body, one actually leaves the physical body to take a look at the worlds beyond.

Here he gains confidence, courage, and becomes acquainted with the other worlds, so that when the time comes, he moves through the transition very smoothly, very naturally. Death loses its sting, the grave loses its victory.

Once we leave the physical body permanently—if we are advanced to any degree at all—there need be no concern for this life on earth, for we have moved into a far greater expression of it. Our divine evolution is a wonderful thing.

If you have any questions, I would be glad to answer a few.

The Sound Current

Q: How do you distinguish between the Sound Current and other noises, such as ringing in the ears?

HK: You will definitely know the difference. The Sound is simply the action of the Holy Spirit coming into Soul, uplifting and purifying It for a greater level of understanding.

The Sound and the Light are the two aspects of the Holy Spirit. The Light generally comes first, and then comes the Sound, which is more important. It is the Sound that will carry you into the higher worlds.

Q: Is there a technique to open up to the Sound Current?

HK: Sit or lie down, close your eyes, place your attention on the Spiritual Eye, and chant HU. As you chant, listen carefully in a gentle way. Use the creative imagination. Try to visualize the Sound as golden musical notes flowing down from a place above you. As you see them, know that each golden note has an accompanying sound. Listen for the melodies as they pass into and through you in a continuous stream.

Visualize something connected with the music that strikes a definite image on your mind, perhaps a stringed instrument, a flute, or woodwinds. First try to see and then try to hear the golden notes flowing down from this musical instrument. Know that you are listening to the melody of God.

Try this technique for twenty minutes a day. If it doesn't work after a week or two, try another creative technique.

Transition to Higher Worlds

Q: What is the transition like when we leave here at death and go to the next place?

HK: In most cases, as we make the transition we are totally unconcerned about it. As bright as the sunlight appears to our eyes, this physical world is a dark, small, mean place compared to the other worlds. You will see settings similar to those on earth, but larger and with a lot more light.

There will be a lightness and spaciousness about the body that you wear there. Soul is once again wearing a body, but It is on a higher plane. It is so natural that generally you don't give it a second thought. And you are always greeted by someone you know and love.

People who are of a higher character have an easier time going across than those who have been mean in life. If they have cheated others and selfishly extracted everything they could get, they usually don't have someone so happy to meet them on the other side. But for people who love truth and love God, it's a smooth change. The key really is love.

Sometimes the transition is made so gradually that the person who is near death finds it a pleasant experience. I remember the way my grandmother would sit by her sewing machine and seem to be talking to herself. But she wasn't at all. She was speaking with friends and relatives from the other side, already able to see them.

This often happens with people who are about to die. The transition is very gradual, and you know they are in good hands. The person who leaves this plane generally does not miss it. There's no reason to, once you realize the continuity of life.

Guardian Angels

Q: What is your opinion of guardian angels?

HK: Do you have one?

Q: Yes. He has been coming to me for years. He wears a long robe. He's the one who told me to come here tonight. If he turns me over to the ECK Masters, what do I do with him?

HK: Whether it appears as a guardian angel, Christ, the Inner Master, or anything else, what you are seeing is merely the form that the Holy Spirit uses to manifest in your inner worlds through the vision of the Spiritual Eye.

The Holy Spirit takes on a form that fits your state of consciousness, so that It can make Itself known to you in the form of someone you feel comfortable with and have learned to trust. This guardian angel will stay around until it is time for you to go to another state of consciousness. Then he will turn you over to the individual who can take you on the next phase of your journey.

Q: But what will happen to my guardian angel then?

HK: You really don't need to worry about him. Remember, these masters you see on the inner are actually the manifested Holy Spirit. It is omnipresent, which means It is everywhere at once. It's a little hard for the mind to understand, but in the Spirit body, your guardian angel has the ability to work with an unlimited number of people at the same time.

Psychic Dangers

Q: If one practices psychic phenomena, will he get into some kind of danger?

HK: Most of us don't have a full understanding of the laws of Spirit. Because of our ignorance about what we are doing, we pay the price. Sometimes it's a small price, sometimes a large one, but it's always within our capacity to handle. I'm not saying the psychic is necessarily bad. A lot depends on how a person works with this area.

Psychic Healing

Q: Are you saying when used for good, it's all right?

HK: Let's put it this way: You will find that many of the psychic healers are in poor health. They generally burn out before the age of forty, especially if they are heavily involved. This is because they haven't learned that people with health problems have earned them through spiritual ignorance.

When you take away a person's symptoms, you actually deprive him of the opportunity to learn what he needs to know in order to avoid the karmic patterns that caused the illness. He is just going to keep on doing the same things over again.

Psychic healing is quite often an individual's real attempt to serve his fellowman in some way. However, without an understanding of the consequences of that form of service, it is a double-edged sword.

At some point the psychic healer will realize that the toll on his own health is too heavy and that people don't really appreciate or grow from what has been done for them. The healer can then step back from that practice, look seriously to his own forward progress, and learn how to serve as an agent of God in a clean way so as not to take on karma. There is a way to do that.

Q: What is the alternative? Should we not heal?

HK: If someone asks for help, then it is our choice whether or not to give them whatever information we have. But so often the people who do healings, especially those who know nothing about the laws of Spirit, take it upon themselves to pray for a sick person to get well. That is actually a violation of the spiritual law, but many people feel they are doing it for God and therefore it's right.

Do it if you will, but because you are interfering with another person's spiritual beingness, you are going to pay the price. This is one of the areas in which the orthodox

98

churches have failed the people. They constantly encourage praying for someone else to change their state of consciousness—to find Jesus, to be healed, or whatever.

If these prayers are directed toward a person of greater spiritual evolution, one who is protected by a higher force, there will be consequences. These prayers are really only psychic forces that are shot toward the white light that surrounds the protected one. When these prayers hit the protective light, they bounce straight back to the sender. You will find that the people who do a lot of praying for others usually have plenty of problems themselves. Money doesn't come in right, health isn't good, and family problems arise.

One family back home made it a cause to pray for me to come back to the church. I didn't want to go back to the church. They might as well have been praying for a fourth grader to go back and be a first-grade pupil again. People do this in the mistaken belief that it makes them more spiritual.

Every Sunday night I would get a headache. These headaches persisted until I finally figured out what was happening and surrounded myself in the white light of Spirit. The headaches went away, but that family continued to pray for me.

They were determined to change my consciousness. They went through some very bad experiences, but that was their choice. They may not learn from it in this lifetime, but they'll be back to try again—until they do learn.

Self-Healing

Q: What is a good technique for self-healing?

HK: There isn't any one healing technique that will work for all of you. As your state of consciousness changes, as you unfold spiritually, you are going to find that the old healing systems don't work for you anymore. A lot of things won't work anymore.

This is why the creative imagination is so important, as well as your willingness to stay open to life and to the Holy Spirit. When the old remedies don't work anymore, Spirit is going to show you something new that does work. But if you are rigid in consciousness, you won't even notice the solution; therefore, you'll suffer, sometimes even to the point of death.

The path to truth is like a two-edged sword. You have to stay open; you have to be willing to give up your preconceived notions about right eating, what is right for your health—all those things. At some point, whatever was right for you in the past will no longer work.

The old rules become completely powerless to do anything more for you. But Spirit will put in front of you a new and better way, and once you pick it up, you are a new creature.

The Physical Realm

Q: Some of the ECK books mention life on Venus. Do people actually live on Venus the way they do here?

HK: On Venus, no. On some of the other planets, yes.

Q: Is Venus a spiritual realm, or is it physical like earth?

HK: It's actually part of the physical, but it operates at a higher vibratory rate than earth. It's like the difference between ice and steam; both are part of the physical realm, but one is solid and the other is vapor. The properties are different.

The Physical Plane has various ranges of composition, ranges of consciousness, and ranges of heaven and hell. Even the other planes, such as the Astral and Causal, have ranges of heaven and hell. The earthbound spirits are actually in the lower part of the Astral Plane, but sometimes their vibrations are so coarse that they can be seen here by people who are spiritually sensitive to a high part of the Physical Plane.

The veil becomes very thin, much like a filmy curtain which allows you to see ghostly images on the other side. But most of the time the veil between the Physical and Astral planes is more like a solid wall that you can't see through.

Understanding the Spiritual Laws

Q: Once you are initiated into ECKANKAR, can someone still interfere with your consciousness?

HK: It can still occur. Some people are better at the path of ECK than others. Some people's defenses can be gotten through simply because they don't keep up with the spiritual disciplines or the spiritual exercises, or because they don't fill themselves with love.

Q: Why do people interfere with another's consciousness in the first place?

HK: Why do people cheat each other in business? It's the old idea that you can get something for nothing. The Physical Plane is exactly the place where they can work this out of their system.

People who do not understand the spiritual laws don't realize that you pay for everything you get. Some people are just not as far along on the spiritual path as others. Those of us who know better have the consciousness to keep out of their way. In the same way that you can't cheat an honest man, you can't take advantage of someone who is strong in spiritual consciousness.

Wherever you are and whatever you do, you should live life to its fullest in the way that is most comfortable for you. If you can do this, you will find that the Angel of Love will unveil its face for you, and it will be a happy meeting.

Evening with ECK, Auckland, New Zealand,
November 13, 1984

The foreign writer was tricked into feeling guilty for making the Indian pedal so hard, and he overtipped the cyclist.

7

The Garden of Spirituality

Soul in the lower worlds needs every experience before It can become a Co-worker with God. As we become exposed to the different aspects of the ECK teachings, such as Soul Travel, the ECK-Vidya, or healing, we have experiences of all kinds. We have to go through the baptism of fire so that we can learn how to get ourselves out of it.

Experiences of All Kinds

One evening while out to dinner with friends, one of our companions excused herself and went to the ladies' room. She returned to the table a few minutes later with an amusing story. While she was standing at the sink in the restroom, somebody began pounding on the door. A young man poked his head in. "I've got to come in," he said.

She wasn't quite sure what to say. He pointed at the floor. "My lizard is by your foot." She looked down, and sure enough, there was a lizard by her foot. She didn't know how or when it got in, but she was glad this young man was the one who found it. If she had come upon it unexpectedly, the entire restaurant would have known about it.

These things come up as you go through life. Sometimes you wonder, Can this really be happening to me? When they're funny experiences, we can enjoy them; but every so often life takes a turn on us.

ECKANKAR is a step on the path to God. It is often presented to the public as the Ancient Science of Soul Travel, a descriptive phrase that arouses people's curiosity. It also gives an indication of at least one of the powers of Soul, which is movement.

I Am Soul

The orthodox religions in our society have misled people for centuries by presenting the concept of Soul as something one possesses. When they say, "my soul," who do they think is saying "my"? Is their physical body claiming to have a Soul? Such a viewpoint is a perversion of truth.

In ECK we know it is the other way around. Therefore we say, "I am Soul, and I have a physical body." When we come to the realization that we are Soul, an eternal being, and that we have a body, a temporary vehicle that eventually wears out, it changes the way we look at life.

While we live in the human body, it is a temple of God, to be kept clean and used here on earth in the most useful and uplifting ways possible. But really it is a vehicle, a medium that Soul uses to come into the physical world and get experience.

Soul is not able to gain experience in the lower worlds except by using a body that matches the substance of the plane It is on. This holds true for the Physical, Astral, Causal, Mental, and Etheric planes, until you come to the Soul Plane.

"The Ancient Science of Soul Travel" is an easy way to answer someone who asks, "What is ECKANKAR?" You'll get one of two reactions: Either the person will want to hear more, or he'll raise his eyebrows and try to figure out how to get away as fast as possible.

A Window for ECK

The consciousness has lifted considerably since 1965, when Paul Twitchell brought out the teachings of ECK. In those days a window was created because of the Vietnam War. People were exposed to the realities of death. So many American young men were sent off to fight for an ideal they sometimes didn't even understand, and nobody seemed to appreciate it when they made the ultimate sacrifice of their lives.

There was an openness in the consciousness in the United States and throughout the world—a need for new ideas. Thus, ECKANKAR, the Ancient Science of Soul Travel, was able to slip into the twentieth century almost unannounced.

In the years since then, the consciousness has grown. People have come to know that there are techniques by which one can enter into the Kingdom of Heaven in this lifetime. This means attaining the state of God-Realization.

Although God-Realization is a possibility for each individual, only those who are ready will find it. It is not a good idea to say, I am a God-Realized being; come and hear what I have to say about it.

When you find a religious teaching that suits you, live it to the fullest. Be the best you can in it. You owe it to yourself to be fully alive. All too often, church members who pride themselves on being followers of God approach their religion as a Sunday-morning occupation. The rest of the week God is mostly forgotten.

In my travels I visit a lot of bookstores. I have found that the good books on any subject not only endure through time, they make their way to the ends of the earth.

In South Africa, which is about as far south as you can go in that part of the world, I've seen some good books on religion and philosophy. The people are knowledgeable and, in a way, proud of the isolation that has forced them to rely on their own resources. If they have a problem, they have to work it out for themselves, not only as individuals but even as nations.

In the United States we are used to having close neighbors. There's always somebody nearby to bounce ideas around with. We have more interaction with the nations around us. But when you get to the ends of the earth, some of this communication slows down.

I went into a bookstore and had to fight my way through the overwhelming scent of incense. The shelves were loaded with books on out-of-body travel, Krishna, and Christian Gnosticism. The owner played a tape of guitar music, and I enjoyed it as I leisurely browsed the shelves.

As I was heading out the door, the owner came over and started a conversation. "Are you in town on business?" she asked.

"Well, sort of," I said.

"What's the name of your company?"

I said, "ECKANKAR."

That drew a complete blank. "What's that?" she asked.

I said, "The Ancient Science of Soul Travel."

Two things happened at once. First of all, she took a step back. Secondly, it was as if a visor or an iron mask surrounding her head suddenly split down the front and opened all the way, allowing a light to come flowing out of her. It was interesting to watch as the hardness in her face turned to softness.

She just stood there looking at me. Finally I said, "Well, I'll probably see you sometime," and then I left. There is plenty of opportunity for her to find out more about ECKANKAR. If she's the least bit inquisitive and if she is supposed to learn more, she'll find a way to take the next step.

Levels of Consciousness

Not long ago, we had an Evening with ECK in New Zealand. The people in the audience were somewhat skeptical. They seemed to have more of an interest in the occult than the spiritual aspects of the path of ECK, such as the Light and Sound of God.

I tried to explain how the Holy Spirit works through different levels of consciousness, such as the Christ Consciousness, Buddha consciousness, cosmic consciousness, or Krishna consciousness. Another level that we know in ECK is the Mahanta Consciousness. When you do the Spiritual Exercises of ECK, the Mahanta, the Inner Master, appears at the Third Eye, usually in the Light body or as a shining Blue Light.

This being has the power to bring you the Light and Sound of God. These two aspects of the Holy Spirit enter into the human body and the individual Soul, and they uplift and purify the mind for the freedom of Soul. This is the sequence that must occur—first the purification of the mind, and then comes the liberation of Soul.

I also spoke about death. I pointed out that if you can gain the Kingdom of Heaven here and now, you will be ready to go over very smoothly and easily when the time comes. But if you have no knowledge of the life hereafter other than what you have read in books and the Bible, you might find it more difficult to make the transition.

What Does Death Mean?

Death used to bother me when I was about four or five years old. In our country church, nothing was hidden from the children; funerals were accessible to grown-ups and children alike. When my grandfather died, the undertaker came out to the house, took the body away, and brought it back a day later all dressed up in Sunday best with cheeks rouged to a lifelike pink. Then the body was kept on display until the funeral.

The next morning, a bunch of people came to the house to view the body in the casket. "What a fine job they did on him," everyone said. "Doesn't he just look alive?" I didn't know what they were talking about. Grandpa looked stone-dead to me.

The funeral was handled very smoothly. The casket was loaded into a hearse, and everyone headed for the church. There, the opened casket was placed at the front of the church so that everybody could get a last look and have a good cry.

The attitude concerning funerals and death is based on a misunderstanding about the nature of Soul, which exists even beyond eternity. When we cry at funerals, we cry for ourselves. I've cried at funerals, too, and I'll probably do it in the future. Naturally we miss our loved ones, but the fact is, the loved one who has left here is delighted to be gone.

As a five-year-old boy back in Wisconsin, I tried to grasp what it meant to be dead. I'd pinch my skin until it hurt, thinking that one day it wouldn't hurt at all and wondering if they were going to put *me* in that dark hole in the ground. I didn't like that idea at all. Ashes to ashes, dust to dust—how depressing to think my life would end like that.

The Purpose of ECK

I searched for years through a lot of different things before eventually finding the answers to my questions, but that doesn't necessarily mean ECKANKAR will answer yours. The Ancient Science of Soul Travel is designed for one purpose: to take you by your own path, at your own speed, back to God. We all want to go at our own pace, and we all will.

During the talk in New Zealand, one woman said she'd had a guardian angel for as long as she could remember— a man in a long flowing robe. The reason she came to the ECK talk was because he told her this was her next step. She went on to say, "What do I do with my guardian angel once he transfers me to the ECK Masters?"

I had been trying to explain to the audience about the Inner Master, and this lady's experience provided an example. I assured her that she didn't have to worry about her guardian angel: he had plenty of others to work with.

I reminded her that consciousness forms a matrix; and whether it shows up as a guardian angel, the Christ Consciousness, the Mahanta Consciousness, or any other state of consciousness, it is merely a form which the Holy Spirit, the ECK, uses to reach each person at his present level. When you are ready for a higher step on the path, then Spirit—the master who brought you to that point—will turn you over to somebody who can take you further.

The masters you see inwardly do not conflict with each other; they work in harmony with each other. Even the negative power, sometimes called Satan, known as Kal

Niranjan in the ECK writings, is working for the divine cause. Each of these beings, no matter how positive or negative, is bringing about some degree of purification of Soul at some level. That is why we never concern ourselves about someone leaving the path of ECK.

Following Only One Path

You can really follow only one path at a time. You owe it to yourself to choose only one, whatever it is. It's not possible to follow two paths at the same time and do yourself justice.

Each religious or spiritual teaching is made up of its own unique energy currents. If you try to follow more than one path at the same time, these currents begin to pull on the inner Emotional and Mental bodies. Eventually the different currents will tear you apart with doubt, cause health problems, and other things like this.

If you are a member of a particular church, follow the teachings with your whole heart. When you grow out of it, when you are able to weather the storm of attacks by people who would try to hold you to that church, then you can take the step beyond it to a new way of life.

This step will be difficult for some of you. For others, who have fewer attachments to people of their old denomination, it is easier to move on quickly and freely. The fewer attachments you have to the things of this world, the easier it is for you to move forward into the worlds of God, into the high consciousness, into receiving the Light and Sound of God.

The Workings of Guilt

While doing some research at a library in New Zealand, I came across a story about guilt. Guilt is a curious thing. It can be caused in many different ways, and a person who wants something from us will often use it as a tool to make us work against ourselves.

A writer of books on the occult and Eastern religions was traveling in India. He had to get to the train station by a certain time, but the cab he had ordered didn't show up. He spotted a pedicab, which is a pedal-driven tricycle with a hooded carriage that carries passengers, and quickly negotiated a fare with the cyclist.

The writer loaded his baggage into the pedicab, climbed in back, and the cyclist went pedaling off. After a while, the writer noticed that the cyclist had to labor harder and harder to keep the pedals turning. He started to feel very guilty. The farther they went, the worse it got, until it began to look like the man was going to work himself into a heart attack. Just as the writer was about ready to yell, "Stop! You ride, and I'll pedal!" they arrived at the train station.

Several Indian men were sitting around watching as the cart pulled up and the weary cyclist dismounted. They recognized the game and couldn't help wondering how much their countryman was going to make from the unsuspecting foreigner. The writer was so guilt-ridden that, naturally, he generously overtipped the cyclist. The Indian men sitting outside the station chuckled and winked at each other. It was obvious they admired the pedaler's cunning and scorned the traveler.

Realizing he had been tricked, the writer made an interesting observation. "Guilt," he said, "was the meat of this transaction."

So often you find this is true. You go into a restaurant, get bad service, and overtip because you are expected to leave 15 percent, and you'll feel guilty if you don't. It would be working against the social consciousness, and you might feel as though you hadn't done your duty.

Guilt is bred into us, and not just in this lifetime. The unconscious memories from past lives come with us, too. Wherever we walk, whatever we do, we have clouds of guilt hanging over us. They are chains on Soul that make us waste our resources and do things against our will. With all that energy being diverted from our spiritual goals, is it any wonder that there is so much unhappiness and poverty?

Liberation Takes Effort

ECKANKAR does not promise to make you healthy, wealthy, and wise, but the Spiritual Exercises of ECK will raise your state of consciousness. However, it won't happen automatically; it will take work on your part. Most of us want something without putting in any effort.

This is the age of instant foods and the microwave oven. But certain skills require that you put in your time. For example, I don't know anybody who can teach you how to swim instantly. To win a race of endurance, you have to practice. In some manner you have to pay in the true coin, or you will never have a chance at victory.

This holds true in every endeavor. You can fool yourself by saying the instant foods are as nutritious as the vegetables you get from your garden. But it is a mistake to try to transfer this concept to your spiritual life, to take the attitude that if somebody can promise you instant success and an immediate cure for your pain and unhappiness, then you will follow him to the ends of the earth. Not that it wouldn't be nice—if somebody could really do it.

Positive Thinking and the Psychic Element

In the early 1950s, Norman Vincent Peale wrote books on the power of positive thinking. His techniques brought upliftment to many people. But the power of positive thinking is temporary; someday it will reverse and fall back on itself.

The principles that work for a while will eventually fail, because they deal with the psychic element. Prayer and psychic healing are also based on an unstable force.

There's a gentleman who does healings using the psychic force. Although he has cured several people, his own health has taken quite a beating. But he doesn't seem to mind. He has chosen to use his own body as a laboratory for learning more about life and the things that try to curtail it. People who do psychic healings have asked me if it's OK to keep doing this. Even if I advised them to stop, they would continue to do it anyway. This is just how people are.

We do what we want to do because we feel we know ourselves better than anyone else. We think our life is built on the principles of truth. But our way is often based on bad habits, ignorance, and any number of other things which cause our ailments.

Health Situations

A woman came up to me in New Zealand and complained that she had a great deal of congestion in her head. She was all stuffed up. Generally I don't comment to people about their health, but every so often I throw out an idea and see if they catch it. I said, "Have you had any of the dairy products while you've been here in New Zealand?" Some people are highly allergic to dairy products.

"Oh, yes," she said. "They are just wonderful!"

In an oblique way, I tried one more time. "I've heard that dairy products can cause congestion."

"That can't be the problem," she said. "We live on a farm, and I eat dairy products all the time."

115

I dropped it then. She didn't realize that although she had built up her tolerance to a certain level, the travel and change from her customary eating habits had thrown her system out of balance.

She could have remedied it very quickly by laying off the dairy products for a few days, but she was so sure she knew better that she didn't listen. It would have been easy to take her by the shoulders, shake her, and say, "If you want to get rid of that problem, stop eating dairy foods for a few days, and you'll see an improvement." But I can't do that, and I don't want to do it.

Knowing the Laws

When we operate in ignorance of any law—whether spiritual, physical, nutritional, economic, or any other kind—we are going to suffer for it. We like to kid ourselves that our difficulties arise because we are unfolding so fast spiritually, or because of psychic attacks from other people, but that isn't necessarily so.

When you are on the true path to God, you still have to pay the piper. You're paying your own debts, not somebody else's. The main difference is that now you are paying them faster than you would have before.

The path of ECK is a path of total responsibility for every action that you take. Actions have consequences. When you start practicing the Spiritual Exercises of ECK, you begin to learn how to dry up the stream of karma. These exercises start working to open the inner body to a direct pipeline to the Holy Spirit, so that the Light and Sound can enter into an individual and bring changes. But you have to keep up with the exercises or nothing will happen.

It is not enough just to do them mechanically; you have to put all your heart and love into any approach to God.

116

When you want to approach the Lord of all worlds, you must come in pure humbleness of Spirit. Too many of us are unwilling to do that. Often we don't even know what it means. We already think of ourselves as humble, and we'd be very angry if anybody tried to ruin our self-image.

A Disturbing History

The history upon which some of the churches are built is disturbing. The Inquisition started around the thirteenth century. It might seem that such ancient history wouldn't have anything to do with us today, but it does.

Many of us lived in the Middle Ages and went through the Inquisition in one way or another, either as victim or persecutor. Maybe we testified against a defendant and caused his doom. This was often done for a price or to gain favor with state or church. Sometimes out of fear of being accused of heresy, a person would point the finger of guilt at someone else. Memories like these are imbedded in our consciousness, and so we walk around in a swirling sea of unconscious guilt complexes, frustration, and anger.

The path of ECK brings the Light and Sound of God into the human consciousness. Thus begins the purification process whereby these aberrations pass off into the Audible Life Stream, which is the Holy Spirit. When you have the Second Initiation in ECK after two years of study, the chances are very good that you will have some experience with either the Inner Master or the Light and Sound.

Working Toward Initiation

You are not given the ECK initiation as soon as you walk in the door. People are often quite disappointed to learn that they have to study for two years before the initiation comes. But someone new in ECK needs time to strengthen his spiritual legs.

The First Initiation, which takes place in the dream state, actually comes within a year. It is done purely by the Inner Master, which is a manifestation of the Holy Spirit. This individual is there to escort you into one of the inner heavens, a plane very close to earth, to give you an experience that fits your spiritual unfoldment at that time. Mainly it is to provide you with proof that you are Soul, that Soul exists beyond life in the physical body, and that as Soul you can conquer death.

Like Gideon's Three Hundred

The ECK Masters look for people who are like Gideon's army of three hundred from the story in the Old Testament.

Gideon was to lead the Israelites in battle against the Midianites, but the Israelite army was far greater in number than the enemy's. Jehovah, the God of the Old Testament, knew that if Gideon went to battle with so many soldiers, it would be a sure victory, and the Israelites would want to take all the credit for it. They would never believe they were helped by a divine force.

Jehovah is only one of the lower lords, incidentally; a servant of the SUGMAD, the highest God. Jehovah was to put the Israelite soldiers through a test—a purification process—to help them realize their victory was achieved not of their own will but because of the divine power. The first step was to reduce the size of the army.

Jehovah instructed Gideon to announce to the soldiers that anyone who was afraid could go home. Two-thirds of the army left.

The remaining soldiers still outnumbered the Midianites. Jehovah then told Gideon to bring the men down to the river and have them drink some water. Most of the men set aside their shields and weapons, got down on all fours, and put their heads to the water to drink.

But three hundred of the soldiers were more careful. They knelt down on one knee, cupped the water with one hand, and held on to their shields and swords with the other—all the while keeping an eye out for the enemy.

Jehovah had Gideon tell all the others they could take the rest of the weekend off. By now, of course, the Midianites vastly outnumbered the Israelite army.

Three hundred men can't just march out and take on an army of two thousand, so they had to make careful plans. First, Gideon and one of his men snuck into the enemy camp to look it over. They returned to their own camp with a great strategy. The three hundred soldiers were divided into three companies of one hundred, and each man was provided with nothing but a trumpet in one hand and a pitcher that hid a blazing torch in the other.

The Israelites surrounded the enemy camp. When every man was in place, Gideon gave the signal. Each soldier began to blow his trumpet as he broke his pitcher and held up a blazing torch. Then all at once, the three hundred soldiers shouted a deafening battle cry.

You know how it is when you're startled awake in the middle of the night. The Midianites didn't know what was going on. They were so confused by all the lights and the noise that they began to run wild, bumping into each other and whacking away at each other with their swords.

Meanwhile, the Israelites stayed on the hillside around the camp and kept blowing their trumpets and yelling. Every so often some of the enemy soldiers would try to escape, but the Israelites easily handled them.

Creative Imagination

This was a curious way to illustrate a lesson—that the real help in life doesn't come from our human state of consciousness; it comes when we contact the divine state of consciousness. In ECK we call it the creative imagination.

It sounds paradoxical, but when we have a problem, we don't call on God to solve it for us. We dig into our own resources, knowing that the solution to every problem is hidden within the problem itself. This is all there is to it.

Most of you may not believe it, but if you're poor, somehow you have the ability to pull yourself out of the hole. For too long we have been led to believe that some omnipotent power might miraculously appear and hand us a million dollars. People like to dream about winning a big sweepstakes, and occasionally some do.

But why waste your life dreaming about someday when you can be building your own world now? This is something you are going to have to learn before you can leave the lower worlds of karma and reincarnation.

The only way we can buy our way out of here is by the accumulation of good karma. In ECK this means doing all things in the name of the Mahanta—or in the name of God. You can simply say, "I am not doing this action for my own benefit or for the benefit of anyone else; I am doing this in the name of God." Then you go and do it, and you don't worry about it.

Drying Up the Karmic Stream

This is the way we start to dry up the karmic stream that runs through us. As it dries up, the conditions of our life have to change. It won't always be for the better at first, because as we begin working off karma, we also gain the capacity to work off more. By the time one reaches the Second or Third Initiation, which usually means after two to five years in ECK, much of the karma has begun to work off. We find that we are better able to live this life and to move forward with happiness and confidence as we make our way to God.

I wish I could promise you a smooth and easy way to God, but it's not true. Anything worth getting is won the hard way. You have to earn it. And once you have earned it, the way is opened for you to find the path.

Inner Link

I don't shake hands with you too often because the outer touch is not really needed. The real link on the path of ECK is with the Inner Master. It is the image you see when you shut your eyes and go into contemplation. Each evening or each morning, for twenty minutes, simply close your eyes and sing HU or one of the other names of God. Sing it quietly to yourself. And do it with love.

If you wish to approach God, you must first be filled with love. If you are filled with fear, frustration, or any of the lower negative states, you will have nothing but failure.

The Importance of Love

One way to fill yourself with love is by recalling the image of something from the past that brought great happiness to you. Use this as a conductor for love. Ask yourself, Where is the key to love? This is a discipline and you must find a solution for yourself. But if you start looking for it, you will find it, and the way will be different for each of you.

Without love, you cannot take one step on the path to God. You've got to have at least a little love before you can even begin to accept the teachings of ECK. But as you get a little and persevere with the teachings of ECK, you are given a talent. Use it well and you will be given another, and another.

If you start with a little love, as you grow you will get more and more. One day you will become a Master who has had the God-Realized state, and perhaps gone even beyond to the Akshar state. Beings of this nature are filled with love and compassion to a degree that we find hard to believe.

Their love and compassion is so great that if they walked among men, the reaction would be to attack them, without even knowing why. The human consciousness isn't able to withstand the full power and love of the Light and Sound of God. This is why most ECK Masters generally stay in the background, in seclusion.

No matter what path you choose, don't go around half-conscious or unconscious. You owe it to yourself to give this life a good whirl, to put everything into it, and to make it worth living. You owe it to yourself as a spiritual being to enjoy the richness and fullness of this life.

Hawaiian Regional Seminar, Honolulu, Hawaii, November 16, 1984

Like the fellow with the hang glider, if your fears are holding you back, unconsciously you will tip the wing too high in the wind, go bouncing back, and end up in a tangled wreckage.

8

I Came Here to Fly

The title of this talk, "I Came Here to Fly," means I came here to learn how to live right—to go forward instead of backward.

Wealth and health are areas of concern for many people. Part of my job is to show how the spiritual principles can be applied to any part of this life. When we have bad health or not enough money, it's too easy to say, "It's because the Kal is attacking me."

The Law of Economy

We can kid ourselves all we want, but the spiritual law is that we have to pay, in some way, for everything we get. This comes under the Law of Economy, which operates in the lower worlds up to the Mental Plane. Higher laws, such as the Law of Love, prevail in the spiritual worlds, but down here we are in the worlds of dichotomies—lack or plenty, highs and lows, riches and poverty.

Karma and reincarnation come under the Law of Economy. If you direct your spiritual energies in the most straightforward way, always keeping in mind where you

125

are going, you will get through these rebirths faster than if you get sidetracked.

You pick a goal, such as God-Realization. Then you open yourself to the Holy Spirit, the ECK, and make your way directly through life to accomplish the goal. There will be help along the way. You take it as it comes, even though it may not seem to fit into your beliefs up to that time.

The Law of Economy starts down here in the physical. Many times we are broke simply because we don't use our resources correctly. Once at dinner I saw a good example of the Law of Economy. A friend and I were having soda water. All of a sudden he said, "Squeeze the straw."

I said, "Why should I squeeze the straw?"

It seems this fellow likes to get the most from everything. He had discovered a way to enhance the taste of a drink while fooling the body into thinking it was getting more. Whenever he gets a soft drink, he squeezes the straw on top and takes big, long drinks to force the liquid through the smaller opening.

After looking around to make sure no one was watching, I tried it with the soda water. Sure enough, by the time I drank an eighth of a glass, I was full. And it really tasted good.

Leaks in the Dike

Sometimes we are broke because of leaks in the financial dike. Picture a little Dutch boy standing in front of this huge dike. All of a sudden he sees a leak, so he runs over and plugs it with his finger. The water is so cold that he starts turning blue. But the little boy is on a mission to save his country, and he will not leave the dike.

In the meantime he begins to notice more leaks. Pretty soon he's wondering if it's worth it to try to hold back one leak. Now it looks like the whole dike might come crashing down around him. This is when he pulls his finger out and runs screaming through the town, "Leaks all over the dike! Leaks all over the dike!" This brings help from other people, of course, so his effort alone doesn't save the day.

That's how it sometimes happens with money. It dribbles away here and there—we don't actually know where it all goes. And when we can't stop the flood, we pound on the doors of Spirit, "Oh Holy Spirit, I am poor, I am broke. Please, *please* change my luck." We do this when we haven't learned the law of Spirit that says, Whatever you get must be earned in the true coin.

Changing Conditions

If you are in a bad financial position, it's not going to change overnight. The mental conditions you have grown up with, that you have let strengthen over the years, don't just magically disappear. Even if someone comes up to you with a way to start pulling yourself out of the hole, you won't recognize it if your mind is still filled with blocks against the blessings of the Holy Spirit.

When you wear the mantle of heaven, everything begins to straighten out. I don't mean to say this is the path of total opportunity and no problems; it's not quite like that. But there is a way to get yourself out of poverty and into the richness of Spirit. And once you get yourself into this state, it will begin to work its way down into all the worlds, into every department of your life. It can't help but do that. As above, so below.

This doesn't mean that each of you is going to be satisfied with the same amount of richness as another person. Some of us have fewer needs, so we can be happier with a lot less. But whatever the case, we have to realize

127

that what we have at any given time is exactly what we've earned up to that point. We might as well accept that fact; otherwise we are living the great illusion—playing a trick on ourselves.

We are not the victims of luck or anything else. What we are today is the result of our own actions and thoughts. The best that we have ever been in all of our lifetimes sits here now. And this is not always easy to accept. It certainly upset me the first time I thought of it that way. I couldn't help but think back to lives where I was taller, handsomer, and richer, and I said, You mean this is it? The greatness of all the lifetimes sits here?

It Helps to Ask

If you want something from life, first of all you have to earn it. But you also have to be open to the gifts life is willing to give you, and that means you have to ask for them.

All too often we don't like to ask. I'm often that way, even when it comes to simply asking for assistance from a sales clerk in a clothing store. People who go shopping with me don't hesitate to walk right up to a sales clerk and say, "Do you have blue slacks in a certain size and blend of material?" It's much quicker than the process I go through. As soon as I walk into a store, I begin to study the layout, check to see what kind of lighting system they have, and other things that most people consider nonessential. But I like to get the flavor of the clothes I'm going to wear.

A friend of mine was going on a trip, and his wife drove him to the airport. Since they had a little time before the plane left, they decided to go to a pizza parlor at the far end of the terminal and have a pizza.

128

As luck would have it, after they placed their order, the proprietor came out of the kitchen and said, "The oven isn't working. We're trying to get it going now, but it will be at least fifteen minutes before we can even put your pizza in."

That wouldn't have left the man enough time to make his flight. But instead of mumbling and grumbling about it, he jokingly said to the proprietor, "Well, this ought to be worth something."

The proprietor responded immediately. "How about next time you come in, you get a free pizza?"

"That would be fine," the couple said. The proprietor validated the offer by handing them his business card with a note on it good for one complimentary pizza.

When my friend returned from his trip, he and his wife took the card in, presented it to the waiter, and got a free pizza. The proprietor was happy because he was able to satisfy the customers, and the customers left happy; so they were all served well. It never hurts to ask, because somebody just might say yes.

Life might say yes, too. A lot of times the bounties of the Holy Spirit are held back from us simply because we don't ask. We want something to come into our life, and we just sit around and wait.

But if you ask for it, be sure you know what you're asking for. You may have to earn it, even the hard way; but by asking, at least you have opened the door. And if it is not for your well-being, the Holy Spirit in Its infinite wisdom will help you to know in some way that this is not for you.

Taking the Steps to a Goal

By making a request, you put it into the ECK, but then you have to take the steps to figure out what you must do to earn it.

An ECKist bought a car. After he took it home and thought about it, he realized he should have negotiated to have a ski rack put on. But it was too late now; the sale was final, and he had no more bargaining power.

So he had a little conversation with the ECK. "I'd really like a ski rack," he said. There's no reason you can't have a happy, friendly relationship with the Holy Spirit.

Soon after that he went to visit a friend. As he left to go home, he noticed a ski rack sitting on top of the trash pile. "Wow!" he said. "You ask the ECK and here it is!" He said to his friend, "Can I have this ski rack?" The friend said, "Sure, but it's not in very good condition." It looked OK to him, so he took it home.

Later, when he examined it in a better light, he saw that it really wasn't in very good condition at all. The rubber molding that fits against the car had torn loose and needed to be reglued, and one of the suction cups had come off. He now had the ski rack he wanted, but he hadn't said how good it had to be.

A few days later he was visiting with his father-in-law. As he was leaving, his father-in-law said, "By the way, I've got this brand-new ski rack. Since I don't need it, I wonder if you would like it." The fellow's face lit right up.

Going Forward

As I mentioned earlier, "I came here to fly" means I came here to do it right: to go forward instead of backward, and to learn how to do it in the most direct way.

When Soul comes into the lower worlds, Its one mission is to gain the experience It needs to eventually become a Co-worker with God. It's that simple. This is the reason for all the things you put up with as you are learning.

Being a Co-worker with God doesn't mean being a servant or a do-gooder. It means when the time is right, in some way you will be able to answer a call that goes out from another Soul within the body of the Holy Spirit. It may be something small, such as giving a cookie to a child, but you do it simply because at that time the child needs a cookie.

A Custom-made Path

Someone asked, "How can I know if I can have God-Realization in this lifetime?" Actually, not everybody is going to get God-Realization in this lifetime, because not everybody wants it badly enough. Most people want it as long as the price isn't too great, and the price of God-Realization is different for all of us.

Each of you is on a custom-made path. The ECK writings give only a guideline. Each person sees the same words, but the difference is in the individual perception that you have as Soul, as a unique spark of God.

This understanding comes from an area that is beyond the mind. As an individual spark of God, your understanding of what you read will be based on the sum of the experiences in your life, not someone else's. And because your perceptions are unique, your way back to God is going to be made-to-order.

So in answer to the question, "How can I know if I can have God-Realization in this lifetime?" all I can do is point to the Spiritual Exercises of ECK.

Recently I requested that introductory discussion classes on the ECK books be limited to six weeks. Some people feel these classes should go on for a year. But what good are you doing for yourself or for other people? The class members should have an opportunity to move into another area. When you're getting close to the end of the discussion class, just say, "This is going to be over in about two weeks. Let's start thinking about what we want to do next. If you want, we can have another book discussion class for six more weeks. Which book do you want to use?" In other words, don't get locked in to anything.

Soul enjoys change. We in the human body tend to resist change because we are usually under the control and power of the mind. When change comes into our life, such as the loss of a job or a death in the family, we don't like it.

But while we struggle in the human consciousness with the problems of change, in the highest sense we, as Soul, are delighted. Our emotions and our mind may be distraught and upset, but Soul is a happy entity. It knows there is never really any separation of Soul from Its loved ones or any beings in the worlds of God.

Breaking the Web of Illusion

Misunderstandings about gods and lords often come to us from the traditional religious teachings. For instance, Jehovah, whom we know in ECKANKAR as Jot Niranjan, is the lord of the heaven immediately above the earth plane—not a very high one at all.

There is a lord assigned to each plane. He is in complete charge of that particular plane, and he also designates the lord of the next plane below. Each of the lords sets up a whole chain of command to carry out the duties of seeing to the education of Soul.

All kinds of psychic waves are thrown loose in the world for this very purpose. We get caught up in these waves. They lead to fears about nuclear war, worry about the ecology, and plans to save the whales. I doubt if anyone tried very hard to save the dinosaurs. They chomped away at a lot of us in our past lives—and so today we don't like lizards.

Jehovah, the angry God of the Old Testament, is an entirely different being from the loving God of the New Testament. The Christian is taught that they are one and the same God, but their characteristics are completely different.

We take things so seriously because the lord who rules over this plane is able to throw a web of illusion over us. He rules by fear. Like the Wizard of Oz, he stands off to one side. He's like a little old man controlling his kingdom with his voice amplified to sound loud and powerful. He has everybody so shook up that they're not sure if they want to go down the yellow brick road or not. And it's the same way with the gods of the other planes.

Many ECKists have the ability to rise above this web of illusion through Soul Travel, the movement of Soul in Its state of consciousness from the Physical Plane to other planes. You go first to the Astral Plane. Once the essential things have been learned there, you go on to the Causal Plane to learn about the past lives that have an influence on you today. Then you go beyond that to the Mental Plane, and so on. Once you begin to learn about the hierarchy that exists on the other planes and its place in God's plan, then you no longer fight or resist it but learn to work with it.

People today are trying to understand the role of Satan in relation to the Christian idea of God, and it's kind of a standoff. Who's going to win? Well, ultimately we know that God will win. But we wonder, Why is Satan so strong? The negative power is strong because it is a servant of the Divine Power, and its sole purpose is to train Soul. This is why we are run through the mill in every way—given hardships, tempted, cheated.

There is an old saying, "You can't cheat an honest man." But you can always cheat somebody who is trying to get something for nothing. It happens a lot when you think you're saving money on a bargain. You find out real quickly that the bargain clothes don't fit or the cheap car doesn't run.

You learn that you have to pay for the quality you expect to get; but you can be wise enough not to get cheated into paying more than it's worth. On the spiritual path, your discrimination becomes finer.

Finding the Pearls of Wisdom

Once upon a time, Jot Niranjan went on a long journey to the outer reaches of his worlds. When he returned home, all of his servants were feasting in the great banquet hall. The negative power is very good to his helpers.

He had been away from his kingdom on the Astral Plane for quite a while. Now that he was back, he saw through new eyes, and it was clear to him that his subjects had been stealing from him while he was gone. Jot Niranjan was really disturbed, but he didn't show it. He had taken on a very benign appearance for the party; his servants saw him as a small, kindly old man. But his intense blue eyes roamed continually up and down the long banquet table, and they didn't miss a thing.

The servants were unaware that their lord had something on his mind. They just went on having a good time, drinking his wine and eating the abundance of food on the table.

When the meal was over, he called for their attention. He sounded very serious. They began to suspect he was displeased about something, and everybody became nervous. Remember, their comfortable stations in life depended upon pleasing this lord.

Jehovah began to speak, and his voice sounded a warning to them. "First I took you in," he said. "I lifted you from the gutters, gave you work, and provided you with plenty of food, good clothing, and enough to take care of your loved ones. But was that enough for you? No!" His subjects were trembling by this time.

He went on: "Next you wanted me to take care of your spouses. OK, I did it. But then you wanted me to care for people who didn't even live under the same roof—your uncles, aunts, nephews, nieces, and even some cousins. All right, I'm easy—I did it.

"But were you satisfied with that? No! Now you want me to include your cats and dogs." His voice rose in anger: "This is too much! I won't do it!"

He stood up and waved his arms over the table. "And look at all this food. You've wasted half of it!" He was talking about the Law of Economy, and people on the Astral Plane have to be approached at the emotional level.

He was trying to make them understand that life extracts an exactitude from everyone and everything in it. You can call it karma or anything else, but the fact is, you are going to have to pay for everything you get in the true coin. Now his very own subjects were wasting his resources.

He said, "You know, you would be better off if you had to go down in the tunnel to see how the meat is slaughtered. If you saw both the good and the bad, and you had to work with that mess up to your knees, you would realize that these things don't come so easily."

The people just sat there very quietly now. "Uh oh," they said, "the old man is mad. We'd better cool it." As quickly as possible, they left the table.

One Soul alone remained seated. He was no longer interested in preserving his position of wealth in the kingdom of Jehovah. He approached the Lord. "You mentioned a tunnel that goes down to where all this good food came from," he said. "Is there really such a place?"

"Why, yes," said Jot Niranjan, obviously pleased with the man's question, "there most certainly is." He can be agreeable at times; he's not always the angry God as depicted in the Old Testament.

"Well, where is it?" the subject asked.

Jot Niranjan said, "The entrance is in that storage shed over there. But it's all jammed up with old equipment."

The subject said, "I'd really like to see it."

"Are you sure?" Jot Niranjan was testing him now. "It's like a sewer in there—full of filth and scum. You have to scrunch over to get down in there. Think about it. Are you sure?"

"Oh, yes," said the servant. "I really want to see it."

Jot Niranjan led his subject over to the shed. He began to remove a huge stack of old bags and trunks that were piled up on top of a heavy metal cover. He then slid back the cover to reveal a dark hole in the ground that was every bit as foul as he had described.

But this particular Soul was determined to know what was down there. Bracing himself, he crawled into the hole. Jot Niranjan called after him, "Head east, and just keep going."

The individual moved cautiously, bent over to keep from scraping the roof of the tunnel. He felt his way along the walls and tried not to fall down into the slime. Finally, after what seemed like a very long time, he saw a light at the end of the tunnel. He continued to make his way

136

toward it until, at long last, he stepped out of the darkness and straightened his back.

This tunnel was a path, masked behind a facade of dirt and filth, that led to a higher world. Those who were interested in the easy life would never have considered looking for it, and even if they found it, they wouldn't have walked through it. But this Soul wanted God-Realization. He knew there had to be a way out of the Astral Plane, the first heaven, and he found it.

As he came out of the tunnel, into a beautiful kingdom of pearls and diamonds and light, the voice of Jot Niranjan echoed behind him: "The pearls of wisdom in my kingdom are put where only the humble in station will find them." This Soul was now ready to become established on the next higher plane.

This is how we make our way through the different worlds of God. There will come a time when our attachment to the pleasures we find around us is broken. But we can still enjoy them, simply because life is giving us all of its bounty. If we are the good stewards of what it gives us, then eventually we can find our way to the spiritual worlds. The way is always through the Spiritual Exercises of ECK.

The Fallacy behind Some Biblical Stories

Too many are willing to follow Jehovah with blind faith. They completely miss the fallacy behind some of the Biblical stories, such as the sacrifice of Isaac by his father, Abraham, the patriarch of the Old Testament.

Life was good for the people of Abraham. Everything was going smoothly. Then one day Jot Niranjan, or Jehovah, called down to him.

"Abraham," he said, "I need a sacrifice."

137

"No problem. I've got a couple of extra rams around here." Abraham was a good sheepherder.

But the Lord God Jehovah said, "No, I have something else in mind this time."

"Anything you want," said Abraham. "Just ask so that I can show you that I love, trust, and believe in you."

"All right," said Jehovah. "This time I want you to sacrifice your son, Isaac."

"Oh, no!" said Abraham. "Not Isaac!"

Jehovah said something like, "I have spoken," and went away.

This didn't make any sense to Abraham. He had been given a vision of how, from his son, an entire nation would come into being which would last throughout the centuries. If God wanted him to sacrifice his only son Isaac, then what would become of his vision for the future? Yet, if that was what God wanted, he would do it.

Abraham and two of his manservants loaded up a couple of donkeys with the wood that was to be used on the altar, and along with Isaac, they began the three-day journey to the land of Moriah, where the sacrifice would take place.

On the third day of their journey, Isaac turned to his father. "You know, Dad," he said, "we've got the firewood, and we can always find stones to build the altar—but we don't have a lamb."

Abraham's heart was heavy with sorrow as he looked at his son, but all he said was, "Don't worry. The Lord will provide." Isaac, being a good son, didn't say any more. He figured he was only along for the ride.

When they got near the mountaintop where the sacrifice was to take place, Abraham said to his two servants,

"You just wait here. We'll be back in a little while." He wanted to be alone with his son for the last time.

Abraham and Isaac walked up to the top of the mountain. Isaac, of course, was curious. He looked around and didn't see any kind of sacrificial offering, but he didn't say anything; just went ahead and helped his father build the altar of stone. When all the sticks were laid out around it, Abraham tied his son hand and foot and put him on the altar. Isaac, good son that he was, didn't even put up a struggle.

Abraham reluctantly raised the knife. Just when he was ready to bring it down to end the life of his son, which would prove his love and trust in God, an angel of the Lord appeared.

"Abraham, stop! Don't do it! Hold your hand!"

"What for?" said Abraham.

"Because now I know that you love and trust the Lord." The angel then explained that Abraham had been tested by God.

The fallacy in the story is this. God, supposedly being omniscient, all-powerful, and all-knowing, surely should have known that Abraham was faithful and that his whole heart was with God. It couldn't have been a real test if God already knew.

God does know, doesn't He?

Maybe the highest God knows, but some of the lower gods don't know; and maybe that wasn't the real reason for the test.

Some people might say, "Go a little easy on these Biblical stories. These are our patriarchs. The man was trusting in God, so leave well enough alone." But if we just take things at face value, sometimes we lose perspective.

Putting It in Perspective

Let's take the same story into modern times. Imagine Abraham living in South Sea Cliff, U.S.A. He wakes up one Sunday morning, looking forward to watching the college football game that starts at 11:00 a.m. Suddenly the voice of the Lord booms down.

"Abraham!"

"Yes, Lord?"

"Before the college playoffs come on, I want you to go into the backyard. Take the stones left over from when you built your patio, and use them to make an altar of stone."

"Yes, Lord," says Abraham.

"Take your son out there with you. He's big and strong, so I don't know how you're going to do it, but tie him hand and foot and put him on the altar. Then pour some barbecue lighter fluid on him."

Abraham doesn't quite understand the reason for this.

"I want you to sacrifice your son," says God. And then He goes away.

"Oh, no!" says Abraham. This doesn't make any sense to him. He'd always envisioned his only son becoming a quarterback in college. Where does this leave his plans for the future? But he loves and trusts God, so he will do as he's told.

Now imagine that you are Abraham's next-door neighbor. That morning you wake up in your upstairs bedroom and go over to look out the window.

What's that crazy Abraham up to now? Why in the world is he building a stone altar? Pretty soon you see him getting out his barbecue equipment. Now he's putting wood on top of the altar. Then, to your amazement, he wrestles his son to the ground, ties his hands and feet, and puts him on the altar.

140

What should you do? Pray to God or call the police?

Abraham reluctantly picks up a knife. When he's just about ready to plunge it into his son's chest, the Lord stays his hand.

"Abraham, hold your hand!"

"Thank God," says Abraham.

About this time the police arrive at the front door. They run through the house and out to the backyard waving their guns. "Hold it right there! Drop the knife!"

Abraham chuckles. "It's all a mistake, officers," he explains. "You see, the Lord told me to do it, but at the last minute He said I didn't have to. It's OK now. You can go."

If that Biblical episode took place today, Abraham would be carted off to a mental institution. And imagine the newspaper headlines: "Man in weird cult tries to sacrifice son! Stopped in nick of time by police! Man claims God said 'Stop!'" Even the staunchest believers in the Bible wouldn't consider it too pious if they saw some nut ready to sacrifice his son.

The real question is, Would a God who knows everything put a man of such true faith in a spot like this? We must learn to contemplate more about the meaning of the stories that supposedly convey truth.

I bring these points up to make you think. You might not agree with them, they might upset you or make you angry—but examine your beliefs. Make sure that what you believe comes from your heart and not from someone else's lips, including mine.

I Came Here to Fly

I know an individual who once owned a hang glider. Whenever he got the urge, he would take it to a cliff, set it up, and go soaring off with the wind. He usually liked to go by himself, but one day he brought along a friend who had never flown a glider before. That day there was a strong wind blowing.

His friend was so anxious to give it a try that he ignored the instructions of the experienced hang-glider pilot. He took off running with the wing tipped too high. As soon as he got to the edge of the cliff, the wind caught the wing and blew him back.

The man who owned the glider repeated his instructions. "When you run into the wind, dip the wing down a little," he said. "Otherwise the glider could flip back on you." Then, almost as an afterthought, he added, "Remember, if you're going to fly, you don't want to go backward, you want to go forward."

His friend seemed to understand. Once again, he backed up and ran toward the cliff; but again, he neglected to keep the wing down. A strong gust of wind sent him somersaulting back across the field, and he and the glider went bouncing off into the distance.

The guy who owned the hang glider went running after him. When the glider stopped, his friend unhooked the safety harness. That wasn't very wise, because with no weight to secure it, the glider blew off with the wind.

The glider owner hesitated. He had a decision to make. Should he help his friend, or should he go after the hang glider? He looked back and forth, first at his friend, and then at the glider—blowing farther and farther away.

Finally he decided his friend would still be there; he was too dazed to walk. He ran after his hang glider, secured it to himself, and brought it back to where the other man was waiting.

His friend was just sitting there shaking his head. "That thing is really dangerous," he said. "You shouldn't go hang gliding by yourself. Look what happened to me. If you had been up here alone, you might have gotten hurt, and there wouldn't have been anyone around to help you."

The fellow with the glider just looked at his friend for a moment. He was trying to find a way to explain to him that he had failed because he wouldn't pay attention to how it should be done. Finally he said, "Look, I came here to fly, not to fall."

His outlook on life was to focus on the moment. First he took the time to learn how to operate the glider correctly and to study the rules of safety. Then he went forward with confidence, never worrying about what might happen if the wind bounced him back.

The Spiritual Survivor

If you came here to fly, then fly. But if your fears are holding you back, unconsciously you will tip the wing too high in the wind, go bouncing back, and end up in a tangled wreckage. It takes courage to do what you started out to do.

If you came here to fly, you must take responsibility for your own spiritual life. That means if one spiritual exercise doesn't work for you, then you try another. First know where you are going, and then do what it takes to get there. Look for the open doors, and know that there is always a way out.

Wherever you go, expect the most from life, and be willing to pay the price. When you can do this, you will have become the spiritual survivor who will survive under any conditions; and when you have finished your experiences on earth, you will have gained an incredible degree of strength and courage. You will be prepared to face the worlds to come with confidence, knowing you are protected by the hand of the Holy Spirit.

Take your share of drubbings, because within each lesson is hidden the seed of truth which is needed for you to take the step that follows. But you can't take the next step until you take the step that is right here. You must begin where you are now. When you can live your life fully, under the Law of Economy and the Law of Love, you will be qualified to take the next step.

If you ask God to show you truth, but you haven't used your talents today, then you can't expect to find the greater talents and the greater truth tomorrow. The way is always through the Spiritual Exercises of ECK.

May the blessings be.

Hawaiian Regional Seminar, Honolulu, Hawaii, November 17, 1984

If we want to succeed in what we are doing, we have to talk the same language as the people with whom we are working.

9

The Common Language of ECK

We are here to learn spiritual survival. And it is not possible to separate material survival from the spiritual. The lessons we get in our everyday life are what make us stronger spiritually and increase our ability to survive in the high spiritual planes as well as on earth.

People have all kinds of notions about how the Living ECK Master operates. When there is something to be done, the ECK, or Spirit, makes it known. Then it is up to me to carry out what I see and figure a way to make it work. I have to find people who are willing to do it, and determine who can do it best.

Doing Things Simply

Interesting things happen as people grow and unfold to their full potential. For example, if you set an imperfectly unfolded being to a task which is meant to help him unfold spiritually, he'll often ignore a simple way to carry it out and manage to find the hard way.

My dad was a wonderful man in many ways, but he insisted on doing things in an old-fashioned way. When all the other farmers had figured out easier ways to make hay, he still used the methods from a generation past. He seemed to think there was something righteous about doing everything the hard way. He continued to haul in loose hay ten years after everybody else began working with chopped hay, a more highly mechanized method. Ten or fifteen years after everyone else got into baling, he finally got into baling.

Dad could turn the simplest job into a real chore, and he made it quite clear to my brothers and me that his way was the right way. If we didn't sweep out the barn to his satisfaction, getting every bit of dust from all the corners, we'd hear about it.

To demonstrate the proper way to do it, Dad would grab the broom, and in a fit of rage, sweeping against the bristles, he would stir up such a storm of dust that within minutes we would all be coughing. Then, in his funny accent, he would proclaim, "Dere, dat's da way!" and throw down the broom. Dad had quite a knack for destroying brooms. I came to think of my father as the perfect vehicle for training in how to do things the hard way.

Ability to Face the World

A common language is needed for the survival of the spiritual community of ECKists. It's true you are going for God-Realization as an individual, but you don't do it in a vacuum.

The fact is, you have to work with the people around you. Somehow you must gain the cooperation of every being on every plane on your way to the high states of realization. This means the petty little tricks of the mind have to go. If you have anger, hate, and jealousy in a group, there is no way to establish a common language, a common understanding, and a common ideal.

The ECKANKAR staff is developing a common language so that we can all work toward common goals. Hopefully this attitude will then spill over into the field so that we can have common objectives in our ECK activities. Some people will think this is a very good idea, others will be upset by it, and many won't understand what it's all about.

No matter which of the three categories we fall into, as we stumble through life the ECK helps us. By divine grace, we come further along the path, closer to the realization that we are looking for, more able to face the world that we have created for ourselves.

When conflict arises in our personal life, we can handle it in one of two ways: accept the troubles as strengtheners from the Holy Spirit, which is the ECK; or complain that life has dealt us too many low cards from a loaded deck, and conclude that there must be some mistake to the whole plan.

Training with Top Executives

A number of the ECK staff, including myself, signed up to take some administrative courses. This not only provided an opportunity to grow, but gave us a common understanding of administrative practices. The intensive administrative training I attended lasted for six days and put me shoulder to shoulder with top executives from very large companies across the U.S. and Canada.

The meeting was held in a hotel. Forty of us sat at a round table so large that it had to be brought in by sections. Some of the attendees were very hard-nosed types. Over half of them filled the room with smoke from cigars, cigarettes, and pipes; the other half were more enlightened.

The chairman opened the meeting by saying, "Let's have each of you stand up, introduce yourself, and tell us what you do."

I try to be prepared for things like this, but as I found out, you are never really prepared. I sat there sweating as they worked their way around to me. How do you keep your dignity while explaining that you are the spiritual leader of a group they're surely going to consider a cult? Inwardly I was wondering, Why did I get myself into this spot?

Many years ago I'd had a conversation with a shopkeeper. When he asked, "What is ECKANKAR?" I gave him a long speech, trying to avoid the subject of Soul Travel for fear he'd start pelting me with tomatoes. Now I wondered what I might have told the man that he could have understood. Why hadn't I tried harder to come up with a good answer then? It was training in survival that surely would have helped me today.

Finally it was my turn. I hemmed and hawed. I said I was the president of a religious organization—they could relate to that—and gave a rather brief explanation of ECKANKAR. When I sat down, they all looked curiously at me.

The chairman of the meeting was a gnarled old administrator who had been around for years. He was so heavy with materialism that he reminded me of a turtle with a heavy shell. The man expressed definite opinions about me and about groups such as ECKANKAR.

The next day he lost his voice. Nobody could understand it, because when this man was scheduled to talk on a program, he always delivered. But now he couldn't talk at all. He finally started to get his voice back during the last couple of days, but he could barely wheeze out his words, so his talks were short.

Good Communication with Others

The point of the training was survival, but even more than that, if we want to succeed in what we are doing, we have to talk the same language as the people with whom we are working. After six days of intensive work, I returned home filled with new definitions for words such as *objective, commitment, goal, strategy,* and *action plan.* But I found when you use a language that has a specialized use, you're like a stranger in your own country. I saw the value of a common language.

We sent more staff to be trained, to learn the language. From these trainings we have a new management tool: people in the ECK Office who can communicate well with each other about administrative procedures.

It is important for us to use the ECK language among ourselves. Our terminology—words such as *SUGMAD, ECK, ECKANKAR, Arahata,* and *Shariyat-Ki-Sugmad*—has a special meaning for us; it is one of our bonds. But when we are speaking with the public, we use their common language, the English equivalents that they are more familiar with—*Holy Spirit, Holy Ghost, God, the Bible,* or *teacher.* While *Arahata* means something special to us because of our unique way of teaching in ECKANKAR, a word like *teacher,* used in a broader sense, might be more meaningful to others.

Work with the common language that is spoken by the people you talk to. We are looking for a common language in ECK, but at the same time, as we go out into the world to learn ways to survive, we come shoulder to shoulder with our neighbors. We learn from them and they learn from us.

Ashamed of ECK?

No matter who you are or what you say about ECKANKAR, some people are going to think well of you and others are going to think poorly of you. It shows up in a number of different ways. During the breaks at one of the administrative trainings, the other participants approached the ECKists and asked, "What is ECKANKAR all about?" Some of the ECKists came up with very good answers, but others didn't quite know how to explain it in a clear, concise way.

One of the seminar coordinators noticed this. Calling the ECKists to task in front of that entire group of business people, he said, "You shouldn't be apologizing for what you are." On the other hand, another coordinator complimented them: "You people are very good representatives for your organization."

When you present yourself to the world as an ECKist, you are going to find some people love you and others don't. You are a mirror for those who look at you. Because some people don't like what they see in themselves, they won't see very much good in you. Others who are unfolding even along the lines of different spiritual paths will also see themselves through you, and these people will like what they see.

How to Run Your Life Better

We work with both inner and outer resources in our planning meetings. We have access to everything that we can obtain through the usual information systems—computers, mail, telephones. But as ECKists, we have something else going for us, which is contact with the inner worlds, with the Mahanta. In some way, through the dream state, Soul Travel, or a knowingness, you are being given directions on how to run your life better.

Understand how the ECK works. If It gives you some knowledge on how to sidestep a problem and you listen, then It will give you still another insight on how to run your life even better. On the other hand, if you get lazy, if you say, It couldn't have meant that, and you don't act on it, the ECK—the Mahanta—will try again.

It will warn you twice, three times, six times. But when you get out of the habit of listening, the voice of the Inner Master becomes weaker and weaker. It's not because he's talking quieter, but because you have turned down the volume on the inner instrument of Soul. Your mind has strayed, and you're not listening to what Spirit is saying— so the resource dries up.

And because you haven't listened to the warning signs that could have helped you to deal with the problem long before, all of a sudden everything that has been building up—due to some quirk in your pattern of doing things— turns into a big problem.

If it becomes a big enough problem, we call it the dark night of Soul. You are pulled into such a deep depression that it seems as though life has taken you to the bottom of the pits. This happens simply because the Mahanta was speaking, and you couldn't hear.

For this reason, I strongly encourage you to continue with the Spiritual Exercises of ECK. Even when it seems they are not working, you may notice that your life is going more smoothly. When you stop doing the spiritual exercises, you lose the ability to know instinctively what you should do to run your life in the best way.

Wearing the Mantle of Heaven

Knowing is the highest form of working with the Mahanta. It's higher than Soul Travel, where you move out of the physical consciousness and look at a problem; or the dream method, where you have to interpret what you see. *Knowing* means it is completely upon you to work it out yourself, using your own abilities and natural talents.

To be in accord with the ECK, we have to be vibrating with the same rhythm as the ECK. This is a common language of the highest kind. It means we are in agreement with the principle and the rhythm of life. The person who wears the mantle of heaven, who speaks the common language of ECK, finds that all things work out well for him.

One of the initiates told me a story about survival training that was given to a certain group of children. "If you ever get lost in the woods," they were advised, "talk to a tree." Shortly after that, a three-year-old boy did get lost in the woods near his home.

Generally when a small one gets lost, he quietly lays down and curls up, and unless you stumble on him accidentally, you probably won't see him. But this little boy remembered what he had been taught. He found a tree that looked friendly, and stood there chattering away to it until someone came along and heard him.

This is what saved the child's life. He was up, moving around, and making quite a racket. Because he found a friend in the tree, he was able to survive.

The Goal Every Person Seeks

People have such a limited understanding of the Temples of Golden Wisdom. There is a major temple on every plane, as well as countless other temples of all kinds in all the different worlds.

Those of you who have visited the inner worlds using Soul Travel know that the heaven spoken of by the clergy is too limited. It has nothing to do with the way heaven really is. The heavens are far broader, with unlimited opportunities for learning and growth.

Another type of inner experience, wholly different from Soul Travel, is a direct encounter with the Light and Sound of God, where it is simply the ECK and you. But whatever kind of inner experience you have, each one is valuable in bringing you higher and closer to the goal that every person seeks, whether he knows it or not. That goal is to return to the heart of God, to the Ocean of Love and Mercy.

Every so often the past Masters will come to you and give you knowledge, wisdom, and understanding. Since he left the physical body, Peddar Zaskq, or Paul Twitchell, continues to work on the inner planes to bring together the common language of ECK in books.

I saw Paul some weeks ago. He was standing in an alcove in the library on the mezzanine level of a Temple of Golden Wisdom. The room was rather dark except for a shining golden light that was glowing over Paul and the book on the desk in front of him.

Paul just stood there, reflecting and thinking. As I watched him, I recognized that the gifts he gave through the writings and teachings of ECK were understood and appreciated by only a very few. He didn't expect praise, and he didn't wait for applause. He just kept doing what had to be done and bringing out truth, without thanks or reward.

He continues to do a number of different things, but he especially enjoys research. He loves to find the hidden truths among us so that they can be shared with the people on all the planes.

Recognizing the Jewel of God

There are so few who understand the truth of ECK, so few who know they have the Jewel of God right in their hand—so they throw it aside. It isn't until they need it for entrance into the Kingdom of Heaven that they realize they left it buried in the mud a couple of miles back, and it's going to take a long time of digging before they can ever find it again.

We have the Jewel of God in our hands, but it is up to us to do with it whatever is needed for our spiritual good. The Mahanta can give suggestions, but it depends upon you. How well do you listen? How faithfully do you do the Spiritual Exercises of ECK?

ECKANKAR International Youth Conference, Toronto, Ontario, Canada, Friday, April 5, 1985

The son knew it would take a lot of hard work, but the farm would once again run the way it should.

10

Steps to Soul Travel

At a business meeting I was put in the position of explaining to forty businessmen what ECKANKAR is. I didn't say ECKANKAR is the Ancient Science of Soul Travel; it wasn't the place for that kind of explanation. To some people Soul Travel sounds frightening, so it's best to explain it in words they understand.

What Is Soul Travel?

Soul Travel is simply Soul's movement to God. This is the same thing they have been looking for in their own religion. The difference is that Soul Travel is an active method of going home to God and a dynamic way of describing it. With all the television commercials and advertisements in the mail bombarding us each day, a less dynamic presentation wouldn't catch anyone's attention.

The ECK teachings must come out and be heard, because they fill a real need. Most of the advertisements that come in the mail fill an artificial need. They work on your self-image—own a new car, buy a new suit, or improve your life by using a certain product.

Some of the ECK initiates have never had a conscious experience with the Light and Sound, and they feel unable to help the newer initiates who are starting to have some experience. *The ECKANKAR Journal* is published to share with you the experiences other people are having in the Light and Sound of God. It's a matter of gaining confidence in and awareness of the experiences that you are having on the inner planes. The key is having an open heart.

How We Soul Travel

Soul Travel, which is restricted to the lower worlds, occurs in two ways. One form is experienced as the apparent movement of the Soul body through the planes of time and space. It is not really movement, because Soul already exists on all planes. What seems to be movement, or travel, is simply Soul coming into agreement with fixed states and conditions that already exist in the lower worlds.

If you can imagine a scene, then you can be there in the Soul body. This is called the imaginative technique. It may feel as though you are moving along very quickly, and this is why it is perceived as travel. Actually it's the process of changing the setting around you.

In Soul Travel, as you begin the Spiritual Exercises of ECK in the physical setting, you may experience a rushing sound, like wind in a tunnel, and the sensation of moving incredibly fast. But really, Soul doesn't move; Soul *is*. Time and space adjust to Soul's state of consciousness, and it is this adjustment of time and space that gives the sensation of movement or speed.

This is one aspect of Soul Travel that frightens people. They fear if they go traveling somewhere, they might get lost and be unable to return to the body. But remember, since you don't actually travel anywhere, you can't get lost.

Keep this in mind when you do the spiritual exercises; it will help to give you the confidence to open your heart and accept the experience that comes to you.

The other form of Soul Travel is known as the expansion of consciousness. This is closer to the state of true personal revelation or enlightenment that we are looking for in ECK.

The ECKshar State

A higher state of the expansion of consciousness comes on the Fifth Plane. This is the ECKshar, the state of seeing, knowing, and being. It may not sound as adventurous as Soul Travel, but Soul Travel is an intermediate step that gets us to the state of seeing, knowing, and being.

The ECKshar cannot be spoken about. Only the briefest mention can be made of what occurs during the experience. This is because the ECKshar consciousness is Self-Realization, and there simply is no way to describe it in words. But once you have the experience, you recognize it again and again. You feel refreshed and happy. In God, in ECK, you are a new creature, and now you must come to grips with it.

When a person becomes a Fifth Initiate, certain duties may be assigned to him by the Living ECK Master. These include the positions of ECK Initiator and ECK Spiritual Aide, as well as other duties which are quieter and less known.

It's best to let a person become established in the Fifth Plane for a year or two before he is approached to become an ECK Initiator. After he has spent some time as an initiator, I may then ask him to serve as an ECK Spiritual Aide.

You need time to absorb the experiences that come to you as a new Higher Initiate. If you take on too much too quickly, many valuable experiences of spiritual unfoldment can be lost.

A Higher Initiate told me he had once recommended someone near and dear to him for a higher initiation. I didn't approve the initiation. The Higher Initiate later realized that when you truly care for someone else, you let that person have his experiences in a natural way, rather than push him ahead before he has had a chance to benefit from where he is now. It's much like depriving someone of the joy of being a child by making him become an adult too fast.

Many of the Soul Travel experiences on the Astral, Causal, Mental, and Etheric planes are highly enjoyable. They represent certain levels of unfoldment that the chela in ECK goes through, and you ought to get the most that you can out of them.

Beyond Self-Realization

Never feel bored with your present initiation or be in a hurry to go further. The planes are so broad that for most people it can be a lifelong endeavor to learn about any one of them. In ECK, of course, we move faster. Before the end of this lifetime, a number of you will reach beyond Self-Realization into the higher stages of God-Realization.

It is important that you know and understand that it is possible to become a God-Realized individual in this lifetime. Otherwise, why try? And the first step is Soul Travel.

Soul Travel in Your Daily Life

In the broadest sense, Soul Travel can be used in every aspect of your daily life. It encompasses much more than merely traveling out of the body. It is the expansion of consciousness which allows you to get along every day with more awareness of the greater wisdom and understanding that is coming to you from the ECK.

Soul Travel is the movement of consciousness. That means in any situation in your daily life, you ought to be able to put yourself into a higher state of consciousness, get above the trouble zone, and not panic. Now you're in a position to stop and think: What is the next logical step to take? And then you take that one next step. You don't try to do it all at once, because you'll just end up stumbling around in all directions.

A Cure for Spiritual Headaches

Rather than expect you to get an overview of the philosophy behind Soul Travel, I try to convey the concepts through stories and examples. You may not remember everything I've said when you go home. The words are imbedded in the Soul body, but in the physical body, you forget.

This is why stories are important. They paint a picture. They're like seeds or little time capsules. When you need to remember a certain spiritual point, these stories come to mind. They can take care of your spiritual headaches in a way that straight philosophy does not.

As we expand our consciousness, we are required to conduct ourselves in a different way in the world around us. This includes our interaction with our families and people at work. In ECK you are a new creature, but this doesn't mean instant transformation. You find a lot of Fifth Initiates do not seem very different from when they were Fourth Initiates.

How Soul Learns

As Soul going through the process of the expansion of consciousness, we have our experiences, take our licks and beatings, then come staggering back to hide and heal. But human nature being what it is, we forget. When our strength returns, we come back as sassy as ever.

This is what happened with our neighbor's little tiger cat, Mitty. Mitty has already used up about three of his nine lives. My daughter is worried that he's going through them too fast. When our neighbors first brought him home, all he did was make an awful meowing sound. He was like Soul trying to figure out why It was in this big cruel world.

Mitty wanted attention; and the more he got, the more he demanded. Our neighbors finally started to put him out in the backyard every day. Little by little, he began to explore the neighborhood.

As Mitty grew to be a young cat, he began to follow the bigger cats around, studying them to learn how to be a cat. But the big tomcats didn't appreciate students or intruders in their territory, so Mitty got beaten up a couple of times.

Mitty had an enormous ego. As he got bigger and stronger, he decided to challenge a big cat, who then proceeded to take him apart—clawful by clawful. One of the neighbors ran out and rescued him, but by the time she got there, he had eight gashes in the chest.

Each time Mitty was injured, the neighborhood kids got together and took care of him. He managed to survive despite their nursing. Before he gets to the last of his nine lives, we hope he'll become wise, patient, kind, and live a long time.

Soul, too, goes out, takes a beating, and then crawls back to spend time healing. The next time It goes out, It takes an even bigger beating, because now Soul is more mature, more unfolded, and can take more.

The further one goes along the path, the bigger the lessons get. But like Mitty, you can always rest in a corner until the fur grows back in—then you go out and try again.

Facing Hardships

As you study the spiritual life, you will find that when you're having the hardest time, you are probably unfolding the most. If you wonder whether you are unfolding, look at how your life is going.

The lower worlds need a balance. If you didn't have negative things happening on the outside to match the spiritual growth taking place on the inside, you would pop apart.

The hardships that you face are not things to run from. It isn't that we are looking for a hard life, but when difficulties come despite our best efforts, it could be an indication from the Mahanta to look on the other end of the scale. You may find that the degree to which you are having outer hardships matches the degree to which you are unfolding inwardly.

I can't promise you an easy time in ECK, and I wouldn't even want to. The higher you go, the bigger the problems get, but the more you unfold. It may take a little longer to heal from the lessons, but you heal better and you come out of it stronger. It's a step in the growth phase.

An Eighth Initiate mentioned how difficult it was for her to move around among the initiates at seminars. She said, "People want to make you something that you are not. They forget that an Eighth Initiate is also a human being learning lessons and doing the best that he or she can." Higher Initiates in ECK often feel more comfortable going about their business in the community without letting other people know who and what they are.

Reality on the Inner Planes

When I go into the other worlds, I am there; it's not a dream. Many of the Higher Initiates also spend time in the other worlds, moving about and doing things. I don't have the words to describe it; the best I can do is show you how to get there and find out for yourself.

The description of heaven given by the orthodox religions is a relic left over from the early days of Christianity. It is a heaven that has stopped evolving—an anachronism, lost in time. The heavens we find today are not as described in the Bible. Rather than wearing long robes, the people you meet in heaven these days are dressed similarly to those you meet here in the physical plane.

At times you may be taken to a paradise. You might have some revelation or illumination during these isolated instances of Soul Travel, but then you have to come back here to earth and learn how to deal with it.

On the inner planes you are also running a body similar to the one you have here. You are not just dealing with people on one plane; you are interacting on many planes, on many different levels.

By operating in the Soul body, one is able to draw experiences from a number of different bodies, or vehicles, at the same time. Some people use only one or two, but others run a number of different bodies, not only here on earth but also in the other planes.

This is especially true of the individual who takes the Rod of ECK Power and becomes the Living ECK Master. Reports come in all the time from people who had experiences with the Master years before his physical body reached the point on the Time Track where he was ready to accept the Rod of ECK Power.

Making Honest Choices

Before birth, there was a certain place—let's say a level of spiritual competence—that you, as Soul, decided to reach before you left this life. When someone leaves ECK, he usually doesn't recognize that perhaps this is the time he chose to get off the path before he even got here. He feels he has to make up all kinds of excuses before he can do it without feeling guilty: he's upset with something a Higher Initiate did, or put off by something he read in one of the books.

It would be more honest if he would simply say, "For some reason it doesn't make sense to me anymore, and I think it's time to get off the path." Then get off and let it be. Those who are not honest with themselves carry bands of anger and a grudge, always wanting to justify their decision to others.

Every so often I run into somebody like that, but occasionally the ECK says this is not a good time to be seen, so I am invisible to that particular person. I got into line at the bank one day when I noticed, about two people ahead of me, there was somebody I had worked with for years.

His attitude about ECK is much as I just described. He went as far as he wanted, and then felt he needed an excuse to stand on the sidelines.

I really didn't have time to get into a conversation that day. He looked directly at me from ten feet away, but apparently the ECK didn't want him to see me. I accepted it; because of this man's feelings, I didn't particularly want to be seen by him at that time. When his turn came at the

167

teller's window, he stood there looking all around. By then I was standing behind a pillar. You can let the ECK do just so much for you, but you don't push it.

I met this person again, this time a few nights ago on the inner planes. Here is what took place.

The Prodigal Son

One dark, cold morning, many years after leaving the farm, the son returned home. He had gained much experience out in the world, and now it was time to claim his inheritance. His father had retired and turned over active operation of the farm to a tenant farmer, and the son was saddened to find the property run down and the animals neglected. A renter doesn't take care of things the way an owner would.

The son got on the tractor and drove around looking for his dad. By the time the sun came up, he found him out in the north fields, talking with the individual who had left ECK.

The father had planted all the crops and done everything he could up until that time to make the farm self-sustaining, to fulfill its productive function. Now he was inspecting the land to determine its potential for growth. Looking over the field, he said to the other man, "The crops that I planted gave the farm property a certain value, but I suspect there's oil underneath here. Look at that soil!" The other person listened attentively to the older man, liking him, believing in him—but he wouldn't even talk to the son. The son didn't mind; he had other things to do.

Father and son looked at the soil together. "There used to be corn and oats and wheat here," said the father, "but

168

just look at this soil. It looks like there's oil under here. It's worth drilling to find out." If this were the case, the value of the land would increase beyond measure.

The son got back on the tractor and drove all around the farm, trying to assess the condition of the property. While his dad had been absent, exploring the greater value of the land, the tenant had let the farm run down considerably. The calf pens were dirty and filled with manure. In front of the barn sat a bunch of people listening to tape recordings of themselves and having a philosophical discussion. Someone scurried around feeding a little hay to a calf here and there, but nobody was taking proper care of the animals. There was no feed in the mangers for the cows when they came in for milking. Everything looked neglected.

As the son surveyed the farm, he saw exactly what had to be done to get it back in shape. The land could support crops in some areas, but in other areas it could also support oil wells. Neglect had done some damage, but that was all right. It could be repaired. For the moment, all he could do was put fresh bedding in for the calves. He knew it would take a lot of hard work, but once it was cleaned up, the farm would once again run the way it should.

The farmer who retired and stepped aside was Paul Twitchell. Paul was the Mahanta. In *ECKANKAR: Illuminated Way Letters,* January 1971, Paul wrote that he was serving as the Mahanta until the time came to appoint an interim ECK Master. This individual would serve as the Living ECK Master until the next Mahanta, who was still in training, was named.

The inner experience ties into the outer experience. Some of you aren't ready to make the connection between the inner and the outer, but others of you are more than

169

ready. Some of you can't remember the inner experience; this is what we want to correct.

How Unfoldment Comes

Your relationship with the Inner Master determines where you go in the spiritual worlds. Unfoldment comes not by merit but by grace—the grace of the SUGMAD. After we spend time learning our lessons here, there is still the step beyond our means and ability that has to be taken.

It is the grace of the SUGMAD that allows us to come in contact with ITS Light and Sound. This is the basis for the ECK teachings, and this is the reason I am here: to help you, in whatever way possible, to make the connection between yourself—right here on earth in this lifetime— and the Light and Sound of God.

Training for Mastership

It takes persistence on your part, and devotion to the Spiritual Exercises of ECK. Problems and worries can be overcome by doing the spiritual exercises every day. This will give you the strength and stamina to not become discouraged.

Work in the realization of ECK and know that as you solve the problems you are capable of solving today, you are growing into the state of being able to tackle greater worlds tomorrow.

You are training for mastership, and mastership means service. It means being a Co-worker with God. To do that, you must be a fully integrated being, able to handle every situation on every plane. You have to be able to generate the spiritual energy to overcome every problem that tries to knock you down. You have to learn how to work with the energy of Soul.

May the blessings be.

ECKANKAR International Youth Conference,
Toronto, Ontario, Canada, Saturday, April 6, 1985

In a sense each being on every plane is the Mahanta; and in some way the Mahanta is expressing some degree of truth through every person we meet.

11

Mahanta at the Door

A transition from the old to the new happens gradually, in stages. As we turn a corner, we gain momentum. The spiritual direction and forward action taking place now are very necessary at this time. You will start to see it more clearly as you look to the inner and work with the different creative techniques and spiritual exercises.

Myths and Gods

One of the ECK initiates said that when he was a child, his parents tried to convince him that the Easter bunny came every year and brought eggs. As he got older, he told them he didn't really think there was such a thing as the Easter bunny. But they went out of their way to convince him that there was. So he believed them.

Eventually the boy's parents admitted that there actually wasn't an Easter bunny after all—but there was a man who rose from the dead. To make the story more complicated, they also told the boy that after the man who rose from the dead was born, Santa Claus began bringing presents to families all over the world. By this time the

173

little fellow was thoroughly confused. These people didn't make any sense at all.

The boy never quite fit into that family, anyway. They always thought he was rather strange. He used to try to tell them about these invisible people who came to his room and talked to him. "That's nonsense," his parents said. "Nobody comes into your bedroom and talks to you." And yet they expected him to believe their stories about the Easter bunny, Santa Claus, and the man who rose from the dead.

Too many myths and pseudogods are associated with the different holidays. Interwoven into all of it is a real deity, but it's surrounded by so many lies that children become confused.

By the time the parents are ready to go past the Easter bunny and Santa Claus and tell their children about the man who rose from the dead, they have lied so much that the children are no longer listening. And parents wonder why the children don't want to go to church.

Why Some People Sleep in Church

Ministers worry about why people sleep in church. If someone in the audience falls asleep during one of my talks, I figure he's getting what he needs from the inner at that time. But ministers don't work that directly with the inner, so they probably feel their sermon is failing when somebody goes to sleep.

Recently on a radio talk show, a woman caller told the host that she never could figure out why she used to fall asleep every time she went to church. As long as she had to stand up, sing, or get on the kneelers and pray, she was fine; but as soon as the minister started his twenty-minute sermon, she went to sleep.

One day it occurred to her that several of the women sitting around her in church were wearing cheap perfume. She also realized that each time she visited a friend who sold beauty-care products from her home, she felt sick or tired. She began to suspect she might be having some kind of an allergic reaction.

She decided to study the effect of scents and odors on an individual. Her research revealed that expensive perfumes made out of natural ingredients didn't cause these symptoms. But the cheaper perfumes that utilized synthetic substances bothered her. Considering the effect of all that cheap perfume on top of a dull sermon in a stuffy, airless church, the lady concluded that she really couldn't help it if she went to sleep during church services.

Spiritual Pollutants

Soul also has spiritual pollutants that surround It. One of the worst is anger. Wild, unbridled anger causes Soul to fall into a sleep state.

There simply is no such thing as righteous anger. The ECK doesn't recognize any distinctions between anger for a cause and anger for no cause. Through the Law of Karma, the ECK impartially doles out justice whenever there is any imbalance of the emotions.

Anger is an imbalance of the emotions which arises from a mental passion. Whatever the provocation, when emotions such as anger, jealousy, or greed go out, like ripples on a pond they affect the people around you, who then carry those emotions home with them.

When we indulge in anger or any of the other passions of the mind, we are simply passing it down the line. The higher our initiation, the greater the influence and the broader the circle of people we affect.

175

The ripples go out as far as the energy of our anger can carry them, and then they start to come back. This energy may return a little at a time, so that little things go wrong. Since we don't know why it's happening, we blame it on everything but ourselves. Occasionally it comes back in a huge chunk, perhaps showing up as a catastrophe.

We blame our problems on the Kal Niranjan, which, of course, is our own base nature. To put it another way, the Kal is our indulgence run free. It is perhaps more honest to look at Kal Niranjan, the king of the negative world, as something of our own creation which has no life or energy except what we give him.

In other words, I'm pointing the finger right back at the person—which is usually ourself—who sends out the blast of energy to other people. We are responsible for all the ripples created in others by our anger, as well as the ripples they in turn pass along to the next group. The higher you go as an initiate in ECK, the greater your responsibility becomes. The Law of Love becomes very exacting.

We do not get away with indulging in things such as anger. It always comes back home; but because it comes in disguise, people are often able to blame it on someone else, thus making it easier to live with themselves. Some people simply would not be able to handle it if they had to take full responsibility.

When someone wants to believe that the cause of his problem is some outer source, I generally don't take away his delusion. He needs it for survival. But whether he admits responsibility or not, the penalty is paid.

Soul Travel and the expansion of consciousness make us consciously aware of the effect our words and actions have on other people and ultimately on ourselves. We make our own heaven; we make our own hell.

Adapting to a Fast-paced World

Times have changed so much since the early days of ECKANKAR. We must now adapt our spiritual exercises to an even faster-paced world than we found twenty years ago.

Husband and wife are both working these days, and it's becoming harder for a family to survive than ever before—not just financially, but as a unit spiritually. Time is more consumed in the workplace than it was twenty years ago. That means both husband and wife come home tired.

The spiritual exercises where you sit quietly for twenty or thirty minutes may work for many of you. If not, try something like this one. I call it "The Mahanta at the Door," and it's an exercise that is meant to be practiced during the waking hours.

Mahanta at the Door

Throughout the week, somebody is always knocking on your door or ringing your doorbell. Each time it happens, say to yourself, "It will be the Mahanta, the Living ECK Master." Be very aware of what you are doing at that moment—where you walk, what you touch, and what you see. When you open the door, no matter who it is, be conscious and aware of what the person looks like and what he or she is wearing.

Let's say you're in the kitchen washing dishes when the doorbell rings. Observe your movements. You reach for the towel, dry your hands, walk to the door, and open it up—and expect to see the Mahanta.

It might be the little child from next door, but this is the ECK in expression at a certain level. It's bringing something for you. In a sense, each being on every plane is the

Mahanta; and in some way the Mahanta is expressing some degree of truth through every person we meet.

When you go to bed that night, review three or four of the experiences you had with visitors. Retrace your steps from the moment you heard the knock until the time you opened the door: The person knocked several times; you noticed this or that on the way to the door; you knew it would be the Mahanta. Who did you see when you opened the door? It was the newsboy collecting for the paper. Remember details: What was he wearing? What did he say? This is a spiritual exercise that you can build into your daily life.

Create your own spiritual exercises along with those you find in the ECK discourses. Experiment with them; work back and forth. Try "The Mahanta at the Door" during the day. The energy you have put into this will carry over and help you at night.

You are going to get very used to opening the door and expecting to see someone that you want to see standing there. This helps to open the heart so that you can open the door with love. Because unless you do, you will never see the Inner Master. If you can open the door with love, the Master will come to you, because the Mahanta is always there.

In Search of Sudar Singh

We have begun a search for records that will document the life of Sudar Singh, the ECK Master who served before Paul Twitchell. He was an elusive Master, and it's not easy to follow his trail.

A few months ago I sent two individuals to India to see what they could find out. These ECKists found two businessmen who knew something about Sudar Singh.

One of them remembered him as a very old man giving sermons in the marketplace. It was rumored that when Sudar Singh began his sermons, even the birds would stop singing. He had an eloquent manner of speaking, and his audiences were always attentive.

Another person who had been a student of Sudar Singh said the ECK Master later left India and fled to Canada because of a political uprising similar to the one that took place after Indira Gandhi was killed.

Some would like to believe Sudar Singh didn't exist, because then it would be easier to claim that there is no ECK history. So I'm looking for physical records, but I'm letting the initiates find the information for themselves. There are initiates looking all over, trying to establish a physical history for the lineage of ECK Masters. Each time we find a record of one, we get a lead back to the one before him, thereby constructing the history back as far as we can.

Soul Going Home to God

But these outer checkpoints and verifications really have nothing to do with your spiritual unfoldment. The only reason for the ECK teachings is for you to make an inner connection so that you, as Soul, can go home to God.

It makes no difference how many Masters have been here before; none of this is important. Nor does it matter whether or not other people are able to have experiences with the Light and Sound, but only whether you can. Even if the whole world is ignorant of ECK, what matters is that you know about ECK and can participate in the Light and Sound of God.

The path of ECK becomes an individual undertaking of the highest degree. We have an ECK history and an

ECKANKAR Office that sends out membership materials. But ultimately it comes down to one basic fact: your relationship with the Inner Master. For those of you who care more for spiritual enlightenment than you care about your little self, it becomes as important as air for breathing.

The definition of Soul Travel is simply Soul going home to God, or the movement of Soul to God. To be a Co-worker means that no matter what you are doing, you make it easier for the next person. As you begin working at any endeavor, keep in mind that you are smoothing the way for others.

The Bubble of Protection

One of the initiates observed how often the Temples of Golden Wisdom are depicted as being domelike. The dome over these temples is the protective energy of the ECK which surrounds the structure beneath it.

When I started working at the ECKANKAR International Office in 1975, I would notice an entirely different feeling on the freeway as I drove to and from work. Driving home at night, I could tell when I was coming out from the ECK Office's bubble of protection. It was a sphere with a perimeter of perhaps two miles, that surrounded the ECK Office.

There is a similar little dome, extending perhaps a block or two, around the home of each ECKist. It's much smaller for each of us because there isn't such a concentrated flow of ECK as there is in the ECK Office. Animals are quick to pick this up. A dog will perk up and start looking around when you arrive within a block or two of home, because it can sense that it has entered the atmosphere of the home. This spiritual circle that surrounds the home is the protection of the Master.

Relighting Your Inner Light

Each seminar builds toward the next one. They are geared toward the needs of the individuals who attend, and the needs are always changing. Each stage leads to a greater and greater circle, even as individually we move from one circle of initiation to a greater one.

When you return home from a seminar filled with the love of ECK, you are like a bubble of light going back out into the world. The light shines brightly for about a week.

Be very careful to get yourself down to earth when you get home by immersing yourself in the duties at hand. If you fly too high for too long, there comes the time of reckoning when the bubble goes away.

You can't stay in heaven as long as you have a body on earth. You can go into the heavenly state but you have to come out of it. What makes you different as ECKists is the fact that you know you can go back into it again and again.

The ECK seminars help to relight your inner light that may have dimmed. If you can't afford to take advantage of them due to the cost of traveling, you can put special attention upon the seminar at home. The weekend it occurs, go into contemplation and visualize whatever you can about the seminar, using the descriptions of the program you've read about in the preregistration brochures. Put yourself on the inner planes and say, "I'm seeing myself with my friends at the ECK seminar; I'm seeing myself in the audience listening to the Master."

If you do this before sleep, keep a journal of the things you remember from your dreams; even if it's a feeling, write it down. This helps you to develop the discipline to make it easier for Soul to work Its way through the mind and the lower bodies to bring a conscious awareness of the inner planes down to earth. If you can remember the experience, you can work with these inner enlightenments from the Mahanta.

The whole purpose of everything we are doing is for you to learn how to have heaven on earth.

May the blessings be.

ECKANKAR International Youth Conference, Toronto, Ontario, Canada, Sunday, April 7, 1985

The concepts of heaven held by the orthodox religions are so outdated that when the followers get to heaven, they don't know where they are.

12
How It Is in ECK

J ust before I came out here, one of the stagehands said I could choose between two chairs. "Do you want to use the white one or the blue one?" he asked.

I walked over to the two chairs, and without even giving it any thought, I plunked right down in the blue one. "This one feels good," I said. He then informed me that it's the chair I used at the World Wide of ECK in October of 1981 when I accepted the position of Living ECK Master. No wonder it feels good.

A Creative Challenge

We want to learn how to live life in ECK with a creative spirit. Even things like chairs can provide a creative challenge. I've been at seminars where the chair barely held up, and it took creativity to figure out how to keep the talk flowing while maintaining my balance on a wobbly chair.

Sometimes new chelas feel that since they are now on the true path to God, everything ought to work out easier than it did before. Actually, life is probably a little bit harder than before, because Soul learns better when It has to put Its shoulder to the wheel than when It's riding in the wagon.

The whole purpose of the path of ECKANKAR is to teach us about the Light and Sound of God. It's easy to deal with this concept when you read about it in *The Shariyat-Ki-Sugmad* and other ECK writings. The books explain that if you sit in contemplation and do the spiritual exercises, sooner or later you will have an experience with the Light and Sound of God.

Let's say you do have an experience with this Sound Current, the Voice of God, which manifests as Light and Sound. Then you have to figure out how to apply it to everyday living.

The person who comes to ECK feeling that this path is supposed to be easier than the religion he came from, or have more meaning than a life without religion, might wonder how to live the life of ECK. A simple answer is: with a lot of creativity.

Are You a Soul Traveler?

We are working all the time to become a Co-worker with God, and so we find ways to share the ECK. I gave a blue-and-gold Soul Traveler patch to my daughter, who is now a preteen. One day, as she was getting out of the car, I noticed that she had used it to cover a hole in her jeans. She had gone to a video arcade with her mom a few days earlier, and while she was in the middle of a game, two boys from school came up to her.

In a challenging tone, one of the boys asked, "Hey, are you a Soul Traveler?" Instead of saying yes or no, she threw the question back at him. "Are you?" she asked. That was a good way to handle it. If she had said yes, they would have said, "Well, prove it." And if she had said no, they probably would have asked why she was walking around with a patch like that. After she threw the question back, the two boys backed away and went to play another video game, but they kept looking over at her rather strangely.

The moral of that story is that the Soul Traveler patch can be used to tell other people about ECK and also to patch holes.

When we become a vehicle for Spirit, we go out in life and do the best we can. Even if you don't have a Soul Traveler patch sewn on your clothing, people can tell there is something different about you.

Carriers of Love

The most effective Vahanas—the message carriers of ECK—are those who simply carry the love of ECK within themselves. They don't sermonize about ECK to people who don't ask; this is about the worst way to present ECK. When people don't care to hear it, you've wasted your time and theirs. Yet they can tell when the love is flowing through you, and even if they don't ask about ECK, they want to know who you are and what's special about you.

Learning to Do Things Easier

In ECK we eventually learn how to do things the easier way. While driving past a shopping center one day, I saw a shoe store that had huge red-and-yellow going-out-of-business signs in the window. I decided to take a look.

Inside the store, I picked through the remaining shoes on the racks, but none of the styles I liked were available in my size. I was just about to leave when the curtain to a back room parted and a man in his midsixties came out. As we talked, I found out he was a sales consultant who traveled around the country helping small stores put on going-out-of-business sales and stock-reduction sales. I asked him how he got started in the shoe business.

Just out of high school, he had taken a job as a salesman in a local shoe store. On his first day at work, a woman and her teenage daughter came into the store to shop for shoes for the daughter. He invited them to sit down, and after some discussion about size and style, he brought out a pair of shoes for the girl to try on. They weren't quite what she wanted. The salesman set the shoes aside, one shoe in the box and the other on the floor.

The girl tried on a second, third, fourth, and fifth pair of shoes. Soon there were more open shoe boxes all over the floor, some with both shoes left out of the box. It took over half an hour, but the young man finally made the sale. He was really pleased with himself.

When the customers left, the manager called the salesman into his office. "I see you made a sale," he said.

"Sure did," said the salesman.

The manager asked, "Do you know how many pairs of shoes you showed her?"

The salesman said, "No, just that there were quite a few."

"You showed her twenty-three pairs of shoes," the manager said. "And you left twenty-two pairs of shoes lying all over the store."

The young fellow didn't see what was so important about that. "I made the sale, didn't I?"

The manager said, "While the twenty-two pairs of shoes remain off the shelf and lying around on the floor, they're unavailable to the other customers. No one else can buy them. Not only that, but when you put them back in the boxes, you mismatched several pairs."

The salesman was beginning to get the point.

The manager continued: "Did you notice which pair of shoes she finally bought?"

"It was one of the first ones I showed her."

"Right," said the manager. "It was the third pair."

The sales consultant learned some valuable things from his first selling experience. He learned to put the shoes back in the box and return them to the shelf, and to show no more than three to five pairs to a customer. He found that if a person was really interested in buying, he or she would generally select one of the first three pairs.

The Only Sin against Soul

As Soul, we are in a similar position. We go through life doing everything the hard way. Our difficulties are our own fault in the first place, and we compound them by opening more boxes than necessary to find the solution.

This is how it works when Soul is resting in an unconscious state. If there is a sin against Soul, it's unconsciousness or lack of awareness. The teachings of ECK awaken Soul to the reality of living consciously every day. We learn to recognize that the ECK is trying to show us the simpler way, to open three or four boxes instead of twenty-three. Eventually we learn how to do things the easier way.

How Karma Is Worked Out

We are living among different states of consciousness. No matter how you see something, the person sitting next to you will look at the same thing from an entirely different viewpoint, and his or her actions will be based upon that outlook.

I drove into a crowded restaurant parking lot a few days ago. Spotting a man getting into his car, I pulled up to wait for his parking space, leaving him plenty of room to back out. About the time he finally got the car started, a woman in a little compact car came zooming around from behind me, saw the man pulling out, and apparently never gave a thought to why I was sitting out there. She stopped her car in front of me, backed up practically against my bumper, and waited for the other car to pull out.

I leaned on my horn. The woman looked around with a puzzled expression, no doubt wondering why this guy behind her was honking his horn. When I saw she wasn't getting the point, I honked again.

By then the other driver was backing out, and the woman in front of me got ready to pull into the spot I had been waiting several minutes for. The person I was with couldn't take it anymore. He reached over and leaned on the horn—really blasted it.

Realization finally dawned on the woman. She stuck her head out the window. With an inquiring look, she pointed at the empty spot as if to say, "Oh, you mean that's for you?" I honked the horn again in reply: "Yes!"

The lady pulled away and drove over to the restaurant door. I watched in amazement as she double-parked, blocking several other cars, and ran inside. A few minutes later she pushed her way through the crowded lobby to the exit, never saying excuse me, then got into her car and drove away.

She was one of the insensitive people that you run into occasionally. The different states of consciousness are what we are working with, and this is how the karma is worked out between people.

We often think we'd get along really fine in this world if it weren't for other people. Yet, these are the kind of experiences that help us to unfold spiritually. Sometimes we wonder, Why not get some kind of an exotic problem instead of the dull, irritating ones that just wear us down for no purpose? But the troubles we run into are exactly what we need for spiritual unfoldment.

We learn about consciousness by becoming aware of the difference between ourself and the next person.

Creating Our Own Worlds

The concepts of heaven held by the orthodox religions are so outdated that when the followers get to heaven, they don't know where they are. Some of the heavens are very similar to the existence you are living here on earth.

Like your present existence, heaven is a reflection of your attitudes, your likes and dislikes. All put together, heaven is your state of consciousness, just as the world around you is your own creation. This is the highest form of the creative arts.

Often we don't like the world of our creation because we've made it with an imperfect consciousness. The teachings of ECK raise our state of consciousness. We can then create a world more suitable to our desires, not in the lower sense of earthly desires, but the spiritual desire for God. We create and build the world that we want with our thoughts and with our actions.

Helping on the Inner Planes

An ECKist went through a difficult period of life, but she didn't complain. "Through it all," she said, "I never felt that the burden was too much to carry. For some reason I felt I was doing exactly what needed to be done as a vehicle for the ECK."

She had, in fact, been helping out on the inner planes during this time. I showed her some of the things that she had been doing to help other initiates. Then she was able to see exactly why she was going through those particular troubles.

The Creative Process

Whether you are a writer, musician, or business person, you work with the creative process in some way. We face challenges all the time. Some things don't have solutions, and the best you can do is hope to control them.

An office manager, for instance, has to deal with situations such as employees who come in late. Good managers are capable of gaining cooperation, while others have nothing but dissatisfied employees who make life very rough for them.

How well your world runs depends on how well you tune in to the ECK. None of us likes to hear that we create our own troubles, but it's true. Nor can you tell somebody in thirty-five words or less how to undo the attitudes acquired from a whole series of lifetimes.

Meeting a Deadline Creatively

When a writing deadline comes up for me, I don't expect to instantly produce a masterpiece. I mark the deadline date for the article in yellow on my calendar. As the date gets closer, the ECK starts pouring ideas into me. Putting the ideas into words and meeting the deadline are things I have to do myself.

Sometimes I have so many things to do that I'm not the easiest person to live with right before a deadline. One time I had three or four articles that had to be completed. Everything hit at once.

One of the articles was on a short deadline for the *ECKANKAR Journal*. For a couple of weeks before I got to work on it, a thought kept coming to me: Where did the old religions go wrong? After mulling it over for a while, I realized the answer: they forgot the Light and Sound of ECK.

The ECK gave me this basic idea, and now it was a matter of writing the article around it. But nothing came to me.

As the deadline got closer, the idea kept building and building. Finally it was Saturday, the day I had set aside to work on the article.

I had gone to bed early the night before and stayed in bed a little longer in the morning, so I'd be well rested. Then I decided to take a nice long shower so I'd feel even fresher. In the meantime, this idea kept boiling around inside—What the old religions forgot: the Light and Sound of God.

I sharpened my pencils, emptied the wastebasket, and had breakfast. Suddenly I remembered a couple of things I really needed, so I went out and did some shopping. By the time I returned, there was no getting around it; I simply had to get to work on that article.

I thought about writing it in expository form, which is like preaching a sermon—but who's going to want to wade through a sixteen-hundred-word sermon? What good is a bright idea unless you can present it in a way that others will read? Then all of a sudden a new picture took form and began moving along the inner screen:

For the first time in several millennia, Sat Nam sent a message down to the Kal Niranjan. The king of the negative worlds can run things pretty much the way he wants to, but now came the big moment—a directive from on high: Find out if the old religions still teach the Light and Sound of God.

The best way to conduct such a massive investigation was to get all the various representatives together in one place. The Kal Niranjan called a convention. The religious leaders from all the worlds on every plane were instructed to gather in the Great Hall of the palace.

By this time I was so inspired that I couldn't type fast enough.

The next morning, without any delay tactics at all, I sat down and wrote the next article—two thousand words about the razor's edge, that delicate balance between the social consciousness and the spiritual consciousness.

Reading People and Their Motives

Sometimes the ECK can create a miracle. Last week I drove to the grocery store. When I pulled into the parking lot, in the space next to me was a late-model car. In it sat a man with his son, who looked about five years old. The man caught my eye as I got out of my car; he held up an empty one-gallon gasoline container and waved it out the window. "I ran out of gas," he said.

I was short of money, felt under the weather, and maybe I didn't feel real spiritual at that moment—or maybe I did. I had a feeling this guy was a panhandler, but even if he was out of gas, that big gas-guzzling car wouldn't get very far on one gallon of gas. "Are you sure the tank is empty?" I asked.

"Oh, yes," he said. "It's empty."

When someone is asking you for money, why not check it out? I said, "Do you mind if I see your gas gauge?" He turned on the ignition, and the needle moved just above the empty mark. "Your needle is still above empty," I said.

194

"But I live twenty miles away."

"Well, you're not going to get twenty miles on a gallon of gas," I said. "You're going to need more than that."

"Three dollars would sure help me a lot," the man said. The little boy looked at him proudly, obviously impressed with the way his dad earned money.

The man was flat-out lying to me. I shook my head and said, "Sorry, no."

I got back in my car and drove away. Two minutes down the street, it dawned on me that I had forgotten to go into the grocery store. I made a quick U-turn, and in another two minutes I was back in the parking lot. The other car was gone. A miracle! I thought, chuckling to myself. He was able to run his car with an "empty" tank.

Sometimes we have to use our creative faculty to determine whether or not people are being honest with us. As you become more in tune with the ECK, your consciousness unfolds to the point where you can read people and their motives very clearly. This enables you to steer yourself around troubles, trickery, and anything else that is thrown at you.

Keeping Your Eyes Open

In Utah, a church official had large oil-and-gas holdings. Because of his wealth and position in the church, some of his fellow parishioners believed him to be spiritually greater than the average person. Many felt they could multiply their savings by investing their money with this man.

Unfortunately, things didn't go as planned, and he lost their money. They couldn't complain to the president of the Mormon church that their neighbor took them for several thousand dollars. Instead, they had to go to the additional expense of seeking justice through the court system.

This is a situation ECKists could also be faced with. Too many people are willing to line up like sheep behind someone else's prosperity programs, looking for a new opportunity to be laid out on the sacrificial altar.

When someone comes to you with a really creative scheme on how to get rich, remember this: If it sounds too good to be true, it probably is. Put your money down—if you can afford to lose it.

Occasionally I hear about Higher Initiates who misuse their spiritual position. Perhaps they are ignorant of how other ECKists look up to them, assuming they have some special "in" with God and that dealing with them will make everyone filthy rich.

Steer yourself around get-rich-quick schemes. They can lead to problems. If someone that you know approaches you with this sort of proposition, look at his deal as if it were coming from a complete stranger. Don't make a decision on the spot. Go to the Inner Master and check it out.

Be willing to walk away from any scheme even if it was presented to you by an ECKist. Use the creative faculty that you have within yourself—you'll be a lot better off.

An ECKist should not use his association with the ECK to make a living for himself. There's nothing wrong with taking advantage of an honest opportunity, but many of the people who offer these big programs are just dreaming. Keep your eyes open. This is a lesson in creativity that some may have to learn the hard way.

May the blessings be.

ECKANKAR International Creative Arts Festival, Anaheim, California, Friday, June 14, 1985

The bully tried to jump the sandbox too, but tripped, skinned his knee, and fell down.

13

The Razor's Edge

The Living ECK Master keeps his eye on cultures and the latest trends in society; he doesn't just sit in a room by himself and contemplate. I read different executive newsletters and reports in order to keep up on what's happening today. Radio talk shows also are good indicators of what the people in our society are thinking and feeling.

There really is a very fine line, if any, between the outer and the inner life. And you simply can't draw a line and say that this side is administrative and that side is spiritual. The principles of the spiritual life are embodied in everything you do. If not, it is simply because you cannot see them or haven't recognized them.

The Razor's Edge

Paul Twitchell referred to the razor's edge as a kind of precarious walk. He likened it to the life of the Cliff Hanger, one who looks down on the crowds from a precarious position on the side of a cliff, watching the folly of mankind yet not taking part in it. But his grip on the spiritual cliff is such that he is barely hanging on. If he falls, he lands right back down among the masses, in the material consciousness.

The Razor's Edge, by W. Somerset Maugham, is actually a study of the conflict between the spiritual and the social consciousness. The story is set in the 1920s, the booming years right after World War I, when America's image changed from that of a country bumpkin into a world power. All the forces of America were focused like sunlight through a magnifying glass, and the United States suddenly found itself a young giant with incredible strength. Every citizen was expected to contribute to America's greatness and continued prosperity. It was in this environment that a young aviator named Larry returned home to Chicago after the war.

Larry had no taste for the wealth and materialism America was hungering for. During the war a friend of his had been shot down while protecting him from the enemy. The aviator never talked of this, but he carried deep scars from his friend's death. Larry was a quiet, reticent young man, always charming but elusive. One moment he was seen standing there with a smile, and the next he was gone like a sunbeam dancing in the afternoon shadows. Nobody could hang on to him.

When he first came home, family and friends urged him to get a job with a good future, but he kept putting them off. Only war veterans could understand that the young men who saw combat were no longer the same as before they left home. Life had grabbed them by the neck and shaken them, the way a dog will sometimes shake a cat. If the cat survives, it's never quite the same.

This man, who cared nothing for the social values, got engaged to a young woman he had grown up with. Being from a wealthy family, his fiancée loved the fine trappings of society—the parties, the latest fashions from Paris, the social whirl. But Larry wasn't yet ready to settle down. He explained that he wanted to go to Paris for two years. He needed the freedom to search for truth.

The girl agreed to wait for him, with the understanding that if he didn't find what he was searching for at the end of two years, he would return home, take a job in the business world, and fall in line with society.

Quest for Truth

Before he left for Paris, Larry spent his days in the library searching for truth in books such as William James's *Principles of Psychology*. This is where W. Somerset Maugham, in a cameo appearance, happened to run into him. When the author sat down next to Larry and glanced over to see what he was reading, the young man quickly covered up the book. Larry didn't feel that anyone could understand his need for truth.

Two years later his fiancée and her mother traveled to Paris with the expectation that Larry would return home to Chicago with them. Larry instead tried to convince the young woman to stay with him, promising to show her a life greater than anything she had ever experienced. He said they could travel to different parts of the world to study the people and learn what's important to them. He saw this as a way to gain spiritual freedom.

His fiancée protested. She wanted to travel, but Larry had only a small income and she didn't want to go third class. And anyway, she said, she wanted to have babies. Larry didn't see that as a problem. "We'll take them with us," he said.

His fiancée didn't understand him at all. She asked Larry just what he was looking for.

He explained that he wanted to find out if there really is a God. He wanted to know the source of evil and whether death meant continued existence or the end. He wanted to find meaning beyond the social values.

Unable to agree on a common goal, the couple broke their engagement. The young woman returned to Chicago and married the son of a millionaire, and Larry went off to search for truth. The young man had had to choose between the social consciousness and the spiritual quest. He chose an uncertain life that offered the vibrancy of existence, which his fiancée rejected in favor of material security.

The story moves ahead ten years to the stock market crash of 1929. Larry turns up in Paris looking lean and youthful and at peace. Ironically, the rich family that the young woman married into lost all their money, and the material security she sought was swept away.

In ECKANKAR no one is expected to give up material possessions, but in time we give up our attachment to them. This way, if they are ever taken away from us, we don't crumble and fall because of the loss.

We look for the Light, and we listen for the Sound of ECK. With these as our inspiration and guide, our pillars of strength, we can take any hardship in life; we can accept this life as an opportunity for Soul to reach God Consciousness.

The social-minded person never sets his goals toward God Consciousness. He seeks social recognition, power, and money—all the things that don't matter, all the things which are left behind at the death of the body and sometimes even before.

Walking the Line

We walk our own razor's edge every day. It shows in little ways as we attempt to keep a balance between the spiritual and the material viewpoints while living in a physical world loaded with heavy materialism. Sometimes we wonder how to keep this balance.

When you go into a public place, people are drawn to you, and it takes a little longer for you to complete your business than it did before. Grocery stores seem to fill up faster when I enter them now than they did before, and whatever checkout line I'm in seems to get longer and run into more delays. If you don't have the insight to know what's happening, you'll see these things as hindrances.

Even a simple thing like getting gas for my car is filled with delays. About two weeks ago I drove into a service station, filled up my tank, and took my credit card inside to pay for the gasoline. The attendant filled out the credit slip and handed it to me to sign. I looked over the figures and saw that he had written in a larger amount than I had pumped into my car. "Is this some kind of special price?" I asked.

"That's your car on the other side, isn't it?" he said.

"No," I said, "that's my car on the side with the cheaper price."

The woman whose bill I almost paid came running in and got in line, followed by several other people. Within minutes there was a long line behind me. This time I was the one holding up the line.

The attendant wrote out a new sales slip, and once again he put the same wrong price on it. "You've still got it wrong," I said. The people in line were scowling at me by then, especially the lady right behind me, wondering why I was holding them up. The attendant tore up the second slip, ran my card through the machine for the third time, and this time he got it right.

Driving down the freeway later, I thought to myself that it wasn't right for a man to have to go through such resistance every day. Where's the ECK when you need it?

Just then, an ECKist pulled in front of me. On her car was a bumper sticker that said, "I'd rather be Soul Traveling." She stayed in front of me for about two or three miles. It was as if the ECK had responded to my thought by saying, "Do you ever wonder if I'm here?" I suddenly felt very happy.

A Gift of Prophecy

The razor's edge comes into play in our tests on the spiritual path. A young lady talked with me about her ability to see the future. Ever since she has been in ECKANKAR, she periodically has prophetic dreams or an inner voice tells her something is going to happen. Her test has been whether to talk about it or keep silent. She chose to obey the Law of Silence, and she wanted assurance that she had done the right thing.

The first time she became aware of the inner voice was during a contemplation. She was told that her mother-in-law had a terminal illness. The ECKist couldn't help wondering if she was supposed to take some action. Should she, in a very general way, suggest that the woman see a doctor? But her inner direction said don't do it, so she didn't.

On another occasion, in her inner vision she saw one of the ECKists in her area receiving the Fifth Initiation. Since it was good news this time, she wondered if she should say something to the person. Again she kept silent.

The young woman wanted to know if she had done the proper thing by keeping these glimpses of the future to herself. I pointed out to her that this had been a test from the Mahanta. What good would it have done to tell her mother-in-law about the illness? The woman didn't have the state of consciousness to accept a healing, spiritually or from medicine, that would have saved her life. Nor did she have the state of consciousness to follow a prophetic warning.

The ECKist knew about her mother-in-law's illness for three months before the doctor found it. To tell the other woman about her illness would have paralyzed her with fear, which may have sped up the degenerative cycle. Studies have shown that when a patient has been informed that he or she has a terminal illness, there is a marked drop in the person's vitality. Suddenly the individual develops worsening symptoms.

By keeping her silence, the young woman passed a test. This was actually another form of walking the razor's edge.

Why do you have to go through tests for which you don't have the spiritual maturity to know the right answer? If you are spiritually mature enough from the experiences you have gotten in life up to this point, you will make the right decision. If not, you may have to face the same test again.

This is the nature of life. You continue to gain more spiritual experience until you know what the right decision is. This is simply the educative process which leads to the maturity of Soul.

The ECKist actually had a choice between taking the path of love or the path of power. If she had told others of her visions, at first it would have been an innocent expression of a miraculous prophecy that astounded her as much as anyone else. After a few more prophecies, she would notice people looking at her with new eyes. "Look at her," they would say. "She's really something special. She can see the future!" Eventually the gift of prophecy is taken

205

away, and what do you do then? Some have been known to make up stories anyway, because of the attention and admiration this ability attracts. This is the trap along the razor's edge.

Will you go the way of power or the way of love? The way of ECK is the way of love, and love conquers all.

The Golden-tongued Wisdom

The ECK-Vidya is called the Golden-tongued Wisdom, because when it speaks, the message comes through clearly and directly. If it comes by way of the written word, the words jump off the page and seem to be a foot wide, painted in gold.

When the ECK-Vidya comes through correctly, there is no mistaking the message. The charts and other guidelines found in the book *The ECK-Vidya* introduce the individual to an elementary stage of this facet of the ECK works; but by becoming engrossed in the study, one might find the true ECK-Vidya.

A Way to Handle Feelings of Revulsion

The razor's edge also means trusting your inner guidance, even when you are too tired to want to, too tired to care.

For nearly three years, every time a certain High Initiate went to a laundromat near his home, a woman with cysts all over her face would also be there washing her clothes. To balance out his feelings of repulsion at her appearance, each time he saw her he would say to himself, "In the name of the SUGMAD."

One night after attending an ECK class, he had clothes to wash, but he was so tired that he decided to put it off. Suddenly he got a very strong inner nudge from the ECK to go to the laundromat. He didn't feel like going out again, but the nudge was so strong that he went anyway.

When the Higher Initiate walked into the laundromat, he got a surprise. There was the woman, and her complexion was completely clear; her skin was smooth and healed. As he looked at her, he couldn't believe this was the same woman he had seen all these years. Then he remembered how each time he saw her, he had said in his heart, "In the name of the SUGMAD."

The Higher Initiate had not said the words so he could heal this woman. To do so would have been a violation of her psychic space. He blessed the situation in order to keep himself in balance and so that he would not take on her condition in some other way for himself.

The ECK led him to the laundromat that night for his own education, for his eyes to see. It showed him that if you are a true channel for the ECK, miracles will take place around you.

Bully on the Playground

One of the ECKists works as a detention officer for juveniles. Before he became a Second Initiate, he thought he had to take a very strong position with these kids; otherwise they would get completely out of hand.

Whenever a child broke a rule for the first time, he would send him to his room for a certain period of time. The second time the child broke the rule, he would have to stay in his room with the door shut. A third offense meant the offender would be locked in his room. With each offense, the punishments got tougher. The officer made it clear to the children that if they got too wild, he would ruin their day.

Later, after he became a Second Initiate in ECK, his attitude changed. He began to realize that natural cycles of energy occur and that cause-and-effect cycles have to run their course. A detention officer is trained to interrupt the cycle before it gets out of hand. Normally, if the kids got into a fight, he would pull them apart to stop the cycle. But now the ECKist began to view things differently.

One afternoon there was a commotion on the playground. The ECKist and another officer saw the playground bully chasing a smaller boy. The ECKist made no move to interfere. The other officer said, "Hey, aren't you going to stop them?"

"No," said the ECKist. "Let's watch and see what happens."

The little guy ran out to an area where a bunch of kids were swinging. He darted through the moving swings. The bully came charging after him, misjudged his position, and got hit in the jaw by one of the swings. It knocked him flat.

Now the bully was really mad. He scrambled to his feet and took off after the other boy. The smaller boy headed for the sandbox, jumped over, and kept on running. The bully tried to jump it too, but tripped, skinned his knee, and fell into the sandbox. Madder than ever, he picked himself up and continued the chase.

The two detention officers watched the smaller boy make a fast turn and run out into the middle of a large empty field. "What a dumb kid," they said. "It's all over for him now."

The other children in the playground had also been watching. At this point the consciousness of the group united, and they all took off after the bully. Several boys jumped on him and beat him up, thus saving the smaller child from the bully's wrath.

But the cycle still had not ended.

One of the kids among the rescuers, feeling really strong with the might and power of the group, took it upon himself to dole out even more justice. While the bully was walking away crying, the other boy ran over and tackled him from behind, whereupon the bully turned around and beat up his attacker. So the other boy learned that you can carry a rescue just so far; it doesn't pay to add your personal vendetta to it.

The bully later blamed the detention officers for the whole string of troubles that came upon him. If the officers had interrupted the chase to begin with, he said, he would not have ended up getting beaten up himself.

As the ECKist watched this whole chain of events unfold, he realized that the bully had hoped someone would stop him, to prevent him from hurting himself. When no one interfered, the bully ended up taking his licking, and then turned around and pointed a finger at the detention officers.

That's how human nature reacts when it runs into trouble. As soon as a situation we have created works its way back to us, we look around and point to the first handy person to blame for our difficulties.

When a Mockingbird Sings

Every night when I go to bed, a mockingbird sings outside my window. He works an incredible shift that seems to last all night long. Each night he repeatedly goes through his entire repertoire of about twenty different songs.

Have you ever noticed how something nice can turn sour when you're not feeling well? For a couple of days I was under the weather, and his songs began to irritate me.

I was hoping he would take a night off, but as soon as I got into bed he started singing the same twenty songs, over and over, all night long.

Usually I find listening to the mockingbird a wonderful spiritual exercise. I recognize and accept the beauty of the music that the ECK has provided.

Mockingbirds like to sit up high in a tree or on a light pole. Maybe they like to get above everything so they can look it over. I don't know if the bird that sings outside of my window does it on purpose to tease the cats, but sometimes it sounds like he's saying "kitty-kitty-kitty-kitty." When a cat starts up the pole, it sounds like the bird is singing "naughty-naughty-naughty-naughty." At other times he seems to be singing "come here-come here-come here" or "teddy bear-teddy bear-teddy bear." Occasionally he likes to imitate a frog— "ribit-ribit-ribit-ribit." When the mockingbird feels really happy, he'll sing "pretty-pretty-pretty-pretty."

When you go to bed, listen in a gentle, calm way to the night sounds. Sometimes you'll hear the night birds, the sound of the air conditioning, the traffic outside, a helicopter flying overhead, or the soft rumble of voices. Just lie in bed and listen. You hear these different sounds so often that you unconsciously erase them from your mind. Put some attention on them now.

While you listen to these physical sounds, chant HU, and then listen for the sacred sounds of ECK. They come in many forms, sometimes as the ringing or tinkling of bells or the sound of musical instruments.

Try to identify as many different physical sounds as you can. Go to sleep with these sounds in your consciousness, all the while knowing that they are part of the HU, the universal Sound which embodies all others. Listen carefully, because in these sounds you will find the secret name of God.

May the blessings be.

ECKANKAR Creative Arts Festival, Anaheim, California, Saturday, June 15, 1985

It's best to tell a series of stories, preferably based on your own experiences, and then add a little bit of philosophy.

14

How to Give an ECK Talk

It requires a lot of creativity on my part to come up with subjects for talks for each seminar, to present them in a way that others would want to hear. These days, with the demands of keeping up with my daily work, I sometimes have only twenty minutes to prepare a talk. You have to trust the ECK—a lot.

Preparing for a Talk

I continually gather material as I go, but sometimes I use up everything in my notes. An ECK leader faced with giving a talk has to prepare for it under any circumstances that come up. A method that always helps me to bring it into focus is to take a shower.

I set the time when I'm going to prepare the talk, take a shower beforehand, and usually the most interesting ideas start pouring through. But then I can't write them down.

Declaring Yourself a Vehicle

The first thing to do before an ECK talk—or before doing anything important—is to declare yourself a vehicle

213

for the SUGMAD, the ECK, and the Mahanta. It's a time of letting yourself surrender entirely to the Inner Master, to the inner force of the ECK love.

Do it carefully, slowly, and quietly. Say: "I declare myself a vehicle for the SUGMAD," and then pause for a minute. Suddenly you can feel a certain distinctive force of the ECK coming in. When it seems to have settled after a few seconds, continue: "for the ECK," and you'll find that an entirely different current comes through. Finally you say, "and for the Mahanta." Again, still another energy comes through, this one happy and light, like a little lamb dancing along on musical feet.

This is the consciousness that can help you to relate to people, in an everyday way, a connection to the high principles of ECK and the SUGMAD.

Two Ways to Give Talks

There are two ways to give talks. The less desirable way is to give a speech about the philosophy, metaphysics, and spiritual principles of ECK. Philosophy is fine when you're talking one-on-one with somebody who just wants an explanation of ECK. But an audience is a group entity with a life of its own, entirely different from that of an individual. So the worst way to give a talk is to preach philosophy and then tag a couple of stories on as illustrations.

It's best to do the opposite—tell a series of stories, preferably based on experiences that you have gone through yourself, and then add a little bit of philosophy.

The Power of Parables

The better speakers throughout history have found stories and parables a more effective way to hint at the spiritual principles. Jesus told his followers that the parables were for the people outside the close inner circles, with the true mysteries given only to those within the inner circles. This is only half true.

A story is like a time capsule that contains a little spiritual bomb. It sticks with a listener. Weeks after he has heard it, the point of the story suddenly comes back to him; a little poof goes off inside, and now it has a special meaning. The story may come to mind during contemplation or while you are working, but it always comes in a nice, gentle way.

Whenever something out of the ordinary happens to you that has any kind of an impact, there is an ECK principle hidden in it. Even the most mundane activity, such as dealing with a used-car salesman, contains spiritual principles. How did you handle it? What did you learn? What ECK principles did you use?

Recently I had an experience that illustrates what happens when a person with a scientific understanding sees his facts fall down, and the inventive reasons he comes up with to cover the fallibility of science.

Purification Cycles

About two weeks ago, I wasn't feeling well. Those of you who are leaders in ECK may also notice that just before certain seminars, a purging takes place, causing impurities to come to the surface. This benefits not only yourself but the consciousness in ECK. You are helping in the Mahanta's work: to purify and bring about a cleansing throughout the body of ECK.

We don't make a big deal about our troubles; everybody has them, and their purpose is for us to learn. I had a sore throat, but I figured it would go away on its own. I tried my own home remedies, and in the meantime I kept working. Several article deadlines came up and other administrative matters had to be taken care of so that I could prepare for this seminar.

But the soreness in my throat didn't go away. The lymph gland on the left side of my throat began to swell, and pretty soon the swelling crossed over to the other side.

I don't often go to doctors, but when the chips are down, medicine can help you out of a hole. Then you can figure out the reason for the illness later. I used to be very down on doctors—my apologies to ECKists in the medical profession—but I found that healings from the ECK come in many different ways, and you take what you need at the moment. The ECK gives it to you, and you need only open up your consciousness to accept what is there.

It doesn't pay to be a purist about the medical profession or anything else. True, doctors don't have all the answers, but if the ECK nudges you to go to a doctor, then go to a doctor. You have the illness for some reason, so go and learn what you can about it. Then maybe you can take care of it on your own.

My throat got so swollen that I couldn't eat or drink, and I began to lose weight. This went on for several days. That's when I learned the pleasures of groaning. When everything hurts, groaning offers some relief.

I groaned for three days before finally deciding to go see the doctor. When I got to his office at the appointed time on Friday morning, he looked worse than I did. He practically staggered as he led me down the hall to the examination room. This man's not well, I thought. Maybe the ECK brought me here because *he* needs help.

The doctor took my temperature, and using the tongue depressor, he looked down my throat. "My, my, my," he

216

said. They like to say things like that. "I'm going to give you some pills to take. Consider yourself contagious, and stay home for a while." Great, I thought, the seminar is coming up, and I'm contagious.

He took a culture from my throat and sent it to the lab. It was diagnosed as beta strep, which is usually quite painful. He offered to prescribe pain medication, but I declined.

When I got home, I crunched up one of the antibiotics, steamed some vegetables, and mixed it all together in the blender. With my sore throat, it took me over an hour to finish a small bowl. Later that afternoon I was lying down for a while when suddenly I felt a strange sensation, like something was stuck in my throat. With no warning, the infection had broken, and a stream of impurities came out. When that was over, I noticed that my sore throat was gone and I could swallow again. It happened almost instantly.

By Monday morning, except for a little remaining weakness, I felt fine. I had an appointment with the doctor to find out the results of another test. When I got to his office, I was pleased to see that he now looked in good health.

"Open your mouth," he said. He peered in and found that my throat looked pretty good.

"Does it still hurt?"

"No," I said, "it doesn't hurt a bit." The doctor was very surprised. Beta strep doesn't clear up that quickly.

He walked to the other side of the room and sat down. I could tell from his expression that his mind was working to come up with an explanation. Finally he said, "Well, from all indications, the laboratory test on Friday was wrong. It was a milder throat infection that really doesn't need much treatment."

Then he started to believe himself. As he built his case for scientific knowledge, giving several reasons why it couldn't have been beta strep, he regained his confidence and sat up straighter. I didn't want to discourage him by describing how the infection had broken open in my throat. I figured when he ran out of ways to excuse himself and the failings of science, he'd stop.

He didn't ask me any questions about what had happened with my sore throat, because he didn't want his ideas upset. At the end of his little speech in defense of the fallacy of the tests three days earlier, I politely thanked him for all of his help and assured him I felt much better. He accepted my gratitude graciously. Before leaving, of course, I had to sign the necessary forms for the bill.

I was quite amazed by this doctor's resourcefulness. He had made a diagnosis based on a theory, and it didn't hold up. He then used more creativity to explain why the theory failed than he had in making the original diagnosis.

Defining ECK Terms

As you give an ECK talk, define the ECK terms. Use equivalent words the listener is used to hearing, so that he can make a connection with something that is familiar to him.

People in the audience don't necessarily know that ECK means the Holy Spirit, or the Holy Ghost—that essence which is imperfectly described in the New Testament—so you have to tell them. Otherwise you might as well be talking to yourself.

We often speak about the Light and Sound of ECK. You can explain that the Holy Spirit is actually the Voice of God, which can be seen as Light and heard as Sound. This is the only way that God makes Himself known to man—

not through a voice from the heavens; the lower lords use that method.

When speaking to others, it may be simpler to refer to God as Him instead of IT, as we usually do in ECKANKAR. If you mention the SUGMAD, it means nothing to the uninitiated unless you explain that SUGMAD is a word for God. When using the word "Mahanta," explain that this is a high state of consciousness, similar to the Christ state of consciousness. There is a difference, but at this point a lengthy definition would be confusing to the listener.

Show ECK Principles in Action

At times you will hear stories from ECKists who experienced protection because they remembered to use the word "HU" or "Mahanta." These stories are valuable illustrations of how the ECK works in one's daily life.

Two ECKists shared a story with me which points out that there are certain rules involved in travel. Whether it's on earth or in the other worlds, you have to know and respect the rules that apply in the different areas you are visiting. If you are not traveling with an experienced tour guide, you must accept the responsibility for yourself. On the inner planes, the best tour guide is the Mahanta.

Returning from a business trip in the Middle East, the two ECKists stopped in Greece for a holiday before continuing on to the United States to attend an ECKANKAR seminar. The two young men passed through customs, unaware that they were supposed to declare the large amount of money they were carrying into the country.

Everything went fine until it was time to leave Greece. At the airport they were stopped at customs and searched. The officials discovered that they were carrying a large sum of money, but the two ECKists didn't have a declaration to prove that they'd had it when they entered the country. They were taken to a jail cell, a small, narrow room with one dirty mat on the floor, with the threat of having to serve a minimum six-month jail sentence.

The ECKists were permitted to contact the embassy of their country. An embassy representative said he would try to figure out some way to get them released. "But," he added, "it doesn't look very good for you. You could be here a long time."

After the embassy spokesman left, one of the ECKists began to chant HU. His companion joined him. Later they read from *The Shariyat-Ki-Sugmad*, which they had been allowed to take into the cell.

The purpose of the ECK books is to spiritualize the individual's consciousness. This is why it helps to read from one of the books before you do a contemplation. But if you find yourself in trouble, a good way to spiritualize yourself quickly is to simply chant HU.

The two ECKists read and chanted throughout the night. In the morning, accompanied by the Greek attorney assigned to defend them, they appeared before the magistrates. Their defense was further complicated by the fact that the attorney was not fluent in their language.

The ECKists explained that they hadn't intended any harm, nor did they realize they were being dishonest by entering the country without declaring their money. But justice in the Greek court system is very definite: In cases such as this, regardless of one's motives, breaking the law means a long jail sentence.

After the arguments were heard, the three magistrates retired to their chambers to deliberate the case. When they came back to the courtroom, they declared the ECKists not guilty. Furthermore, their money would be returned and they would be allowed to leave the country. The verdict was so unexpected that the entire courtroom burst into applause.

The ECKists had found themselves in a very bad situation, but they found their way out of it simply by remembering to chant HU and put their attention upon the ECK and the Mahanta. A story like this has good value in a talk because it illustrates how the power of the ECK works in a real-life situation when you follow the true path of Light and Sound, for ECK is the path of life.

The first few years after I joined ECKANKAR, I continued to go to our country church because of the social pressures. I still had to work with other people in the community, and it would have been very awkward for my family if I'd stopped. I didn't yet have the spiritual strength to stop going, but I did the next best thing.

Instead of sitting downstairs with the others during the services, I used to go upstairs and sit in the choir loft, in the back by the window. Away from the others, my mind could wander and have a good time. I would often daydream about some of the stories I'd heard about the farmers in our community.

Tell a Good Story

One of the stories involved an elderly farmer who had a reputation as a skinflint. I always liked him, maybe because I was like him in some ways.

The farmer liked to sit up in the choir loft, too. He always sat in the back of the balcony, where he felt free to smoke his cigars. This was not appreciated by the choir members, who found themselves surrounded by clouds of smoke as they sang their beautiful hymns. The farmer tried to lessen the effect by opening the stained-glass window, but most of the smoke blew all over the balcony, causing some of the choir members to cough during their performance.

One of the baritones decided it was time to put an end to it. One Sunday morning he loaded a cigar with toothpick-size explosives, and offered it to the farmer. He knew the man was so tight with money that he'd never turn down anything that was free.

Sure enough, the farmer accepted the cigar and took it upstairs to the balcony. The rest of the choir were in on the joke, and they giggled among themselves as they waited for him to light up and get the explosion over with. But for some reason he decided not to smoke it right away.

When the choir was just about ready to start singing, the farmer finally reached for the cigar. They all watched as he lit it and took a few puffs. Suddenly, with a loud boom, the cigar exploded and plastered tobacco all over his face. The choir couldn't help laughing as they tried to sing. The people downstairs turned and looked up at them, trying to figure out the reason for the loud commotion, the giggling choir, and the cloud of smoke hovering over the balcony.

There is an ECK principle in this story, of course. It shows that the Law of Karma eventually catches up with those who invade the space of others.

The farmer did not take the joke well, but he caught on fast. Never again did he smoke in the balcony—except for his own cigars.

Creative Solutions

The creative f low goes on all the time. You learn that no matter where you are or what the problem is, the first step to the solution is always within reach. If you don't have the answer yourself, ask around. Somebody near you will come up with ideas to get you started, and you can take it from there.

It sometimes requires a lot of creativity to get to an ECK seminar. Despite your careful plans, an airline goes on strike. So what do you do now? Talking to someone else might turn up a lead for alternate transportation.

You do the best you can on your own, and by tapping into the ECK, It will tell you what to do next. It works; otherwise many of you wouldn't be here today. The ECK works in even the simplest areas of your life.

Choosing Topics

As an ECK vehicle, you have to be careful of what you say. A fire fighter once told me a very funny story involving a fire, and I decided to use it as part of a talk. Halfway through the story, I smelled smoke coming from backstage. I struggled to keep my attention on the talk. All the while I was thinking, Uh-oh, burning wires; this could be a real problem! I reminded myself to choose my topics more carefully in the future. Thoughts and words are very real things.

Later I learned that as I was telling the fire story, some overloaded wires backstage started to heat up. To make matters worse, somebody back there was about to pour a glass of water on the smoking wires.

Just at that moment, the fire fighter whose story I was telling happened along, grabbed the glass of water from the guy's hand, and prevented a bigger problem. He then hurried to the circuit box and shut off just enough lights to relieve the overloaded circuitry.

Travel Opens Up Our Past

Many of you find that as you travel, past lives open up. You learn things about yourself—about your instincts and behavior—that you never knew before. Travel is often a revisiting of places you've lived before.

If you are not able to attend a seminar physically, it sometimes helps just to put your attention upon the place where the seminar is being held.

Why ECK Seminars Are Important to You

An ECK seminar is always a spiritual occasion. It stirs and speeds up the spiritual activity within Soul. This is why it's important to come to the seminars when you can. We have a number of workshops, roundtable discussions, and talks designed to help you to learn how to live the life of ECK. We continually upgrade the programs to keep them fresh, and we appreciate having your input on how they can be more helpful to you.

The ECK path must always be responsive to the needs of the initiate, so that you in turn can be responsive to the person who is new to ECK.

These seminars teach you how to be a better vehicle for the ECK, to reach the people who want news of the Light and Sound of God in the same way you once did. When you are filled with the love of the ECK, you can do nothing else but share it and give it out. Not always in words, but by your presence and by your being. Others will feel the love, and they will respond to it.

As you leave today, you will be carrying the Light and Sound of ECK back home with you. And so on your journey, may the blessings be.

ECKANKAR Creative Arts Festival, Anaheim, California, Sunday, June 16, 1985

The reason the meals tasted so good in that restaurant was because of the love that was put into making and serving the food.

Nov 09

15
What Is Love?

In *The Shariyat-Ki-Sugmad* there is a sentence that says, "The capability to love is the most noble of all qualities of Soul, for to love is a greater ability than to rule over one's fellowman."

A Matter of Perception

Yesterday while driving past a river, we saw a man fishing from the shore. Beside him stood an enormous bird, almost as tall as the man, waiting to be fed. It looked as if the bird was keeping his eye on the fisherman while he worked to get the bird its food. The people in our car made a joke about it, wondering if the fisherman were actually the servant of the bird.

It reminded me of the attitude of some people who come onto the ECK path saying, "What can ECK do for me?" They are somewhat like the fisherman who thinks he's fishing for himself, not knowing he's really doing it for the big bird. They don't realize that the real question is, "What can I do for ECK?"

Earlier today, it was raining heavily. The man once again stood on the shore fishing, but the bird wasn't

227

anywhere in sight. Since the fisherman was willing to do all the work, why should the bird be so foolish as to stand out in the pouring rain?

The man who asks, "What can ECK do for me?" is actually a slave, in a sense, mindlessly fishing in the rain. He's doing it the hard way, and he's doing it for the wrong reason. In his relationship with the ECK, he thinks he's fishing for himself; but actually, everything he does has to be for the ECK, because until it is, it's done for nothing.

The Gift of Healing

When we have love, the protection of the ECK comes through and helps us in our daily life. If we don't have love, there is no way for the power of the ECK to strike our consciousness; therefore, we never know when the help is there. So we cry and say, "I am in trouble, and the Lord is not healing me. God has forsaken me."

A man came up to me at a seminar about a year ago. He said his wife had died, or translated, several months earlier; and he complained that I didn't even send a card. He was very angry.

"The Mahanta was there," I said, "but you weren't listening. You were too angry and upset to let him heal you." It took another couple of weeks before the lesson finally got through to him that the Mahanta had been there all the time, waiting to heal his heart.

Earth is an impermanent place where everything is subject to change. Each of us goes through the sorrow of separation. The moment comes when our loved ones must translate and leave earth. Our hearts are broken as we feel the empty spaces that used to be filled by someone who shared the meals and quiet times with us.

These spaces will remain empty for a while, sometimes for a couple of years, before we are open enough to heal the heartache of separation. The ECK has already given us the gift of healing; all we have to do is open ourselves to accept it.

Everything we need is always here. If there is a time when you feel you are without the blessings of God, or the blessings of ECK, ask: Am I open to the love of ECK?

Recognizing the Needs of Others

When we have the love of ECK, we have Its protection. As vehicles for the ECK, we can help others. We can give advice if it is wanted or asked for, or we can just be there to give a helping hand to someone in their time of need.

People who come to an ECK seminar for the first time usually aren't looking for advice; they are looking for someone who will just listen to them. But some of the new people have found that the ECKists they met never stopped talking about the philosophy of ECK.

It didn't occur to these ECKists that by listening they could learn what the new person's needs were. Sometimes it's best to simply ask the other person: What would you like to know? Maybe the person has problems and just needs someone to talk to. By listening, you are giving.

And when you listen—when you are open to the ECK and you have the love of ECK—the protection is given to you in any number of ways: to help you in your diet, to help you chart out your future course of business. It helps even in the smallest areas of your life.

A Protective Sleep

On a plane trip to Holland, the flight attendant served my meal in the usual little square plastic dish. I was hungry enough to eat it all, but decided I'd better not touch the sugary dessert. The plate also contained cheese and some sausage. I don't do well with dairy products anymore, but I wanted some cheese. The sausage looked good, too, even though I know what they use to make it.

I was just about ready to dig in when I saw some movement out of the corner of my eye. The only fly on the entire plane chose my cheese to land on. Just then, the person sitting next to me put down his fork. "Don't eat the meat," he said. "It's spoiled." That took care of any intention I might have had to eat any of that meal.

Many times the ECK brings a blessing to us, but because it comes in the form of depriving us of something that looks good to us, we complain. But the ECK was actually saying: This food is spoiled, and it will make you very sick. The fly stayed on my plate long enough to deliver the message, then it flew away and didn't come back.

After the meal I fell asleep. Later I learned that I had slept right through another danger without even knowing it.

One of the people traveling with me wanted some orange juice. He decided I'd probably wake up thirsty, so he ordered a glass for me, too. After he drank his juice, he saw that I was still asleep, and it appeared that I wasn't going to wake up until we got to Holland. Rather than let my juice go to waste, he decided to drink it. He took a sip, but it tasted funny. He realized it was spoiled.

When I awoke, he didn't say anything for a long time. Finally he told me what had happened. "During the night I ordered some orange juice for us. But yours turned out to be no good, so I sent it back."

Even while I slept, I had a juice taster looking out for me. The protection of the ECK works in subtle ways. "Thank you for checking out my orange juice for me," I said.

"Think nothing of it," he replied graciously.

Putting Love into Your Day

ECK is found in the very things that we do every day. Here in Holland, I found a little Dutch restaurant that was very good. The prices were reasonable; the food was simple, tasty and plentiful; and the waiter very accommodating when I asked to substitute the dessert with more vegetables. The food was light and easy to digest. I couldn't help wondering why such a simple meal tasted so good.

The next time I returned to the restaurant, I noticed there were a couple of birds—a parrot on a high perch near the ceiling and a large exotic bird in a cage with no door. The owner of the restaurant occasionally stopped what she was doing, lifted the parrot from its perch, and spent a few minutes playing with it and stroking its feathers. When she was ready to place the bird back on its perch, it would resist for a moment, not wanting to leave her because of all the love she was giving it.

Several of the other employees would occasionally pause in their work to lovingly stroke the feathers of the bird in the cage. Later I noticed the owner carefully arranging flowers in small vases for the dining tables, and all the flowers were fresh. Her great love for living things was obvious.

The meals tasted so good in that restaurant not because of the ingredients that were used, but because of the love that was put into making and serving the food. The owner had the ability to select employees who had the capacity to love. Even the background music was soft and tasteful, and I could tell it had been chosen with care.

If you are preparing a meal, or performing even the smallest task, do it in the name of the SUGMAD or in the name of the ECK. Put love into it instead of the frustrations of your day. Because whatever you put into the food is a reflection of what you have inside yourself. It goes out to your family, it goes out to your friends, and it makes a very real difference.

An Experience with the Light and Sound

When an individual begins to ask, What is love?—even if it's years before he comes in contact with the teachings of ECK—in some manner a demonstration will be given of the Light and Sound.

Years ago a college student had stayed up two nights in a row cramming for finals. On the third day, after she took the last exams, she could hardly wait to go home and get some sleep. But her body was so exhausted that when she lay down, she immediately went out of the body.

She stood off to the side of the bed and looked around. Seeing her body laying there, she thought she must have died. She even considered phoning her mother to let her know. That made sense to her at the time, because when you are out of the body in full consciousness, you are more alive than you've ever been.

People who have an experience such as this, even years before coming into ECKANKAR, never really fear death again. They are curious now and want to have the experience again. It haunts them and guides them. Without knowing from where or why this power came, they can actually feel it. They accept that in times of trouble or peril there is a Master or a guardian angel standing by to help and protect them. Where love exists there can be no fear; and where there is fear, there can be no truth.

When a person is ready to ask, What is love? and has asked in sincerity—in the spirit of humbleness and a desire for truth—then love will come to the individual in a way that is necessary.

This was the young college student's first out-of-the-body experience. She didn't know that the Mahanta, the Living ECK Master was standing by to see how she would handle this experience of expanded consciousness.

As she stood by the bed, something caught her attention. She turned and looked out the bedroom window. Suddenly there appeared a shaft of brilliant blue-white light, probably six to eight feet in diameter. With it came a sound almost like a rushing wind, but more of a pulsing, electrical sound.

Then she found herself back in bed, united with her body. It was many years before she met the Master who had been with her during her first experience of the Light and Sound of ECK.

This is one way in which the truth of the Holy Spirit, the ECK, is brought to some people. We aren't frozen in time; the miraculous religious experiences didn't stop occurring after the biblical times, nor were they limited to a few isolated saints.

If a spiritual teaching is true and alive, experiences of the Light and Sound of God are a very real part of the follower's life. In ECKANKAR there are probably more people who have this type of experience than on any other path on earth.

This doesn't mean that every person will have such an experience before he comes to ECK, or within a year or five years after he comes to ECK. Most of us have spent lifetimes coming to the point where we have earned the right to ask the question What is love? and get an answer.

What Is Love?

What is love? ECK is love; God is love. But God is not an individual who walks among men in the human embodiment. So when the answer comes that ECK is love, which is to say the Holy Spirit is love, we then ask, How can I know love? And the answer is, through the Light and Sound of God.

The question then is, How can I get the Light and Sound of God in my own life? The answer that has been given for ages is simply: through the Spiritual Exercises of ECK. They are simple, and there are many of them.

Anytime a certain exercise no longer works for us, it means we have unfolded beyond the scope of this particular spiritual exercise or personal, secret word. It's time for us to use our creative abilities to go a step further, to find another word or another spiritual exercise, so that we can tune in to the higher level of spirituality which we have attained in the spiritual worlds. Then it is up to us to become aware of it in the physical state of consciousness.

A housewife took a job as a teacher. She soon found that every minute of her time at home was spent cooking meals, cleaning the house, grading test papers, or preparing lessons for her class.

She often thought about an experience of many years ago in which she had seen the Light and heard the Sound. When she first heard about the teachings of ECK, she said, "This is it!"

But just saying "this is it" is not enough. She was too busy to do the Spiritual Exercises of ECK, to take another step on the path which would allow her to unfold toward truth, to a fuller expression of love.

One night Peddar Zaskq, or Paul Twitchell, came in the Soul body and took her out of the physical body. Together they went downstairs to the kitchen. As soon as they sat down at the table, he said to her, "You're not serious enough."

When she woke up, she couldn't understand what the experience was all about. Wasn't she working from morning until night, taking care of all kinds of duties? Everybody else thought she was *too* serious. Why would the Mahanta say she wasn't serious enough? The fact is, she was serious—about all the things that didn't matter.

There's a biblical story in which two sisters, Mary and Martha, received Jesus in their home. While Martha ran around preparing the food, Mary sat quietly listening to Jesus, who was a master.

Martha complained to Jesus that her sister had left her to serve the food alone and asked Jesus to get Mary to help. Jesus replied, "But one thing is needful." He was trying to tell her that there is something more important than physical food, and that is spiritual food. She was running around taking care of food for the physical body while the spiritual body went hungry.

Paul was trying to tell this individual that she wasn't serious enough about wanting truth and wanting to learn about divine love. When the understanding eventually came to her, she began to do the spiritual exercises, and then she found the Light and Sound returning to her. Once again she began to have the experiences she was looking for.

Accepting the Gift of Love

I had a conversation with an individual who, with great sincerity, said he wanted love to enter his life. He asked if I could give him a definition for love.

I thought about the immensity and scope of ECK and divine love. Finally I said, "I really can't give you a definition for love at all. If you want to open your heart, you can read *Stranger by the River*. If you really want to know what love is, the answer is going to have to come to you in the form of another human being. But when the love comes, you will have to be open enough to accept it."

He then said he wanted to learn how to give love. I agreed that was a very good thing to learn, because giving is the first step. The hardest part is to learn how to give love; but once it is learned, the second step, which is more important, must be to accept love. Until this is done, the full gift of love has not been received or enjoyed.

"If you want love," I said, "the ECK will bring you someone to show you what love is, and this will be the definition for you." But, I added, when it comes, it's not something that can be taken for granted; it's something you are going to have to earn day by day. Like a high state of consciousness, it must be rewon every day. You can't rest on your laurels.

When one asks in sincerity "What is love?" and opens his heart, the ECK will bring the gift that is already there and has been there all along. But the individual must do the spiritual exercises to stay open to the guidance that is needed every day to preserve and nurture that love.

Living ECK Every Day

This same individual then asked, "What can I do to serve the Living ECK Master? I have so many blessings from ECK, but what can I give back?"

I said, "What you are doing already is the proper service for the Holy Spirit. You are doing everything that is needed for now. But when love enters your heart more fully, you will know what to do, and you'll be able to give more and better."

It's fine to distribute the ECK brochures, as this man was doing, but when others can see and appreciate the

Spirit of ECK within you, they will ask, What is ECK? Without knowing it, they are really asking, What is love?

ECK is not something you just talk about; it is a life to demonstrate and live. As you live it, others will see and know it. Soon they will come to you and ask, What is ECK? and all the other questions that follow as they try to find out more about what makes you the way you are.

It isn't so much what ECKists say, but what they are. They carry the Light and Sound, and they live their religious teaching.

What really comes through is the Light that shines from ECKists. They are a living testament to ECK and the teachings of ECKANKAR, just as you are when you carry the Light and Sound home with you from the ECK seminars. People can see and feel and know that there is something different about you.

The Give and Take of Love

As a gift of love is given, it must be returned. An ECKist recently wrote to tell me of an incident that took place many years ago when he worked at a paper mill in a remote town near the U.S.-Canadian border. To do their shopping, the townspeople had to drive quite a distance along a deserted stretch of highway to get to the nearest city.

One weekend the man started the trip to the city to pick up some supplies. On a stretch of road that ran through the forest he saw parked cars and a group of people gathered around the path that led to the woods. There wasn't much excitement in that remote area, so naturally the man was curious to see what had drawn so many people. He parked his car and walked over to join them.

As he worked his way through the crowd, he saw a big black bear sitting on its haunches, its front paws up in the air. Right away he spotted the problem: The bear had thorns stuck in his paws.

Being a practical sort, the man hurried back to his car and got a pair of pliers. He then returned to the bear and pulled out the thorns. As soon as he finished, the bear got back down on all fours and sprinted off into the woods. Gradually the people got back in their cars and went about their business.

The man continued on to the city and did his shopping. Three hours later he started back home along the same route. When he reached the spot where he had seen the bear earlier, he again noticed a bunch of cars parked at the side of the road. I wonder what's going on now, he thought. He parked his car, worked his way through the crowd, and found the very same black bear, this time intently examining the face of each person before him.

Suddenly the bear saw the man who had pulled the thorns from his paws. The curious crowd watched as the bear turned and ran a short distance into the woods, went behind a bush for a moment, and came running back with two pails of blueberries dangling from his mouth. He went right over to the man and stood patiently in front of him, the handles of the pails clasped between his teeth, until finally the man got the hint and took the pails from him. His deed accomplished, the bear quickly turned around and headed back into the woods.

Truth is stranger than fiction, and these things do happen. But where would a bear get two pails of blueberries? A bear in the woods can get anything he wants. I suspect there's another story behind this one that may someday be revealed.

It has to do with a berry picker out in the woods alone who suddenly sees a huge black bear standing nearby on its hind legs. With a ferocious roar, the bear probably says something like, "Sir, may I have those blueberries, please?" And being an openhearted person, the berry picker no doubt replies, "Certainly; I can pick some more later"— and runs off screaming.

The man who helped the bear didn't have any fear because he was filled with love. When one of the creatures of ECK was in need of help, he gave it without hesitation. Once given, the gift of love had to be returned—and so it was.

As to the question "What is love," I don't have a definition for you. Until you can find the answer for yourself, you are living the letter of ECK, but you have yet to find the Spirit of ECK.

ECKANKAR European Seminar, The Hague, The Netherlands, Friday, July 19, 1985

When the young ECKist used this spiritual exercise, she
went out of the body in full consciousness and found herself
in a video arcade in the other worlds.

16

The Mahanta's Hidden Ways

Until one finds the way to love, to love *truly*, he will never understand the Spirit of ECK. Unless he understands the Spirit of ECK—or better, can accept It—he will have difficulty with Soul Travel, with the spiritual exercises, and also with his dream experiences.

The Mahanta, the Living ECK Master uses many different methods to try to get through the individual's barriers or resistance. One spiritual exercise or another is tried, and then another, to approach the individual's state of consciousness from a number of different ways.

Opening the Doors of Love

The love of the ECK is in our lives. It is simply the lack of recognition which causes us to feel that the Master is not there to take us into the other worlds and that we are not being given the spiritual help we need or deserve.

So the first task is to open the doors of love for the individual. This is often difficult to do, because the time spent by Soul in the lower worlds has been devoted mostly to power—the acquisition of power under the guise of love or any of its qualities.

241

This is love misunderstood and not correctly seen. This is where relationships are entered into for one's own gain rather than to give the spirit of life to another or to experience loving another as much or more than oneself.

Power takes and love gives, and Soul has spent centuries taking. Little by little, in the lifetimes leading to this one, the ECKist finds that he has increased his capacity for love. Now he is looking for a greater ability to love. Once he acquires this ability, the worlds of God are opened, the protection is recognized for what it is, and his way is made clear.

The communication between Soul and the Mahanta must be understood and seen clearly: Soul is made of the ECK, and the ECK is the Mahanta. At some point the recognition must come that a person is one with the ECK. This can only be realized through love.

A Question of Perception

In the discourses that Paul Twitchell wrote, he wove intricate, delicate thoughts that almost go beyond the mind's capacity to understand. In fact, the only way to grasp the concepts about the Mahanta, the ECK, and the SUGMAD that he's trying to give Soul is through the faculty of spiritual perception. But sometimes there is a gap in communication, and we don't perceive correctly. This reminds me of the story of the little boy who colored everything black.

Every time the teacher asked her class to draw a picture, the children would use a variety of crayons—red, green, blue, yellow—except for one little boy who colored everything black. The other children drew pretty, colorful rainbows, but this little boy made them black and white.

The teacher found this very disturbing. What was wrong with this child? Perhaps a trauma had occurred at home that had caused some psychological damage. She began to watch him very closely, but over the next few weeks nothing changed: he continued to color everything black. She decided she'd better mention the boy's problem to the school psychologist.

The psychologist visited the classroom to observe the boy. She saw for herself that while the other children used all the different colors, this child colored all the pictures with his black crayon. The psychologist later consulted with a few colleagues, and together they came to the conclusion that the boy probably had deep-seated problems stemming from some trauma suffered in infancy.

The next step was to question the boy's parents. The psychologist arranged to have them come to her office to discuss the problem, but the parents could think of nothing that would account for the child wanting to color everything black. The psychologist suspected the parents weren't owning up to what they had done to the child to create such an aberration.

The psychologist decided on a course of action that would help the child out of his psychological problems. She called him in to her office to begin the program. After several probing questions, she finally asked the big one: "Why do you color everything black?"

The boy answered immediately, "Because it's the only crayon I have."

We are like this when we judge another person. We tend to judge him on the one color or one aspect that we have seen from our own limited view of him.

When an individual does this with the Mahanta, the individual evaluates the ECK works from his limited view. He concludes that ECK is this or ECK is that. Maybe he says ECK is not what he would have liked it to be, so ECK has failed him. The lack is actually in the individual's perception.

A gentlemen told me that, in the past, whenever an accident happened to him, it was regarded as something to become angry about. He would say, "Why did this happen to me? It must have been a psychic attack."

But this individual has learned how to look for help from the Mahanta behind these so-called accidents. He has gained the ability to look for the silver lining in the cloud and to see why the ECK brought this apparent misfortune to him.

Now he says, "Maybe there is a good reason for this problem. Maybe it is necessary for my spiritual unfoldment. If I look a little closer, I'll become aware of what the Mahanta has done for my benefit. I simply don't recognize it because of my limited state of consciousness."

Attitude and Awareness

A young lady visited her grandmother. The elderly woman lived in an older home with a steep, narrow staircase leading to the second floor. The granddaughter carried her bags upstairs to the guest room and left them on the bed. As she was coming back downstairs, the carpet on the stairs slipped out from under her foot, but she was able to grab the handrail in time to prevent a tumble down the stairs.

It didn't even cross her mind that someone might be sending her a psychic attack, but she did wonder about the reason for the accident. After considering it, she thought, What if Grandma, in her advanced age, had stepped on the loose carpet? Without the agility of youth, she would have fallen down the stairs and seriously hurt herself.

The young woman checked the carpet all the way down the stairs and found a few other loose nails. She got a hammer and new nails and secured the carpet tightly, insuring that her grandmother could walk up and down the stairs in safety.

This woman recognized that behind the apparent accident, in which no serious injury had occurred, there was a message to look for a deeper problem. She felt the Mahanta had used this near accident to prevent serious injury to her grandmother. Instead of cursing the carpet or the loose nails, she repaired the problem before it became serious. This is one example of the hidden ways of the Mahanta.

When an accident occurs, many people waste time looking for someone to blame. All the while the help of the ECK is nearby. The Mahanta is there saying, "I am always with you," and the protection that you have earned is yours. But because our limited state of consciousness lets us see only a small circle around ourselves, we assume that everything that could occur has happened within the circle of our awareness.

This brings us to the purpose of the circles of ECK initiation, which are literally like circles of awareness. A person in the Second Circle may not have seen the real reason for the accident. But later, after the Third Initiation, he would work from an expanded circle of awareness and see a little deeper into life. This is why the initiates of the higher circles are able to look behind the layers and see facets of life which are completely unknown to the average person who has yet to begin the studies of ECK.

Recognizing Protection

Years ago, before gasoline shortages of the early seventies prompted restrictions on speed to save gas, an ECKist

245

was driving along a desert highway. Traffic was moving about fifteen miles per hour over the posted speed limit. At one point the line of cars crested a hill, but they couldn't see the radar trap that awaited them when they came down the other side doing eighty.

As soon as the drivers spotted the police car, they hit the brakes and slowed to sixty-five—except for the ECKist. She had always felt that honesty is the best approach in life, and she wasn't about to become a hypocrite now. Instead of hitting the brakes, she lifted her foot from the accelerator and coasted to a slower speed.

If you were a traffic officer clocking everybody at sixty-five miles per hour, except for one car that was gradually coasting down to seventy-five, who would you stop? The officer pulled this individual over to the side of the road and walked over to her car. "You were going way over the speed limit," he said. "I'm going to have to give you a ticket."

"But everybody else was speeding, too," she said.

"Maybe so, but not when I clocked them," he said.

"What's the difference?" she said. "We were all speeding."

"But they were smart enough to step on the brakes."

They went back and forth about it for a while, and finally he relented. "All right, instead of giving you a ticket for going fifteen miles per hour over the speed limit, I'll make it five miles, and the fine will cost you only $15.00." The ECKist still didn't think it was fair that she had been the only driver he'd stopped, but she had no choice but to accept it.

A mile down the road, still upset by the incident, she pulled in to a service station. The attendant filled the gas tank, checked the oil, and put water in the radiator. When

246

he checked her brand-new tires for air, he discovered that the left front tire had much more pressure in it than was safe. He immediately let some air out of the tire, explaining that traveling on the hot desert road at such high speeds could have caused that tire to blow out—which would have been a disaster.

As soon as she got to her destination, she mailed her ticket and the $15.00 fine to the police department. Along with it she included a thank-you note to the officer who had ticketed her, saying if he hadn't stopped her when he did, she likely would have been in a serious accident.

Someone else might have taken care of the tire without making the connection and continued to curse the policeman for the ticket. How thankless can some people be in life when life is standing by to protect them? You can be as thankless as the narrowness of your state of consciousness, or you can be as thankful as the expanded state of consciousness which you enjoy. And the expanded state of consciousness always depends upon the factor of love.

Expanded Consciousness

Only love can open the heart to reach out to the circles beyond the one in which the individual is established. For instance, a Second Initiate is established on the Astral Plane, and this is where he travels and moves with other initiates of the Second Circle. But with the expanded consciousness or Soul Travel, an individual is able to visit circles, or planes, beyond the Second, including the Third, Fourth, and Fifth—the Fifth being the Soul Plane, the first of the true spiritual worlds.

Regardless of where you are established, through love for the Mahanta, the ECK, or the SUGMAD, it is possible at times to expand the state of consciousness to areas beyond your level of initiation and to receive the love and blessings of the ECK.

The spiritual exercises must be done daily, and with love, in order to build the foundation for spiritual unfoldment and for reaching into the God Worlds of ECK.

Crossing the Borders of Death

As you advance in the teachings of ECK and as love begins to enter your heart, you are able to work with individuals who are ready to cross the borders through death.

An ECKist changed jobs and moved to another city, promising to keep in touch with an older woman in her hometown with whom she had a long-standing friendship. At first the two women telephoned each other regularly, but as the ECKist began to build a new life and make new friends, she became less inclined to keep the ties with people in her hometown.

Several years after moving, the ECKist heard that the other woman had suffered a stroke. She felt a nudge to give her old friend a call. The two women had a very nice conversation. But the older woman sounded sad as she reminisced about the bridge games she used to enjoy playing with her sister Anna and two of their friends, all of whom had died. On the other hand, she said, she still found pleasure in watching the soap operas on TV every afternoon.

The ECKist had told her friend a little about ECKANKAR over the years. During their conversation she said, "If you like, we can visit in the dream state. All you have to do is ask the Mahanta."

A few weeks later the ECKist got word that the other woman had died peacefully in her sleep a short time after their last conversation. The ECKist had a strong urge to converse with her old friend.

One evening while doing her spiritual exercises, she went into the other worlds and found herself in a setting similar to the physical plane, talking with her friend on the phone. The other woman said, "My sister Anna and our friends are here, and now we four can play bridge again." They talked a bit about the TV soap operas, and then the older woman said, "You know, I'm having a wonderful time here. It's a lot better than it was on earth."

The Christian concept of heaven is outmoded—frozen in time from two thousand years ago. People of the twentieth century are not going to see beings who walk around in robes and sandals; they are going to find themselves in a heaven with people who dress in a modern way. The consciousness of the human race has evolved in two thousand years, and so have the heavens.

Each person goes to a heaven he is in harmony with, although to imply that you go to the heaven where you belong would be considered a sacrilege in some of the orthodox religions. Many people still believe that when you die, your goal is to sit at the right hand of the Lord.

A Mission of Service

As the initiate works to develop in himself a deeper understanding of the secrets of ECK and establishes a closer bond of love with the Mahanta, he begins to serve the ECK. No longer does he serve only himself. He begins to reach out and become a vehicle to bring the message of ECK to people who, as he used to, wonder when someone will come along and bring the light so that they can find their way out of the darkness.

As the ECKist unfolds, he moves into greater areas of service. He becomes a Vahana, either silently or by giving talks. Everything is done in the name of the Mahanta, the ECK, or the SUGMAD. In other words, every action is done in the name of a principle greater than the human consciousness.

An initiate from Africa wrote about an experience he had while traveling to another country to give a talk at an ECK seminar. He explained that travel between African countries can be difficult. Each government has its own set of rules, which sometimes widely diverge from those of a neighboring country.

Due to a series of delays, the ECKist's flight was three hours late, arriving at its destination in the middle of the night. By then the cabdrivers had all gone home. The other passengers decided they had no choice but to spend the rest of the night in the airport and wait for the cabs to come in the morning.

But the ECKist was on a mission of service for the Mahanta, scheduled to speak in the morning at a hotel in a town about thirty-five kilometers away. He knew there was a police checkpoint about a kilometer down the road, and he hoped he could catch a ride from there. And so he began to walk through the night.

Before he had gone very far, an elderly gentleman in a battered old car pulled up alongside him. "Where are you going?" he called out. The ECK initiate named the town. "Get in," the man said. "I shall be happy to drive you." The ECKist quickly tossed his suitcase in the backseat and got in the car.

The old man drove along at a leisurely pace. Neither man spoke, but a wonderful feeling of love and bliss permeated the entire car. As they neared the city, the ECKist could hear the sound of the wind and beautiful music, accompanied by the scent of roses. This is often a sign of the presence of one of the ECK Masters, who in this case was the driver of the car.

The old man pulled up to the entrance of the hotel. "How much do I owe you for the ride?" the ECKist asked.

"It's my pleasure," said the driver with a little bow. "I am very happy to give you a ride."

From that moment on the ECKist was aware of the Light and the Sound, the Music of ECK, being with him. Because he took that extra step to carry the message of the Light and Sound to people who wanted to hear it, the blessing of the Light and Sound came to him.

When the Chela Is Ready

Sometimes an ECKist will complain that nothing ever happens. He has no experiences, he has never been out of the body. But I have to ask, How much have you truly done for ECK? Have you carried the ECK message to others out of love?

It's not enough to do it for yourself or to do it out of a sense of duty. The factor of love is so important for the initiate in ECK, because without love, there is no recognition of the Light and Sound or the presence and help of the Mahanta which are always with the individual.

About ten years ago, a soldier stationed at a military base in the Midwest had a persistent urge to keep a dream journal. He wasn't quite sure why, since he didn't remember any of his dreams. But as soon as he took the step of keeping a notebook and pen by his bed, he began to remember dreams, and he faithfully wrote each one down.

Pretty soon the experiences changed. They were no longer dreams; he was going into the other worlds in full consciousness.

One day, while reviewing the notes of his travels out of the physical body, he realized there was a pattern. Although he was in a state of awareness greater than the dream state, he was not in control of this travel; something else was directing his experiences.

While the soldier was out of the body one night, a spiritual traveler came to him in the Light body. Also called the Nuri Sarup, the Light body is a glittering form that appears to be made of a million little stars. The traveler took him by the hand, and together they soared high above a city. This being then directed his attention to a Temple of Golden Wisdom of such awesome beauty that the neophyte traveler was moved to tears.

There are many Temples of Golden Wisdom. Each houses a portion of the Shariyat-Ki-Sugmad, which contains the secret knowledge and wisdom of the Light and Sound. These works are under the guardianship of one of the ECK Masters.

This individual was eventually discharged from the service and returned to civilian life. Eight years later, while browsing in a bookstore, his friend pulled a book off the shelf and handed it to him. "I think you'll like this one," he said. It was *ECKANKAR—The Key to Secret Worlds*. He took the book from his friend and turned it over to read the back cover.

There he saw a picture of Paul Twitchell, whom he instantly recognized as the being who had taken him out of the body to the Temple of Golden Wisdom eight years earlier. The memory of that beautiful temple came rushing back, and he finally understood the purpose of the experience.

Eight years earlier he had not yet been ready to come into ECK. He needed more experience, he had to overcome his fear, and certain other preparations had to be made before he could take this step to meet the Master. When the chela is ready, the Master appears.

The Mahanta comes in the radiant body that sparkles and shines with a million lights, like twinkling stars. The inner experiences occur more often and with more vividness in ECK than in possibly any other spiritual path on earth, because this teaching has the Light and Sound as living elements.

The Light and Sound are the heart of ECK; they are the ECK. This is why ECKANKAR is the most direct path to God.

Freeing Victims of the Mind

It is the Mahanta's task to overcome the false instruction that Soul has gotten about the Holy Spirit, what God is, and what God is not. All these misconceptions must be put aside, because as they were wrongly built into the lower bodies of Soul, they were imbedded with fear.

"You must do this or that," the priestcraft said. "If you do not practice these rituals, if you do not ask forgiveness, or if you do not take communion, your soul will be damned." These fear factors were tied in with the false knowledge of life hereafter and the nature of Soul.

Because these wrong concepts are held so tightly by the mind, many people have trouble with Soul Travel. The stronger the person's mind, the more difficulty he has with the expansion of consciousness.

A strong mind is like a steel trap, which often makes it harder for a person to break out of this mental cage and have the experiences of God. The true saints of God may have been brilliant men, but they weren't victims of their own minds. They were people who could rise above the mind, its snares, and its doubts and fears.

In the inner experiences, one usually looks for the Master to appear in a long flowing robe and take him to visit a temple made of gold. But some people aren't comfortable with this. The Mahanta works with each person in a way he or she can understand and appreciate.

A very simple spiritual exercise that you might want to use was tried recently by one of the young ECKists, who had an unexpected adventure. She went out of the body in full consciousness, and found herself in a video arcade in the other worlds.

The Master took her over to a game of Pac-Man. The child soon became totally engrossed in the game. "I'm going to play a perfect game of Pac-Man!" she said. After a while she got very good at it.

Then all of a sudden it hit her: "What am I doing playing Pac-Man? I've got to get back to my spiritual exercises." As soon as she thought about what she had been doing in the physical body, she came back instantly, not realizing she had been in the Soul body on the inner planes. Later she figured it out: "The Mahanta had me out of the body, and I didn't even know it!"

The younger we are in consciousness, the less fixed are our expectations of what we should see in the other worlds. If we become as a child in consciousness, the world is an open book; the Mahanta has so much more room to work with us, and the chances of having a successful Soul Travel experience are greater.

In the spiritual works and discourses, there are complicated spiritual exercises and simple ones; some that work on the Light, others that work on the Sound, and still others that use both. I approach it from all different angles, so that anyone who is truly interested in finding Self-Realization or God-Realization can do so.

But the steps must be small and humble in the beginning. If the consciousness were opened to these high states of realization all at once, the person would be destroyed. It would be too much. He would either die on the spot or become useless and end up in a mental institution.

This often happens in cosmic consciousness, when a person is opened for the mental illumination before the preparations have all been made. He may get his split second in eternity. But since he wasn't prepared for it, he could end up a lunatic, commit suicide, or do any number of other strange things.

An individual who has the true cosmic consciousness before he is ready is seldom able to integrate into the community again. He's a stranger forever. He doesn't even know how to play the game of the Kal, how to play the illusions and get along.

Journey on an Ocean of Light

A good spiritual exercise to try is this: Tonight when you go to bed, close your eyes and locate the Spiritual Eye, which is at a point right above and between the eyebrows. Now very gently look for the Light, which can come in a number of different ways.

At first you may see just a general glow of light that you think is merely your imagination. It might appear as little blue spots of light, as a ray of light, or it could look like a beam of light coming through an open window from the sunshine outside. The white light may also show up in any number of different ways.

As you look for the Light, chant your secret word or HU, a name for God which has a power greater than the word *God* for many people. Watch as this Light turns into an ocean of light. Then, as you see It turn into an ocean, look for a little boat that's coming to shore very near where you are standing. At the helm is the Mahanta or one of the ECK Masters, who will invite you into the boat. Don't be afraid; just get in.

When you get to this point, allow any experience to follow that may. Set no limitations on it. You may end up in a video arcade, you may end up near or inside a Temple of Golden Wisdom, or you may have an experience of the Light and Sound of God coming directly into Soul.

May the blessings be.

ECKANKAR European Seminar, The Hague, The Netherlands, Saturday, July 20, 1985

I started working at folding the napkin correctly—and I learned by doing.

17

The Master Is Like All Men

Workshops and roundtable discussions at ECK seminars have a special purpose; they're more than just a place to exchange ideas. They actually let you experience conversing about ECK in simple, everyday terms, so that when people ask you about ECK, you will feel more comfortable discussing it with them. It will come out in a more natural way as you get used to talking about spiritual issues that mean something to you; and if these issues are meaningful to you, you can be sure they will mean something to others.

Caring about the Little Things

The waiter who served our table in a local restaurant had artfully folded the large, square napkins into the shape of a flower. The folded napkin looked like a lily on a lily pad. The four of us at the table took the napkins apart to see if we could figure out how he had done it, but it was such a complicated pattern that we got lost. The waiter noticed our efforts as he passed the table. "I'll be back in a minute to show you how to do it," he said.

As soon as he had waited on the other customers in his section, he returned to our table. Step by step, as if it were the most important thing he had to do, he began to form a napkin into a flower. Very carefully he folded it into many different layers, finally turning it over and pulling the ends out through the back to secure it. "There," he said when he had finished. Then he unfolded it again and generously showed us exactly how he had done it.

What impressed me the most about the man was his ability to give his complete attention to whatever he chose to do. He spent a good five minutes folding and refolding this napkin, until he was satisfied that we had understood.

I made up my mind to learn it well enough to show my daughter when I got home. I like to travel light, and this man's art was something I could carry home with me in my head. Taking a napkin off of a nearby table, I very slowly and carefully began to fold it.

Somewhere in the middle I forgot a step and got lost. But the waiter was watching. He came back over and pointed out the part I had missed. "This is what you do," he offered; then he waited to make sure I knew the rest of the steps. A few minutes later he returned to evaluate my handiwork. "Very, very good," he said. It wasn't nearly as good as his, but he was kind—the expert craftsman encouraging the beginner.

I might have remembered how to fold the napkin correctly simply by watching him, but I knew I'd remember it even better by doing it myself. At the risk of looking foolish, I started working at it—and I learned by doing.

It's the same with the Spiritual Exercises of ECK. We can read in the ECK books about how to do an exercise, but when the time comes to actually do it ourselves, we may be reluctant to try. There's a chance we might go out of the body or move into a higher state of consciousness. Or we may feel it's foolish to even try. We think, This is silly; it couldn't work.

But the only way you can really know is if you try. The first flower napkin you make may not be the best one, but the second and third will probably turn out better. It's a skill that improves only with practice, and it's best learned from someone who knows how to do it.

The four of us at the table thought we were pretty sharp, that we could figure out how to make this flower napkin by ourselves. But we couldn't do it because of the hidden folds that only someone with experience could point out to us. Once he showed us how to do it, it seemed simple.

He did it so well because he really cared about whatever he happened to be doing at the moment. God Consciousness is also attained by those who care about the little things. They know that the little things, the microcosm, contain the secrets of the macrocosm. By learning the lessons of the little things at hand, we can develop the skills and talents to handle the greater scope of the Godhead.

The Secret of Life

There are several different areas that have to be considered when putting forth the teachings of ECK, and many different people are involved in making it all work in a certain way. If one person needs more time to learn, then I have to go a little slower. But there is no hurry; each individual who works closely with the Master has the freedom to proceed at his own pace.

In the physical body, the Master is subject to the physical laws and depends very much upon those who are close to him. I am only as effective as those of you who are working closely with the Mahanta. The strength of ECK in the physical world depends upon the strength of love that individuals have for the Mahanta. If the love for the Mahanta is strong, we will be a strong force for carrying the ECK message into the world; and if the love is weak or uncertain, our efforts to serve the SUGMAD will be the same.

The way to build this strength of love is through the Spiritual Exercises of ECK. If you know how to love and how to put love into the Spiritual Exercises of ECK, you will then know how to live life correctly. There won't be anything more you can learn about it from reading a book, because at this point you will have the secret of life. The secret of life is love.

The SUGMAD administers the worlds through the Mahanta, the Living ECK Master. *The Shariyat-Ki-Sugmad,* Book Two, speaks about the Master being like all men. In the physical body, he of himself can do nothing: "He must depend upon the power of the ECK, that essence flowing out of the Godhead, to use him as ITS channel to reach all that will respond to his efforts to get them to become one with the ECK."

Healings from the Master

When someone asks me for a healing, all I do is open myself as a channel so that a healing can take place if it is for the individual's good. Some people get healings, while others do not.

At times someone with problems in his personal life cries to me, "Please help!" and I reply, "This is a problem only the Inner Master, the Mahanta, can help you with." But when someone is upset by his troubles, sometimes he doesn't make the distinction between the Outer and the

Inner Master. When I say, "You have to ask the Mahanta," I'm telling him to go into contemplation and look to the Inner Master. Instead he looks to me, thinking the Mahanta is the physical body.

The Mahanta is never the physical body; the Mahanta uses the physical body. The physical vehicle that is used by the Mahanta is often given the full spiritual title: the Mahanta, the Living ECK Master. But the Mahanta is the inner spiritual part; on the inner planes it is the Mahanta that you meet. The Living ECK Master is the outer physical vehicle, and in the physical plane it is the Living ECK Master that you see.

Someone said to me, "Why don't you cure me? If you can't, no one can."

"I'm not the one who can heal you," I said. "Only the Mahanta can do that."

He gave me a puzzled look. "But you just said you couldn't."

It's a funny thing to try to explain: It is not me who does these things, but the Spirit within me, which means the Holy Ghost, the Word, the Light and Sound, the ECK. This is true of anyone who carries a high state of consciousness, including those in every level of the ECK initiations.

True Initiation

When ECK Initiators tell me *they* gave an initiation, I say, "That's interesting." The true initiation is given only by the Mahanta, by the ECK. Out here I am the physical vehicle for the initiation, as are the Mahdis who are appointed as ECK Initiators. We are the channels for making the initiation known on the outer, but the real initiation is always given by the Inner Master.

263

The ECK initiation is a unique spiritual relationship that occurs between the Voice of God and Soul, because Soul is made of the substance of the Voice of God. And the Voice of God comes from the Heart of God.

When a Higher Initiate doesn't understand that he is just the vehicle or channel for the initiation, he will try to take credit for it. Humility is something which must be worked on by initiates of all levels, all the time. Pride comes even to those who have reached the higher initiations. When things go well in the works of ECK, they want to take credit for it, not acknowledging that it is the inner power that has brought it about.

As soon as ego gets into the works of ECK, the Light dims. Suddenly the individual has a feeling that he is not in the middle of the Life Stream. The only cure for the person is to go back in earnest to the Spiritual Exercises of ECK, doing them with humility and love, and look within to make contact with the Light and Sound of ECK.

Waking Up Soul

The Master is like all men. I generally go to a gas station in my own neighborhood, but one day while in another part of town I noticed my fuel gauge was almost on empty. I pulled into the nearest service station, where I was greeted by several different islands of gas pumps with various signs advertising Full Service, Self-Serve, Regular Leaded, Unleaded, Super Unleaded, Supreme, and even Supreme-Plus-One. As if that wasn't confusing enough, certain pumps were designated for cash and others for credit cards.

Then there were signs encouraging me to buy various grades of oil, get a tune-up, and so on. It was mind-boggling. All I wanted was gas for the tank, not an education in the petroleum industry.

Cars were coming and going all around me. Just to get out of the way, I drove over to a far bank of six pumps. I studied each one and made my choice. Since I had very little cash with me, I planned to use my credit card. But as soon as I started pumping the gas, I realized I was at the cash pump.

By then I had taken fifty cents worth of gas. What do I do now? Do I take three dollars worth of gas and make believe it's all I wanted? Or switch to the credit-card pump right next to it and fill the tank? Finally I replaced the handle and backed the car to the credit-card pump.

I noticed the young service-station attendant watching me. His suspicious look said it all: He thought I would try to pay only the credit-card amount and not even mention the fifty cents' worth from the cash pump.

I finished filling the tank and replaced the handle. Before I had a chance to say anything, he ran right over and told me how much it was. "I also took fifty cents' worth on the other pump," I said.

"I've already figured it in," he assured me, making it clear he had no intention of letting me leave without paying that fifty cents.

I was curious. "You've got more signs here than a person could read in one afternoon," I said. "Is it possible I'm not the only customer who has pulled up to the wrong pump and started to put a few drops of gas in the tank before realizing he should be at the other pump?"

"Happens all the time," he said.

"This is a very disorganized gas station," I said. "There are so many signs here that it's hard to figure out which pump to use. And you're saying customers come in and use the wrong pumps all the time?"

"Yeah," he said. "The idiots."

"Is it possible that your signs could be confusing?"

"No way," he said.

"Do you enjoy adding up the cash and credit-card totals by hand every time someone makes a mistake?" I asked.

"I hate it," he said. "They're idiots."

"Did it ever occur to you to suggest to the manager that if so many people are making mistakes, maybe the signs could be made a little clearer?" He was furious by this time, but I persisted. "Did you ever do that?"

"Who cares?" he said. "I don't care about that stuff."

Unlike the waiter who took five minutes to show me how to fold a napkin into a flower, this guy just didn't care.

It was on the tip of my tongue to say something like, Young man, you'd never work for me! But I didn't, because feisty as I may have felt, I wasn't looking for a fight. I had said too much already. The man was shaking with anger as he handed me the credit-card slip to sign. Good grief, I thought. Don't say another word.

I often run into all kinds of obstacles and resistance, and usually I handle them with good humor. Realizing this Soul was asleep, however, I felt nudged to try to wake him up. Well, I almost woke him up too much.

Everywhere the Living ECK Master goes, he works with people. I appreciate those who are awake, whether they are in ECK or not. When I see someone who is asleep, I try to engage him in conversation. I try to find out if there is some little thing in life that he cares about. Because if an individual can care for even one small thing, it's a start on the path to God. To do one thing with love—anything at all—is to take the first step toward meeting the Master.

266

As the ECKist goes farther along the path, he takes better care of himself. He looks after his appearance. Whether his life-style is simple or prosperous, his life is in order.

This doesn't mean he always goes through life at a calm, unhurried pace. When the ECK moves you, life goes in cycles of high activity and then rest.

It seems to me the rest cycles are getting very short and the activity cycles are getting longer. I move faster more often than I get to rest. Those of you who are moving into the higher circles of initiation may find the same thing.

The further you go in ECK, the more It uses you, and the more economical your planning has to be. You develop more tolerance and humor as you go along in your daily life, because now you have greater understanding. This means you take more responsibility for whatever happens to you as you go out into life every day. If you are dealing with someone who doesn't understand, you make up the difference. But you only do it up to a point; I'm not saying you have to become a rug to be walked on.

A Measure of Resistance

Like all men, the Master is subject to the physical laws, but he is a channel for the ECK. Without the ECK there is no power for the ECK message to reach out into the world. Today this message of the Light and Sound is being carried into the world to a greater degree than ever before in history. This is often overlooked: As individuals doing our part, we don't see the greatness and splendor of the ECK works as they are presented throughout the world to all of mankind.

This is the greatest era of spirituality the world has ever known. Even during the Golden Age, Soul wasn't learning to Its full capacity, because everything was harmonious. There's nothing wrong with harmony, but Soul is tempered by the hardships of life.

This is why the Kali Yuga, the Iron Age in which we are now, is so important. It gives Soul the opportunity to be tempered to Its final purity so that It can become a Coworker with God. In that sense, the Kali Yuga is the true Golden Age, the age of high spirituality in which the message of ECK can be carried out to the world.

When resistance arises in regard to the ECK teachings, we tend to think that something must be wrong. But there is a saying that a man is measured by the strength of his foes. I'd be more concerned if the resistance were gone. Balance is needed in the lower worlds between the spiritual and negative; greater resistance from the negative forces is an indication that the spiritual forces are stronger.

Keep this in mind as you run into resistance. Put your attention on the Mahanta. Know that the message you are giving out is having a positive effect in the lower worlds, or the negative forces wouldn't have come together to try to stop it.

But don't push against the negative power. There is no reason to. The ECK will open the creative stream within Soul and find a way around the obstacle or resistance. The way of ECK is the easy way.

This also applies to the spiritual exercises. If a certain one doesn't work for you, don't beat your head against the wall for months or years trying to make it work. After a few nights, try another one; and if that doesn't work, look through the ECK works and try still another one.

We learn not to hit life head-on. The Light of ECK shows us how to avoid the pitfalls, to go straight to the Heart of God.

When the ECK Speaks

The love of ECK manifests among the individuals in a group by communication through the inner channels. It works back and forth so smoothly that you instinctively know when something must be done.

At the airport recently, two people in our group went to the check-in counter to take care of the tickets, while two of us stayed with the baggage. The line at the counter was long, and the other fellow and I chatted to pass the time.

All of a sudden I had a strong feeling to get my passport out of my suitcase. I quickly knelt down, zipped open my bag, and pulled it out. I was just about to put it in my pocket when one of the people who had gone to the ticket counter ran over. "I need your passport quick," he said. "The ticket agent is waiting."

The passport was still in my hand. "There you go," I said, handing it over to him without having to waste any time fumbling through my baggage.

Even though he had been on the other side of the room talking with the ticket agent at the counter, the inner communication was so strong that I responded without question. It didn't matter that I was engaged in conversation at the time. No matter where my attention is focused, the ECK is working. And when the ECK speaks, I simply do what It says.

Recently someone asked for a healing. I offered him a suggestion, but apparently it sounded too simple and natural. He proceeded to tell me about a doctor he had been seeing for quite a while. "His treatment seems to be helping," he said.

"That's wonderful," I said. "Glad it's working for you."

Whether or not my suggestion is right for him depends upon his consciousness. Maybe it wasn't right for him at

269

that moment. He may have needed to experience a couple more weeks of pain by continuing with another method of healing. Its his pain and his growth; if he doesn't mind it, it's OK with me.

Soul isn't in a hurry. We have time even beyond eternity. Eternity is only an element of the universes of materialism, space, and time; and Soul is more than eternal. Soul just is.

If you are open to the ECK, you certainly unfold; and whether you recognize it or not, the unfoldment goes with you, the Light and Sound go with you, and the love of the Mahanta goes with you.

Each of you who is open to the works of Spirit will come to see, know, and understand the unfoldment that has occurred within you and the greater vehicle and channel that you are for the Divine Power that resides within you.

On your journey home, may the blessings be.

ECKANKAR European Seminar, The Hague, The Netherlands, Sunday, July 21, 1985

Even though you may have lived as royalty in a past life, what you are today is the greatest and best that you have ever been.

18

The Golden Heart, Part 1

There is a need to put attention on how to work with Soul Travel techniques. Paul Twitchell used to conduct Soul Travel workshops regularly, and people enjoyed them because they got to learn about the great experiences they could have visiting other worlds while out of the body.

Soul Travel is a captivating, enriching aspect of ECKANKAR. Its main benefit is that it gives us the ability to tap into the other worlds twenty-four hours a day. In this way the inner and outer experiences build upon each other. This is perhaps more important than being able to leave the body and come back with the memory of visiting a temple on the inner planes.

We don't rely on a false authority; the real authority always has to come from within the individual.

If you have a Soul Travel or out-of-the-body experience in the inner worlds, you should not have to ask someone else if it was valid. You must be the authority of your own experience and know that it was of Spirit, of the ECK.

Bob Lawton will share a Soul Travel technique with you.

Awakening the Heart

Bob: I've noticed something: You cannot hold what you're told in your heart. The words stay in the mind, but only the experience itself can enter into the heart. This is where we start; this is what opens us up.

But before we can soar into the other realities, where we come to know the truth of immortality, we have to first unlock the door and meet the Mahanta within.

The key to the inner door is the Golden Heart. If you have it, it is very easy to Soul Travel. If you look within and surrender to the Mahanta, you can feel the radiant love. You become aware, very subtly at first, that there is a growing, golden Light that surrounds you.

It caresses your being, flowing around, through, and into the very core of you. This is the gentle guidance of the Mahanta, the Living ECK Master.

Soon you find yourself riding the waves, pulses, and currents of this light. It brings you into the vastness of the cosmic sea, to a place that you have never been before. It's a place deep within your inner being, the dwelling place of Soul.

When you reach this point, you notice that your consciousness has become like a fountain, like a pool of fluid emanating from you, expanding. The depth of it is beyond the conception of the mind. You have traveled beyond the regions of time and space.

Then ever so lightly, ever so slightly, you notice a wind from deep within. It begins to create tiny ripples on the surface of this pool. And you realize that it is the Golden Heart meeting the gentle guidance and love of the Mahanta that brings this stage of awareness.

It seems easy enough to speak of this kind of experience, but words fail us. How do you explain to someone what it's like to hear the single note of a flute as it reaches deep within you? What words could describe the actual experience that accompanies the Sound? There are none. We can try to share the experience, but it's up to each individual to open up that awareness within himself.

Truth is not gained through observation, it's gained through experience. The path of ECKANKAR offers each of us the opportunity to open up to the Golden Heart. We can each feel the love, shimmering in the twilight area, that passes us on from one world to the next, into the higher planes of reality. But the awakening within the heart has to start somewhere.

Meeting the Master

This technique is for Soul Travel. First close your eyes. Breathe in slowly and deeply to relax the physical body and make it comfortable.

Imagine yourself walking down a hallway. As you walk, you notice a Sound. It's a vibrant Sound that rings out true and clear, and you want to hear it clearer still.

Suddenly you realize that the Sound is coming from behind a door. As you get nearer to the door, feel the energy of the Sound; know within your heart that this is truth, this is reality.

Put your hand on the doorknob. Notice how the atoms in it also radiate through your entire being. Feel the pulse of the love that comes from the room.

Open the door slowly. A Light comes flooding out. It totally surrounds your being, and you feel Its golden warmth caressing you. Listen to the Sound that emanates from the room. Inside sits the Mahanta, the Inner Master, waiting for you. He is chanting a name, and the name is Wah Z.

Each syllable is sung from the heart, long and slow and full: *Waaaaaaaahhh Zeeeeeeeee.*

Sit in contemplation with the Mahanta and join him in the chant, knowing that this is where you start—at the temple within, seated with the Mahanta.

When we meet with the Mahanta, we can begin the journey into the multitude of realities beyond this world.

Because we are individuals, no two experiences will be alike. Always give yourself the freedom and opportunity to change the technique to fit your state of consciousness. Keep the part that works and combine it with other techniques that also work for you. This is what makes these techniques so dynamic and allows your experiences to build and expand.

Moving Beyond the Mind

HK: When the guard of the mind is down—usually when one is sleeping or relaxing—Soul can move easily out of the body. It can view the body as it lies sleeping or sitting in a chair and then get back into it.

From that point on, the individual no longer questions whether life continues beyond death. This might not sound logical if you have never had the experience. But when you are out of the body, using the increased perceptions of Soul which originate beyond the mind, you simply know there is no longer any reason to fear death. Now you can go ahead and live a full life, having the experiences you decided on even before being born into this body, with total responsibility for whatever you do.

People sometimes have a skewed idea of what it means to be detached. They interpret it as, I am not affected by this or that. But with this attitude, life actually passes them by.

Expanding the Consciousness

The point of ECKANKAR is to learn how to expand the consciousness into the Light and Sound of God. As these two aspects of God come into Soul, It becomes enriched, with an expanded awareness.

Soul Travel opens the awareness so we can begin to perceive the subtle interplays that occur as the karma around us works out. Soul Travel, or the expansion of consciousness, lets us see the problems that are coming.

When we know a big ball of karmic energy is heading our way, like a huge boulder rolling down a hill, we have the opportunity to avoid it. We can take countermeasures. We can make sure that when the trouble arrives, we aren't anywhere near.

Those who do not have the spiritual awareness to see it coming will be flattened by the boulder. But this doesn't mean we avoid problems all the time, because they are what give us experience.

Concepts of Heaven and Death

Some people still have the concept of a heaven where people walk around in long robes, live in cities of golden light, and spend eternity doing who knows what. These are worn-out images of heaven, frozen in time, that have been passed along by the orthodox thought of two thousand years ago. The ever-moving evolutionary spiral of consciousness has gone beyond that.

Since the other worlds are very unlike the heaven which has been described by the religionists, an ECKist is probably the least surprised individual at the time of death. He has been leaving the body regularly, so he knows the inner life as it really is.

The most surprised people are those who have been misled by false notions about what occurs at the time of translation, or death. Their reaction would be similar to that of a person from the wilderness who travels to the big city for the first time.

The ECKist also knows that the ECK Masters don't necessarily wear knee-length maroon robes and that they are sometimes known by different names. But he recognizes them—the named and the unnamed ones.

In some of the heavens today, we walk along modern-looking streets in cities very similar to those here on earth, except more refined. We interact with people in situations much like those on earth. Sometimes you can't easily tell the difference between a physical experience and one that takes place in the Soul body on the inner planes. The saying "As above, so below" is true. In a sense you see the future, because as events unfold on the inner planes, they occur in some close approximation in your physical life.

Spiritual Readings

Paul Twitchell used to give ECK-Vidya readings, which were a comprehensive, in-depth look at the total spiritual life of an individual. ECK-Vidya readings were different from Soul readings, which looked into one's life in the other worlds, or the Akashic records, which revealed past lives on earth and the other lower worlds.

The ECK-Vidya encompasses both the Soul Plane and the lower worlds. It looks into what is happening now on the inner planes which will manifest in some variation in one's present physical life.

It also looks at past lives to see what forces were set in motion by a person's karmic pattern, causing the circumstances of his life today. Paul's ECK-Vidya readings included suggestions of what one could do about it, but most of the people who got them didn't know how to work with them.

Many Akashic readings tell about a person's past lives as royalty. A person who has an Akashic reading might come away with a big head, overlooking the fact that what you are today is the greatest and best that you have ever been.

A person who comes into this life from a past life of royalty sometimes expects others to serve him, to do his dirty work or carry his luggage. He's so caught up in his own importance that he can't see that other people are also important, that they have also had the experience of being royalty.

We have all been royalty by the time we come to this life in ECK. Some of us have gotten past that vanity, and this time we are willing to carry our own bags. As we gain in spiritual consciousness, we become spiritual royalty. It's foolish to think others aren't spiritually royal too.

Soul Travel—A First Step

When we have an inner experience, we should be careful not to brag about it to those who haven't had any yet, or they may be hurt more than helped by it. But if we can tell our story in a certain way, such as sharing a spiritual technique, we can help them to have an experience of their own.

At a campout, you have left behind many of the worries, cares, habits, and routines of everyday living that put a web around you and close off the door to the inner worlds. So tonight go into contemplation and see what comes. If you need help, call out for Wah Z; this is the name by which I'm known in the spiritual sense. Or you can simply use Z,

279

the abbreviated form. Then just relax and know that help is near. The Inner Master, the Mahanta, will be working with you to bring the experience that is important for you now.

Soul Travel in the dream state can be the first step into the God Worlds of ECK. This is where you gain the confidence and the love that has to come from the Golden Heart in order to move into these planes and universes of God.

Soul Travel Workshop, Connecticut Regional Campout, Friday, August 16, 1985

When the love of ECK comes through, people just can't
keep away from you. You've got to have a lot of patience.

19

The Golden Heart, Part 2

Soul Travel is only an aspect of the entire ECK program, but it is a way for many people to take the first step to God and to the Light and Sound.

Giving to Life

An ECKist observed that she first had to learn to surrender, and then to give. She said that love has come and gone in her life, and now everything she does is for the ECK. But sometimes she feels empty, and she wonders why. Is she doing something wrong?

After Soul Travel and several other intermediate stages, you eventually come to the point where all you want to do is give to life. You enter into relationships with others not to take, but just to give. You have the need to give love.

Working Out Karma in Relationships

An ECKist may be working off the karma of eight or ten lifetimes at once, so it's no surprise that our relationships come and go. When a relationship ends, it's not because you have failed. ECKists are different from those in the orthodox religions where karma works out relatively slowly. It takes a strong person to work through the karma of so many lifetimes in one.

As we work with Soul Travel and the other aspects of ECK, we are trying to find a way to be open to love. Then love begins to open within us, but it doesn't mean that our human relationships will always work out right. Things can go wrong, things can get harder. But in the end, the two individuals in the relationship have unfolded and moved closer to the Heart of God.

A Channel for Love

We are all striving for divine love, and when it comes, it expresses itself through human love. When you fill yourself with love, you are a silent channel for ECK. Other people are drawn to you. Everywhere you go, they try to get close to you.

There are some days I've given so much of myself that I simply don't have any more to give that day. This happens more in the higher initiations. But you know that life will keep giving you more love, and you will have more and more love to give back.

When you are filled with the love of ECK, funny things happen. I had to go into a grocery store recently. Since I was in a hurry to get in and out, I carefully plotted my path: Run in the door, head to the produce section, then to the frozen-food section, and then race to the checkout with the shortest line.

As some of you have found, if you dawdle for even two minutes, the delays start. Suddenly the manager pages an announcement: Will all cashiers report to the front, please? That means lines and more lines, but it also means the ECK is using you to channel Its love out to all these people. So you might as well relax and enjoy it.

Quickly finishing my shopping, I rushed to the checkout with the shortest line. There was only one woman ahead of me, and she had four or five items.

As soon as I stepped in line behind her, the little problems began. She had a vegetable that the cashier wasn't familiar with, and he didn't know the price.

"It's fifty-nine cents," she said.

"Per pound?" he asked.

"Each," she said.

He took her word for it and rang it up.

She thumbed through a magazine she'd taken from the rack while he completed the sale. "That will be $10.12," he said, moving the grocery bag with its four or five items off to the side. I was delighted: This was really going fast.

She put the magazine back on the rack and reached into her purse—and started bringing out one small handful of coins after another. Oh, great, I thought. She's going to pay the whole $10.12 in pennies, nickels, and dimes. Maybe I should try the next checkout stand. But then I thought, What funny trick are they going to pull by the time I get over there? I decided to wait it out.

Ten minutes later the lady had coins neatly stacked all over the counter. "You only have $7.12 here," the clerk said. Only three dollars to go, I thought. She reached deeper into her purse digging around for more change.

About this time a big brawny fellow got in line behind me. He was rough and tough and mean, and you could tell he lived hard. He took one look at all those coins, quickly sized up the situation, and described it with some profanity that I won't repeat. I chuckled, hoping to ease the tension, and then he laughed, too.

285

"I'm going over to the next cashier," he said. "I think I'll be out of here before you."

"You just might," I said.

By the time the woman in front of me finally finished, I had stood in line for fifteen minutes. The clerk rang up my few items, and I headed for the door. The rough-looking fellow was still in line at the next counter.

Ms. Pac-Man Challenge

The ECK will use you to give out Its love to people in ways that you wouldn't recognize if you weren't in ECK. One afternoon, I was tired and decided I needed a game of Ms. Pac-Man. I went with two other people to a bowling alley that had a video arcade with eleven games. Next to the Ms. Pac-Man was a driving game: the kids could climb in, sit down, and pretend to be adults driving cars or spaceships. Nobody else was in the arcade; my companions and I had the place to ourselves. We put our money in the Ms. Pac-Man machine and started the game.

The next thing I knew, a whole swarm of kids was shoving me aside to get to the driving game. Just as I was making an escape with my Ms. Pac-Man, one of them jerked my arm. A few other kids came over to play the machine on the other side of us. A young lady wedged in on one side, the other kids climbed in and out of the car on the other side. But not one person was playing any of the other eight games in the room. Those kids bumped into us, stepped on our toes, stood in our way, and one little guy even hung on my arm. Because of him, I lost another Ms. Pac-Man.

When the love of ECK comes through, people just can't keep away from you. You've got to have a lot of patience.

A Soul Travel Technique

Bob Lawton has a Soul Travel exercise to share.

Bob: A Soul Travel experience starts within the heart; once you have it, it will remain within you throughout eternity. You have been touched by the Light and Sound; it's something that no one can ever take from you.

Doing the spiritual exercises with feeling and knowingness is a creative process. You reach within and stimulate your inner awareness. Many wonderful things lie just beneath the surface of the outer world, waiting to come to the awareness of our conscious self.

But we have to stimulate our awareness with feeling. So when we prepare to do a spiritual exercise, we should be aware of this first step.

In this creative technique, first look at yourself and notice what you are wearing. Develop your outer perception. Notice the environment of your home, the chair, the door.

Then tonight when you're snuggled in bed, prepare for the exercise: Think of someone that you know, trust, and love. Realize that this person is going to take a Soul Travel journey with you.

Begin your contemplation by chanting HU.

Now watch yourself getting up and getting dressed in the same clothes that you wore today. Remember what they look like. Visualize them: See them and feel the texture of the clothes.

Still chanting HU, watch yourself leave your room and walk around your house or apartment. Go to the living room. Remember what it looks like. There you will find the person you trust and love that you will be taking the journey with.

Now visualize the Master coming in through the door, walking over to you both. The Mahanta is radiating love, waiting to take you on a journey to the worlds of God. And from this point, the journey begins.

Surrender to ECK

HK: If you have any questions or comments, or if you would like some extra help, I'd be glad to work with you.

ECKist: How do you surrender to the ECK?

HK: Our society and culture have prepared women to surrender more easily than men. A man is told from the time he's a little boy that he has to be strong; he's told, Don't show hurt, don't cry. So surrender can be a very real problem for some men. Talking with one of the ECK Spiritual Aides might help you to come to an understanding of the concept of surrender in ECK.

Remembering Experiences

ECKist: I know that I am with the Master on the inner a lot, but I can never remember my encounters.

HK: If you know that you are having the experiences, you're doing well. They'll become clearer later.

Spiritual Housecleaning

ECKist: For over a year, I've had an experience of the ECK coming at me so strongly, like a tornado swirling around and trying to pull me out of my chair. I can't handle it; I start feeling sick. I guess it's too much for my human consciousness. Could you help me with this?

HK: How often do you do your spiritual exercises?

ECKist: Usually once a day for about a half hour.

HK: Try doing them for twenty minutes a day. If that doesn't help, back off to every other day, every third day, or once a week. In other words, work backward until you can handle it. As it settles down to where you can handle it, little by little start increasing the frequency of the spiritual exercises again.

The sick feeling is the ECK coming in contact with the human state of consciousness. It's simply cleaning house. The ECK is boring through the human consciousness.

I also used to get a sick feeling when I was beginning with the Spiritual Exercises of ECK. I'd wake up in the morning and feel absolutely sick at the thought of facing the day; the changes that had come about within me made it hard to relate to what I was yesterday. I no longer fit in, but I didn't know what the new spiritual rules were.

So for a short time I was left in no-man's-land. It was the ECK cleaning out the karma in a rather direct way. It goes easier for some people.

Opening the Heart to Love

ECKist: When we were given the technique last night, I felt so much love. But when I went back to the tent and tried it, I found that each time I got to the door, nothing happened; it was like opening a closet door. I thought, Where's all the love that's supposed to be coming out?

Then I visualized the Mahanta in the tent, and that's when I realized that for me, the whole essence of the experience is love. The heart center opened up, and then I was able to flow with the exercise.

HK: It's true the techniques sometimes keep the mind busy, but as you noticed, you had to find a way to open the heart to love. The spiritual exercise works only if the heart center is filled with love. This is called the Golden Heart.

Egyptian Recall

ECKist: I did the spiritual exercise last night. Just before I fell asleep, I started chanting *Wah Z*. During the course of the night I awakened on the inner.

I was in my sleeping bag in the tent, and you were standing at the foot of my sleeping bag. You were talking to the four other people who were asleep in the tent. I didn't know what you were saying, but as you spoke to them, you were gazing at me. Then you told all of us that you were going to take us someplace.

Suddenly the scene changed. I saw a lot of people walking around, and they seemed to be Egyptian. Then I awoke. It was a wonderful experience just seeing you on the inner.

Trying Too Hard

ECKist: I tried very hard to do the technique last night, but I had a lot of pain in my back and arm, and I couldn't seem to finish it. I was up all night; about four-thirty this morning, I just gave up.

As soon as I relaxed and stopped trying, I had a vision of myself riding in a bumper car. There was a big jam-up, and I couldn't steer my way out. All of a sudden I realized that I had been working too hard at the technique. I gave up, and then I felt your love—and finally I was able to fall asleep.

HK: We find out for ourselves the things that work and the things that don't work.

Blue Light

ECKist: While we were driving home last night, I started to concentrate very hard. All of a sudden I saw the Blue Light for the first time in my life. Thank you.

HK: You're welcome.

Dual Consciousness

ECKist: I started the contemplation last night, and soon it felt like part of me was in the room with you while another part was still going through the process to get there. It was a split feeling, and it was confusing.

HK: It's the dual consciousness. Sometimes you can do away with it and just go directly to the experience.

Imagining the Light

ECKist: Sometimes in contemplation I have difficulty imagining the physical form of the Master. Someone suggested that I could use an image of the Light instead. I was wondering if that would be OK for people like me who have a problem with their imagination.

HK: Yes, definitely.

Overcoming Nervousness

ECKist: When I'm Soul traveling I don't have any problems. But on the physical plane, I can't seem to deal with things like cooking or coordinating a lot of activities at the same time. How do I get rid of this outer nervousness?

HK: Some of this goes away later in ECK. You had the courage to get up and ask your question, and that's a start.

When you have a lot going on, you get preoccupied with nervousness. Try to simplify, get it down to one or two things at a time.

People who seem to perform effortlessly are actually thinking of only one thing at a time. If you're trying to do too much, just slow down. Do one thing at a time, and do it well. I think you'll find your life will start to work out better.

Traveling the Path

ECKist: All my life I've been blessed in many ways in the physical, and I feel that I am a reasonably good channel for Spirit. But as far as the inner experience is concerned, I seem to draw a blank, regardless of the spiritual exercise that I try to do.

HK: Someone mentioned the same thing to me this evening. She didn't have experiences on the inner with any of the ECK Masters or the Light and Sound, yet she just knew that she was with ECK. Even so, you can sometimes feel lonely and empty, and you wonder if you've somehow goofed up spiritually.

There are a number of different ways to travel the path to God. Some people need mental techniques. Others just live the life of ECK without having to go through the different exercises. You may be one of them.

Or you may be having actual difficulty seeing on the inner for various reasons. Do you have dream experiences?

ECKist: At one time I attended dream classes. I wrote down the dreams, but they were a hodgepodge.

HK: How often do you do the spiritual exercises?

ECKist: I used to do them morning and night, and then just in the morning. I feel I'm in a rut with the spiritual exercises. I've tried different things, but it doesn't seem to be doing much good.

HK: There are several ECK Spiritual Aides who have been selected to correspond with individuals such as yourself who are having difficulty with the spiritual exercises. If you'd be willing, one of these ECK Spiritual Aides would work with the Inner Master to find the spiritual exercises or approaches needed. Maybe we can help you break through that barrier.

Letting Go of Fear

ECKist: I experience a great deal of fear and self-judgment. I have the awareness of experiencing a lot on the inner, yet I don't allow it to filter through. I think it is being blocked by fear. How can I let go of that?

HK: Fear is one reason people have a hard time with Soul Travel. Even with all of its problems, we're used to this body. We think that maybe it's safer than going into the unknown—because we're afraid of the unknown.

This is why the Inner Master works very slowly and carefully with you. It may take years for some people to have a spiritual experience, simply because they have fear and tension inside, and they are not ready. When they are ready, all of a sudden, they'll find themselves very naturally out of the body.

I wouldn't push it; just let it be. Don't worry about it. If you have fear out here, just recognize that you have it. Acknowledge it and realize that it's a fear of the unknown which is rooted only in the lower bodies—the mental, emotional, and so on—but that Soul Itself isn't afraid.

When you do your spiritual exercises, if you can establish the Golden Heart, which is actually the viewpoint of

Soul, I think you'll find it easier to have inner experiences and to let go of the fear. If you have fear in Soul Travel, you have fear in other things, and it's holding you back in your life.

This is what ECK is about: to get rid of the fear so that you can get involved in life and have the experiences you came here for.

What Is the Golden Heart?

ECKist: When Bob was talking us through that technique to meet the Master on the inner, he said to feel the experience. I wasn't sure what I was supposed to feel. I also wonder if you could explain a little bit more about the Golden Heart, because I feel that is really important.

HK: Somebody who is interested in the Golden Heart might very well not quite understand how to go about the feeling aspect which the technique was working toward.

The Golden Heart means to simply fill yourself with love before you do the spiritual exercise, then carry that love into your life. Some people have to develop it; there are others who have the Golden Heart naturally. They are already filled with love. They have the ability to give of themselves.

These people are the shining lights. They have love and compassion for life around them, perhaps because they have suffered enough either in this or some other lifetime. They can easily put themselves in the other person's shoes; they know how to make things easier for the next person.

The Golden Heart is an attitude. It is thinking of the other person before oneself, giving service, and simply being a channel for Divine Spirit.

It can be a difficult attitude to grow into. Like everything else, it just takes practice; it doesn't come with the snap of a finger or the wave of a wand.

If you ask the Inner Master to begin working with you to understand the Golden Heart, you'll find changes coming about. You can contemplate on the term "the Golden Heart," which is very directly connected with love.

Baraka bashad.

Soul Travel Workshop, Connecticut Regional Campout,
Saturday, August 17, 1985

Glossary of ECKANKAR Terms

Words set in SMALL CAPS are defined elsewhere in the Glossary

ARAHATA.   An experienced and qualified teacher for ECKANKAR classes.

CHELA.   A spiritual student.

ECK.   The Life Force, the Holy Spirit, or Audible Life Current which sustains all life.

ECKANKAR.   The Ancient Science of SOUL TRAVEL. A truly spiritual religion for the individual in modern times, known as the secret path to God via dreams and Soul Travel. The teachings provide a framework for anyone to explore their own spiritual experiences. Established by Paul Twitchell, the modern-day founder, in 1965.

ECK MASTERS.   Spiritual Masters who can assist and protect people in their spiritual studies and travels. The ECK Masters are from a long line of God-Realized Souls who know the responsibility that goes with spiritual freedom.

HU.   The secret name for God. The singing of the word HU, pronounced like the man's name Hugh, is considered a love song to God. It is sung in the ECK Worship Service.

INITIATION.   Earned by the ECK member through spiritual unfoldment and service to God. The initiation is a private ceremony in which the individual is linked to the Sound and Light of God.

LIVING ECK MASTER.   The title of the spiritual leader of ECKANKAR. His duty is to lead Souls back to God. The Living ECK Master can assist spiritual students physically as the Outer Master, in the dream state as the Dream Master, and in the spiritual worlds as the

Inner Master. Sri Harold Klemp became the Living ECK Master in 1981.

Mahanta. A title to describe the highest state of God Consciousness on earth, often embodied in the Living ECK Master. He is the Living Word.

Planes. The levels of heaven, such as the Astral, Causal, Mental, Etheric, and Soul planes.

Satsang. A class in which students of ECK study a monthly lesson from ECKANKAR.

The Shariyat-Ki-Sugmad. The sacred scriptures of ECKANKAR. The scriptures are comprised of twelve volumes in the spiritual worlds. The first two were transcribed from the inner planes by Paul Twitchell, modern-day founder of ECKANKAR.

Soul. The True Self. The inner, most sacred part of each person. Soul exists before birth and lives on after the death of the physical body. As a spark of God, Soul can see, know, and perceive all things. It is the creative center of Its own world.

Soul Travel. The expansion of consciousness. The ability of Soul to transcend the physical body and travel into the spiritual worlds of God. Soul Travel is taught only by the Living ECK Master. It helps people unfold spiritually and can provide proof of the existence of God and life after death.

Sound and Light of ECK. The Holy Spirit. The two aspects through which God appears in the lower worlds. People can experience them by looking and listening within themselves and through Soul Travel.

Spiritual Exercises of ECK. The daily practice of certain techniques to get us in touch with the Light and Sound of God.

SUGMAD. A sacred name for God. SUGMAD is neither masculine nor feminine; IT is the source of all life.

Wah Z. The spiritual name of Sri Harold Klemp. It means the Secret Doctrine. It is his name in the spiritual worlds.

Index

Akshar state, 38, 122
Allergies, 115–16, 175
Alphabets, 82
Angel(s)
    of death, 15
    guardian, 96–97, 111, 232
    of Lord, 139
    of Love, 92, 102
Anger, 266
    and accidents, 46, 244
    bands of, 167
    and change, 45
    and communication, 148
    energy of, 176
    makes you examine beliefs,
        141
    prevents healiing, 228
    problems with, 69
    righteous, 175
    and self-image, 117
    when our religion is threat-
        ened, 80
Animal(s) 168, 180. See also
        Bear story; Bird(s); Calves;
        Camel story; Cat(s); Dino-
        saurs; Dog(s); Easter bunny
        story; Lizard(s); Mockingbird
        story; Sound(s): of birds;
        Turtle; Whales
Answer(s)
    asking for, 222
    finding the, 80, 239
    getting, 234, 236
    to questions, 111, 233
    spiritual maturity and, 205
Apologizing, 152
Arahata, 151
Ascetic, 22
Ask(ing)
    courage to, 291
    God. See God: asking
    for healing. See Healer(s),
        healing: asking for
    for help, 127. See Help(ing):
        asking for
    the Mahanta, 248, 263, 295

others, 222, 229
for something, 129
for truth. See Truth: asking for
Astral
    body. See Body(ies): Astral
        (emotional)
    Plane. See Plane(s): Astral
    travel, 51
    world. See Plane(s): Astral
Atheist, 85
Atlantis, 69
Attachment(s), 112, 137, 202
Attacks, 112
    from Kal, 125
    psychic, 116, 244
Attention, 134, 143
    attracting, 206
    catching, 159, 233
    focus of, 269
    giving complete, 48, 260
    on Mahanta, 75, 221, 252, 268
    on Soul Travel techniques, 273
    on seminar, 181, 224
    sharing, 11
    during spiritual exercises, 95
    wanting, 164
Attitude(s), 114, 149
    aware of. See Aware, aware-
        ness: of attitudes
    changing, 192, 208
    about death, 110
    about ECK, 167, 227
    Golden Heart is, 294
    growing into an, 295
    negative, 90, 276
    old, 57
    reflections of, 191
Audible Life Stream, 87, 117,
        264
Australia, 70
Authority, false, 273
Aware, awareness. See also Con-
        sciousness
    of attitudes, 57
    circle of. See Circle(s): of
        awareness

of differences, 191
of dreams. *See* Dream(s),
    dream state: awareness of
of ECK, 30, 163
    expanded, 277
of experiences, 160, 293
of God. *See* God-Realization
    during initiation, 73, 74, 75
    inner, 177, 287
of inner planes, 75, 83, 181
    lack of, 189
    levels of, 1, 252, 274
of Light and Sound, 251
    open up, 275
    in physical state, 234
    self. *See* Self-Realization
    Soul, 43, 94. *See also* Self-
        Realization
    total, 37
of words and thoughts, 87

Baby, ugly, story, 89–90
Babylon, 2
Balance
    and illumination, 5
    in lower worlds, 165, 268
    maintaining, 75, 185, 207
    out of, 6
    physical, 116
    between social and spiritual,
        194, 200, 202–3
Bank story, 167–68
Baptism, 67–68, 74
    cannot save Soul, 68
    of fire, 105
Bargains, 134
Bear story, 237–39
Being, 84, 161
Belief, 45, 126, 173
    examining, 141
    relying on, 80
Best
    being the, 81, 86, 107, 279
    doing the, 187
Bible, 7, 110
    -carrying Christians, 85

as common term, 151
    and descriptions of heaven,
        166
ECK, 73. *See also* Shariyat-Ki-
    Sugmad, the; *Shariyat-Ki-
    Sugmad, The*
New Testament, 80, 218
Old Testament, 9, 80, 91, 118,
    136, 137
    sayings, 79
    stories of, 44, 137–39, 141, 235
    times of, 233
Bilocation, 26
Bird(s), 179. *See also* Mocking-
    bird story
    exotic, 231
    fisherman and. *See* Fisherman
        story
Birth, 167
Black magic, 4, 69
Blame, 46, 65
    looking for someone to, 245
Bless(ings)
    from ECK, 230, 236, 248
    giving out, 27
    from God, 3, 29, 229
    of Holy Spirit, 127, 129
    physical, 292
    a situation, 207
Blue Light. *See* Mahanta: Blue
    Light of
Boat, 256
Body(ies)
    Astral (emotional), 112, 293.
        See also Emotional, emo-
        tions
    experiences out of the, 71–72,
        83, 92, 108, 160, 163,
        232–33, 234, 251, 252,
        260–61, 273, 293
    human. *See* Body(ies): physical
    imaginative. *See* Imagination
    inner, 6, 96, 116
    leaving the, 8–9, 43, 79,
        82–83, 94, 154, 276, 277
    Light, 73, 109, 252

Body(ies) *(continued)*
  lower, 4, 253, 293
  Mental, 112, 293. *See also*
    Mind
  physical, 18, 19, 26, 84, 106,
    118, 132, 163, 181, 234, 252,
    254, 261, 263, 275
  radiant, 253
  returning to the, 9, 160
  running several, 166
  Soul, 83, 85, 94, 163, 166, 234,
    254, 278. *See also* Soul
  spiritual. *See:* Body(ies): Soul;
    Spiritual: body
  taking care of the, 267
Book(s), 21, 80, 114, 167. *See*
    also ECKANKAR: books
  holy. *See* Bible; Shariyat-Ki-
    Sugmad, the; *Shariyat-Ki-*
    Sugmad, The
  knowledge, 84, 110
  language of ECK in, 155
  learning from, 81, 108, 262
Boredom, 162
Boy who colored everything
    black, story, 242–43
Bridge(s), 34–36
Buddha. *See* Consciousness:
    Buddha
Bully story, 208–9
Bumper sticker, 204
Business(men), 93, 178
  and creative process, 192
  help in, 229
  meeting, 159
Busy, being too, 234–35

Calendar, 192
California Parapsychology
    Foundation, 26
Calves, 54, 169
Camel story, 51
Camera department, 48
Canada, 179, 237
Caniff, Milton, 20

Car(s), 130
  rental, story 32–34
Cashier, 285, 286
Cat(s), 200, 210
  learning to be a, 38, 164
  Mitty, 10–11, 34–36, 164–65
  Siamese, 11
Causal Plane. *See* Plane(s):
    Causal
Cave of fire, 68
Chair story, 185
Challenge(s), 40, 164
  creative, 185
  facing, 192
Change(s), 58, 87, 116, 295
  in attitude. *See* Attitude(s):
    changing
  in consciousness. *See* Con-
    sciousness: changes in
  at death, 96
  on earth, 228
  in health, 88
  ideas, 45
  jobs, 248
  when karma dries up, 120
  Soul enjoys, 132
Channel(s), 87. *See also* Vehicle
  for ECK, 207, 267, 270, 292,
    294
  for God, 92, 262
  inner, 269
  for the love of ECK, 284–85
  purified, 85
  silent, 284
Chant(ing), 87
  HU. *See* HU: chanting
  secret names for God, 52, 57,
    121, 255
  secret word. *See* Word(s):
    secret
  Wah Z. *See* Wah Z
Charity, 38
Cheated, cheating, 133–34
Chela(s). *See also* ECKist(s)
  experiences of, 9, 162
  and four precepts of ECK, 29

and Inner Master. *See* Inner
    Master: and chela
and Living ECK Master. *See*
    Living ECK Master: and
    chela
when, is ready, 253
Childhood, 63
Child(ren), 30–31, 131. *See also*
    Youth
    becoming as a, 254
    and death, 92, 110
    and discipline, 49–50, 207–9
    of ECK, 30, 40
    experiences of, 89, 154,
        173–74
    and families, 174
    joy of being a, 162
    responsibilities of, 63–64
Choice, 265
Choir loft story, 221–22
Chosen ones, 86
Christian(ity), 79. *See also* Jesus
    Christ
    born-again, 85
    church. *See* Church(es):
        Christian
    early days of, 166
    ECKists and, 6–7
    experiences of, 12
    heavens, 38, 155, 249
    mind, 68
    seeks Christ consciousness, 81
    teachings, 133
Church(es)
    becoming the best in your, 86,
        107
    building, story, 93
    Christian, 67
    country, 110, 221
    doctrine, 7
    early stages of God-
        Realization in, 6
    Episcopalian, 6
    failure of, 99, 174
    fundamentalist, 50
    going to, 2, 99, 174

members of, 112
official, 195
orthodox, 98–99, 191
priests. *See* Priest(s),
    priestcraft
searching through, 54
sleeping in, 174–75
Cigar story, 221–22
Circle(s)
    of awareness, 1, 31, 57–58,
        245
    expanding, 1, 43, 181, 245, 247
    of initiation, 1, 175, 181, 245
    inner, 215
    limited, 245
    of people we affect, 175–76
    of protection, 60
    spiritual, 180
Civilization, 80
Clean(sing), 63, 68, 215
    house, 234
    importance of being, 64
    Light and Sound bring, 74
    out karma, 289
Clergy, 155, 174
Cliff Hanger, 24, 199
Clue(s), 33
    from the ECK, 45
Coin trick story, 50–51
Collier's, 8, 20
Color, 242–43
Comfort(able), 12, 79
Comforter. *See* ECK; Holy Spirit
Command, chain of, 49
Commitment, 59, 151
Common sense, 2
Communication, 108, 269. *See
    also* Talking, talks; Write,
    writer(s), writing
    between Soul and Mahanta,
        242
Communion, 253
Compassion, 39
    capacity for, 38
    for life, 294
    for others, 6

303

304

Dream(s), dream state
(continued)
learning through, 153, 154
meeting Master in, 15
messages from ECK in, 1
prophetic, 204
Soul Travel in, 83, 86, 280
visiting friends in, 248
waking, 32
Duty, 113, 161, 181, 235
sense of, 251

Earn(ing), 129
living, 89, 196
money, 195
problems, 98
protection, 245
in true coin, 127
unfoldment, 73, 86, 121, 128
Earth, 2, 106, 114
coming back to, 166
co-workers exist on, 83
ECK on, 27, 29
experiences on, 143
getting down to, 181
heavens near, 118, 132
heavens similar to, 95, 191,
278
as impermanent place, 228
life on, 94
other planets and, 100
paths on, 233
surviving on, 147
travel on, 219
why we are on, 63
Easter bunny story, 173–74
Easy Way, the. *See* Technique(s):
the Easy Way
ECK
activities, 9, 47, 149
child of the, 30
conversation with, 130
Evening with, 109
flow of, 180, 222
how, works, 34, 66, 153, 223
initiates. *See* Initiate(s)

is love, 27, 43, 233
leaving, 112, 167–68
life of, 185, 186, 224, 237
love of, 24, 60, 72, 73, 181,
187, 214, 224, 229, 241, 269,
286
as Mahanta, 53
message of, 19, 27, 71, 249,
262, 267, 268
messages from, 1, 2, 32–34,
45, 46, 147, 230
move faster in, 162
in name of, 231
needing the, 67
open to the, 229, 270
path of, 43, 51, 52, 70, 85, 101,
116, 117, 121, 149, 179, 221,
224, 227, 233, 253, 275
and Paul Twitchell, 18, 24
power of, 72, 73, 221, 228, 232,
262
put it into the, 129
realization of, 170
rhythm of, 154
secrets of, 73, 249
sharing, 186
talking about, 51, 73, 187, 259
talks, 218–19
terms, 218–19
tune in to, 192
in tune with, 195
working with, 33, 76
works of, 264
ECKANKAR
as Ancient Science of Soul
Travel. *See* Soul Travel:
Ancient Science of
aspects of, 109, 273
basis of, 5, 45, 170. *See also*
Light and Sound
books, 1, 43, 59, 85, 100, 131,
167, 186, 220, 252, 260. *See
also ECKANKAR: Illumi-
nated Way Letters;
ECKANKAR—The Key to
Secret Worlds; ECK-Vidya,*

306

308

ECKANKAR: explaining
Expression
    ECK in, 177–78
    of love, 234

Failings, failure(s)
    bank, 4
    causes of, 143, 243–44
    and fear, 121
    in life, 82
    of psychic principles, 115
    of relationships, 283–84
    of religion, 99, 193
    of science, 218
Faith(ful)
    blind, 137
    Christian, 93
    in ECK, 29
    relying on, 80
    and spiritual exercises, 156
    tests of, 137–41
Family(ies). *See also* Child(ren);
        Youth
    death in, 132
    fitting into, 174
    love and, 232
    problems, 99
    relationships, 163, 221
    stories about, 244–45
    survival of, 177
Farm(ers), 93, 147–48, 168–69,
        221–22
Fear(s)
    of death. *See* Death: fear of
    experiencing, 293
    of God, 80, 133, 253
    holding you back, 121, 143,
        205
    and the Inquisition, 117
    lack of, 239
    let go of, 252, 294
    of others' reactions, 150
    and prejudice, 4
    psychic waves and, 132
    and spiritual exercises, 256
    understanding, 70

of unknown, 293
Finances, financial. *See also*
        Money; Wealth
    leaks, 126–27
    reviewing, 55
    stability, 26
    survival, 177
    taking care of, 47
Fire
    exit story, 64–66
    fighter, 223
    backstage, story, 223
Fisherman story, 227–28
Flexibility, 45–46
Fly, 230
Flying, 125, 130, 141–43
Food(s), 17, 134
    cooking, 46–47, 234
    dairy, 115–16, 230
    and diet, 89, 229
    health and, 100, 114
    junk, 19
    and love, 46–47, 231–32
    preparing, 47, 235
    simple, 231
    spiritual, 235
    spoiled, 229–31
Freedom
    capacity for, 38, 68
    to change, 276
    to move at own pace,
        261
    with path of ECK, 72
    of Soul, 6, 68, 83, 109
    spiritual, 57, 201
    steps to, 70
Friends, 248–49
Fubbi Quantz, 39
Funerals, 110
Future
    knowing, 17
    seeing, 19, 69, 204–6
    vision for the, 138

Gandhi, Indira, 179
Gasoline, 203

Heaven(s) *(continued)*
lords of, 132
mantle of, 127, 154
on Mental Plane, 38
modern, 278
on Physical Plane, 101
routes to, 85
and Soul Travel, 26
staying in, 181
travel through, 44
we make our own, 176
Hell
fear of, 80
on Physical Plane, 101
we make our own, 176
Help(ing)
asking for, 98, 128, 262
from creative imagination, 120
from ECK, 58, 126, 149, 228,
232, 245
hand, 229
from Mahanta, 244, 251
in Mahanta's work, 215, 262
from others, 127, 236
others, 47, 131, 143, 180, 192
spiritual, 241
Heresy, 117
Hierarchy, 133
Himalayan mountains, 22
Hinduism, 44, 80
History, 3, 117, 214, 267
Holidays, 174
Holland, 229, 230, 231
Holy Spirit. *See also* ECK
action of, 75, 94
aspects of, 83, 95, 109. *See also*
Light and Sound
the body of the, 131
channel for, 88, 92
as ECK, 1, 53, 55, 73, 218
false instruction about, 253
in form of Master, 12, 97, 111,
263, 291
gifts from, 149
how, works, 109
ideal of the, 55

is love, 234
Light of, 4
nourishment of, 85
open to, 100, 126, 229
protection of, 143. *See also*
Protection: of ECK
purifying elements of, 5, 75,
94, 117
relationship with, 81, 130, 228
serving, 236
truth of, 233
as Word. *See* Word(s): of God
Honest(y)
as best approach, 246
can't cheat an, man, 134
choices, 167
determining, 195
opportunity, 196
about our own creations, 176
Hope, 27
HU
chanting, 12, 86, 95, 210, 220,
221, 255, 287
in daily life, 219
as name of God, 121, 211, 255
power of, 83
Hukikat Lok. *See* Plane(s):
Eighth
Human
body, 18, 106, 109. *See also*
Body(ies): physical
condition, 81
consciousness. *See* Consciousness: human
love. *See* Love(s): human
nature, 164, 209
race, 4
Humility, 117, 137, 232, 255,
264
Humor, 266, 267
Hyperboreans, 3, 4
Hypnosis, 4

Ideal, 81, 86, 149
Idea(s)
of detachment, 276

from ECK, 192, 193
exchanging, 108, 222–23, 259
fixed, 51, 218
need for new, 107
for talks, 213
Ignorance, 4, 116
Illness(es), 209, 215–18
causes of, 16, 98, 175
before seminars, 215
serious, 55
and spiritual exercises,
288–89
telling someone about an, 205
terminal, 93, 204
Illusion(s)
web of, 133
working with, 128, 255
Image(s)
of happiness, 121
of Light and Sound, 53, 291
limited, 44
of masters, 53
on Mental Plane, 82
self-, 117
strike an, 8
Imagination, 255
creative, 58, 85, 95, 100, 120
problem with, 291
and techniques for Soul
Travel, 160, 275
Immortality, 274
Incarnation, 69. *See also* Lifetimes; Reincarnation
India, 113, 178, 179
Indulgence, 176
Information, 1, 152, 179
Initiate(s). *See also* ECKist(s)
in ECK, 70, 101, 173
Eighth, 165
experiences of, 173, 180
Fifth, 17, 161, 163
Fourth, 163
High(er), 11, 16, 58, 165, 166,
167, 176, 196, 206–7, 264
levels of, 263, 264
love and, 251

new Higher, 162
Second, 207, 208, 247
Initiation(s)
circles of, 58
Dream, 68, 118. *See also* Ini-
tiation(s): First
earning, 2
ECK, 58, 67, 68, 101, 117,
264
Eighth, 37
Eleventh, 37
expanding beyond present,
247–48
Fifth, 204
First, 36, 58, 68, 118
Fourth, 36
higher, 73, 162, 175, 264, 267,
284
High Initiate as channel for,
264
importance of, 67
losing an, 79
in lower planes, 73
Mahanta and. *See* Mahanta:
and initiation
meaning of, 37, 58
Ninth, 37
outside of ECK, 68
purpose of, 245
recommending someone for,
162
Second, 36, 37, 58, 68, 72, 117,
121, 245
Soul and, 74
takes two years, 117
Tenth, 37
Third, 36, 58, 121, 245
true, 263
vehicle for, 264
what happens during, 74–75
Initiator, ECK, 161, 263–64
In My Soul I Am Free, 12, 85
Inner
awakening on, 290
bodies. *See* Body(ies): inner
experience(s), 7, 23, 45, 111,

Klemp, Sri Harold, *ix. See also*
    Living ECK Master;
    Mahanta; Wah Z
Knowing(ness), 84, 153, 161, 287
    and working with Mahanta,
        154
Knowledge, 108
    book, 84
    of ECK, 1, 27
    encompassing more, 32
    given by Master, *ix*
    about life after death, 92, 94
    of Light and Sound of God, 74
    from past Masters, 155
    psychic, 3
    scientific, 218
    secret, 252
Krishna, 108

Language(s)
    common, 148–49, 151, 154,
        155
    of ECK, 151, 155
    English, 9, 15
    human, 8
Laundromat story, 206–7
Law(s)
    breaking, 101, 116, 220
    of ECK, 2
    economic, 116
    of Economy, 125, 126, 135, 144
    greater than ECK-Vidya, 19
    higher, 125
    ignoring, 87
    of Karma, 175, 222
    learning, 127
    letter of the, 49
    of life, 2
    of Love, 85, 125, 144, 176
    nutritional, 116
    physical, 116, 261
    of Silence, 204
    of Spirit, 74, 84, 97, 98, 101,
        116, 125, 127
    spirit of the, 49
Leader(s)

    of ECK, 23, 25, 79, 213, 215
    of religions, 194. *See also*
        Jesus Christ; Krishna
    spiritual. *See* Living ECK
        Master: as spiritual leader
Learning
    to build own world, 120
    direct, 130
    about divine love, 235
    about ECK-Vidya, 70
    to give, 283
    how to live life in ECK, 185
    from others, 152
    from problems, 87, 215
    Soul and, 185
    about Soul Travel, 273
    to surrender, 283
    a trade, 81
Lesson(s)
    bigger, 165
    can't learn, from a distance, 10
    in creativity, 196
    daily, 147
    illustrate, 120
    learning, 10–11, 165, 170,
        228
    of little things, 261
    of the past, 5, 70
    teaching, 64
    truth hidden within, 144
    valuable, 11
Liberation
    of Soul, 51, 75
    spiritual, 26, 70
Library(ies), 112
    on inner planes, 155
Lies, lying, 174, 195
Life
    becoming involved in, 5, 122,
        294
    capacity for happy, 58
    after death, 92, 110, 253, 276.
        See also Knowledge: about
        life after death
    of ECK, 5, 186, 224, 279, 292
    end of, 111. *See also* Death

315

Living ECK Master
  becoming the, 166, 185
  and chela, 161, 233, 241
  ECKANKAR as vehicle for, 72
  form of, 52, 291
  inner travels with, 72
  is like all men, 262, 264, 267
  as Light Giver, 74
  meeting, 15, 86, 253, 266
  as messenger of SUGMAD, 29
  mission of, 16, 253
  and modern culture, 71, 199
  how, operates, 147
  past, 56
  Paul Twitchell as. *See*
    Twitchell, Paul: as Living
    ECK Master
  serving, 236
  and shaking hands with
    chelas, 121
  as spiritual leader, 150
  subject to physical laws,
    261–62, 267
  takes responsibility for self, 58
  talks of, 17, 75, 111, 185,
    213–24
  works with people, 266
Lizard(s), 133
  story, 105
Logic, 163, 276
Loneliness, 35, 292
Longevity, 56
Love(s)
  accepting, 236
  for all creatures, 38, 231, 239
  aura of, 60
  capacity for, 38, 227, 242
  chanting with, 57, 121
  conquers all, 206
  definition for, 235, 236
  divine, 54, 235, 284
  doing something for, 48
  doors of, 241
  ECK and, 228. *See also* ECK:
    love of
  ECK is, 53, 233, 234

element of, 34
expanded consciousness depends upon, 247
expression of. *See* Expression:
  of love
feeling of, 86, 250, 274, 289
fill oneself with, 101, 239, 294
finding, 29, 54
flow, 187
gives, 242
giving, 35
God is, 233
human, 53–54, 284
importance of, 121–22
as key to smooth changes, 96
for Mahanta, 247, 249
of Mahanta. *See* Mahanta:
  love of
misunderstood, 242
open to, 284
for other people, 49, 50
pets and, 63
power and. *See* Power(s): vs
  love
seasoning with, story, 46–47
shield of. *See* Shield: of love
spirit of, 52, 59
strength of, 262
of SUGMAD. *See* SUGMAD:
  love of
what is, 232, 233, 236, 237,
  239
Luck, 127
we are not victims of, 128

Macrocosm, 261
Magic, 50–51, 127. *See also*
  Black magic
Mahanta. *See also* Wah Z
  Blue Light of, 109, 291
  chela and, 153, 228, 241, 244
  Consciousness, 26, 81, 109,
    111
  at the Door. *See* Technique(s):
    Mahanta at the Door
  as ECK, 53

Mahanta *(continued)*
  guidance of, 31, 156, 165
  hidden ways of, 245
  and initiation, 73
  judging, 243
  love of, 40, 270
  meeting, 54, 234–35, 274, 275, 294
  in name of, 120, 250
  Order of, 38
  Paul Twitchell as. *See*
    Twitchell, Paul: as Mahanta
  presence of, 251
  and shield of light, 59
  and spiritual exercises, 52, 60, 86, 109, 177, 155–56
  tests from, 204–5
  as tour guide on inner planes, 219
  working with, 154, 254, 261, 280
Mahdis, 263. *See also* Initiate(s): Fifth
Management
  skills, 192
  tools, 151
Manifestation(s)
  of God. *See* Sat Nam
  of Holy Spirit. *See* Inner Master
Manuscript(s), 8
Marketing studies, 21
Marriage, 24
Master(s). *See also* ECK
    Master(s); Living ECK
    Master; Mahanta
  becoming a, 86, 122. *See also*
    Mastership
  Inner. *See* Inner Master
  marks of true, 18
  of other groups, 67
  past, 52, 155. *See also* Living
    ECK Master: past
  protection of, 180, 232
  and recognition, 241
Mastership

path to, 81
training, 170–71
Materialism, 150, 200, 203, 270
Matrix, 111
Maugham, W. Somerset, 200, 201
Medicine, 216
Meditation, 80
  passive, 85
Meeting story, 64–65
Melnibora, 3
Memory(ies), 75, 86. *See also*
    Plane(s): Causal
  bad, 63
  of inner experiences, 252
  of past, 80
  unconscious, 114, 117
  of visiting other worlds, 273
Mental
  body. *See* Body(ies): Mental
  conditions, 127
  institution, 141, 255
  Plane. *See* Plane(s): Mental
  techniques, 292
Metaphysics, metaphysical
  groups, 6, 53, 54
  talks, 214
Microcosm, 261
Microwave oven, 114
Middle Ages, 117
Mind
  beyond, 82, 97, 242
  blocks in the, 127
  and contemplation, 52, 210
  forgets bad times, 63, 80
  guard of the, 276
  impression, 9
  keeping, busy, 289
  keeping, limber, 50
  passions of, 175. *See also*
    Anger; Attachment(s);
    Greed; Vanity
  power of, 132
  Soul works Its way through, 181

318

320

Problem(s), 2, 127
and anger, 69, 176, 244
avoiding, 19, 31, 88, 195, 277
bigger, 153, 165
creating our own, 98, 189, 192
exotic, 191
and get-rich-quick schemes,
196
going through, 80
how attitudes create, 90, 192
learning from, 215
listening to another's, 229
look for deeper, 245
Mahanta helps with, 262
physical, 293
prayer and, 99
protection during, 232
seeing, clearly, 115, 154
solving, 58, 69, 88, 108, 120,
170
with Soul Travel, 253
SUGMAD isn't concerned with
our, 67
with surrender, 288
Prodigal son story, 168–69
Program, spiritual. See
ECKANKAR: spiritual pro-
gram
Promotion, 21, 23. See also Public relations
Propaganda, 4
Prophecy, 204–6
Prophet, 91
Prosperity, 200. See also Wealth
Protection
bubble of, 180
for children of ECK, 29, 59
earning, 245
of ECK, 31–32, 143, 228, 229,
230, 232
for ECKists. See ECKist(s):
and protection
recognizing, 242, 247
of the SUGMAD, 60
for yourself, 51
Pseudogods, 174

Psychic
attack, 60
elements, 115
forces, 36, 99
healers. See Healer(s),
healing: psychic
powers, 3, 69
states, 26
waves, 132
Psychologist, 243
Public relations, 20, 22
Purification
of the mind, 6, 109
process, 117, 118
removes karma, 74
before seminar, 215
of Soul, 75, 85, 112, 268
Spirit brings, 5, 87
Pushing
against negative power, 268
oneself, 19

Quality(ies)
paying for, 134
of Soul. See Soul: qualities of
Quest, spiritual, 202
Question(s), 111, 237
asking God. See God: asking
courage to ask, 291
right to ask, 233
Quest, spiritual, 202

Race(s)
karmic ties between, 3
red. See Atlantis
root, 3
Radiant body. See Body(ies):
radiant
Radio talk shows, 199
Rainstorms, 31, 32
Razor's edge, 194, 199, 202, 204,
205, 206
Razor's Edge, The, 200–202
Reality, inner. See Inner: reality
Realization
God-. See God-Realization

323

Solitude, 65
Solution(s), 69. *See also* Problem(s): solving
finding, 121, 170, 189
first step to, 222
too rigid to see, 100
some things don't have, 192
Sore throat story, 215–18
Sorrow, 228
Soul
advanced, 23, 137
anger affects, 175
body. *See* Body(ies): Soul
concept of, 106
dark night of, 153
dwelling place of, 274
experiences of, 4, 16, 38, 164
fall of, 66–67
false instruction of, 253
and freedom, 57, 68. *See also* Liberation: spiritual
goals of, 167
in higher worlds, 38, 65, 69, 137
infusion of Light into, 74
is made of the ECK, 242, 264
journey of, 65–67, 69, 70–71, 136–37, 276
learning to full capacity, 267–68
lives of, 70, 242
and lower worlds, 16, 65, 105, 241
movement of, 26, 43, 84, 106, 159, 160, 180, 276
nature of, 110
in passive state, 80
Plane. *See* Plane(s): Soul
power of. *See* Power(s): of Soul
proof of existence of, 92, 118
qualities of, 58, 90, 132, 227, 270
recognizes Master's voice, 54
in sleep state, 175, 189, 266
as spark of God, 4, 67, 131
things that hold, back, 114

upliftment of, 109
Soul Travel
Ancient Science of, 26, 45, 70, 72, 106, 107, 111, 159
as aspect of ECK teachings, 105, 273, 283, 284
definition of, 180
difficulty with, 241, 293
as expanded consciousness, 133, 163, 176, 247
experiences, 44, 55, 57, 82, 155, 162, 166, 287–88
explaining, 51, 150
fear and, 159, 294
forms of, 161
Golden Heart as key to, 274
knowing is higher than, 154
learning, 47, 83, 84, 85, 86
learning through, 153
no problems when, 291
opens awareness, 277
philosophy behind, 163
purpose of, 47, 182
restricted to lower worlds, 160
and Saint Paul ("I die daily"), 94
as way to reach Light and Sound, 43
workshops, 26, 273
Soul Traveler patch story, 186–87
Sound Current, 73, 94, 95, 186
Sound(s)
of air conditioning, 210
of bells, 210
of birds, 210
electrical, 233
experience with, 75, 233, 275
as flute, 95, 275
hearing, 52, 79
of helicopter, 210
as music, 75, 95, 250
as musical instrument, 95, 210
during spiritual exercises, 210–11, 254
of traffic, 210

325

Sound(s) *(continued)*
  of voices, 210
  as wind, 75, 160, 233, 250, 274
  as woodwinds, 95
Space(s)
  empty, 228–29
  of others, 30, 49–50, 101, 207,
    222
  planes of time and, 38, 160,
    270, 274
Speeding ticket story, 245–47
Spice jar story, 46–47
Spirit. *See also* ECK; Holy Spirit
  being used by. *See* ECKist(s):
    being used by Spirit
  richness of, 127
  understanding ways of, 55–56
  works of, 270
Spirits, earthbound, 101
Spiritual
  body, 97. *See also* Body(ies):
    Soul
  cliff, 199
  ECK, Aide, 161, 288, 293
  evolution, 80, 84, 88, 94, 99,
    277
  exercises. *See* Spiritual Exer-
    cises of ECK
  experiences, 23
  foundation, 29, 248
  headaches, 163
  healing. *See* Healer(s), healing
  ignorance, 98
  issues, talking about, 259
  ladder, 86
  laws. *See* Law(s): of Spirit
  leader. *See* Leader(s)
  liberation. *See* Liberation,
    spiritual
  life, 49, 59, 81, 114, 143, 165,
    199, 278
  maturity, 205
  motor, 79
  needs, 127, 159
  paths. *See* Path(s), spiritual
  planes. *See* Plane(s)

principle(s), 12, 125, 215
process, 80
program, 2
title, 263
unfoldment. *See* Unfoldment:
  spiritual
Spiritual Exercises of ECK
  adapting our, 177
  are like physical exercises, 86
  create your own, 178, 210
  difficulty with, 52, 241
  and discipline, 86, 114, 153,
    156, 236
  doing, every day, 52, 170, 248,
    288, 293
  in ECK books, 59, 260
  experiences during, 75, 82,
    109, 160, 254
  and freedom, 57
  how to do, 36, 161
  introductory, 59
  and karma, 116
  and Light and Sound, 109,
    160, 234, 235
  and love, 52, 86, 262, 264
  purpose of, 87
  and solving problems, 90
  Sounds during. *See* Sound(s):
    during spiritual exercises
  teach Soul Travel, 82, 85, 249
  trying different, 143, 255, 268,
    276, 293
  as way to find truth, 144
  as way to God, 91, 131, 137
  working with, 173
Spiritual Eye, 12, 36, 86, 97, 255
Spiritual Traveler, 15, 252. *See
  also* ECK Master(s)
Spirituality
  era of, 267–68
  levels of, 234
Step(s)
  finding next, 163
  first, 85, 266, 283, 287
  learning the, 260
  to meet Master, 253

326

on path to God, 106
small, in beginning, 255
Steve Canyon, 20
Story(ies), storytelling
biblical. *See* Bible: stories of
from ECKists, 154
of ECK Masters, 16
enhance talks, 141, 214
like a time capsule, 215
meaning behind, 238–39
moral of, 187
remembering, 163
teaching through, 30, 163, 279
Stranger by the River, 73, 235
Strength(ener)
developing, 6, 11, 87, 88, 118,
127, 143, 165
of faith, 93
from Holy Spirit, 149
individual, 89
of love, 262
man measured by, of foes, 268
of physical self, 19
pillars of, 202
regaining, 164
spiritual, 102, 147, 221
Student, college, 232–33
Subconscious. *See* Plane(s):
Etheric
Success
common language and, 151
instant, 114
reasons for, 2
with Soul Travel, 52, 254
Sudar Singh, 178–79
Suffering, 100, 116, 294
SUGMAD. *See also* God
concept of, 242
forest of the, 59–60
love of, 39, 47
love for, 48
Mahanta as representation of,
52, 262
in name of, 48, 231
put attention on, 75
as reality of God, 29

serving, 19, 38, 39, 118, 262
and Soul, 66, 67
sword of the, 59
at top of hierarchy, 82
Suicide, 255
Surrender, 214, 274
learning to, 283, 288
Survival, 164
of ECKANKAR, 17
family. *See* Family(ies): survival of
material, 82, 147
needs, 176
spiritual, 143, 147
of spiritual community of
ECKists, 148
training in, 150, 154
Sword
of Damocles, 80
double-edged, 98, 100
of SUGMAD. *See* SUGMAD:
sword of the
Symbols, 82, 83

Talent(s), 144
developing, 16, 261
natural, 7, 122, 154
Talking, talks, 50. *See also*
Living ECK Master: talks of
about ECK, 8, 19, 229, 237
giving a, 214
to High Initiates, 58
of Master, *ix*
preparing a talk, 213
for seminars, 17, 185, 250
stories for, 221, 223
to a tree, 154
Teacher, teaching(s)
ECKANKAR. *See*
ECKANKAR: teachings
energy currents in, 112
finding a, 107
of past masters, 45
presence of, 81
secret, 16
Soul Travel, 26

327

Varkas kings, 3–4
Vehicle
  declaring oneself a, 213–14
  for ECK, 17, 76, 187, 192, 223,
    224, 229, 249
  ECKANKAR as, 72
  for God, 86
  physical, 263
  for training others, 148
Veil, 101
Venus, 100
Vibrations, 101
Video
  arcade, 254, 256, 286
  games, 186–87, 254. *See also*
    Pac-Man
Viewpoint
  limited, 106, 243
  material, 203
  other people's, 189
  of Soul, 293
Vision, 58, 69, 97, 138, 290. *See
  also* Inner: vision
Visualization, 86, 95, 287–88,
  289. *See also* Spiritual Exercises of ECK
Voice
  of God, 82, 186, 218, 264
  from heavens, 219
  inner, 204
  of Inner Master. *See* Inner
    Master: voice of
  losing your, 150–51
  of Master, 54

Wah Z, 279
  chanting, 275–76, 290
War
  nuclear, 132
  Vietnam, 107
  World, I, 200
  World, II, 23
Warning, 34, 153, 205
Warrior(s), 3
Washington, D.C., 23, 24, 25
Wealth

ECKANKAR does not promise,
    114
  gathering of, 2
  life-style of, 267
  not enough, 125
  as nuisance, 5
  rejecting, 57, 136, 200
  spirituality and, 195
  waiting for, 59
  working for the sake of, 21
Weapons, 3
Whales, 132
Willpower, 114, 118
Wisdom
  attribute of, 38
  from Divine Power, 59
  ECK, 1, 8, 129, 163
  ECKANKAR does not promise,
    114
  false, 5
  of Light and Sound, 252
  from past Masters, 155
  pearls of, 137
  pool, 37
  receiving, 27
Wizard of Oz, 133
Women, 288
Word(s)
  charged, *ix*
  to describe experience, 275
  as ECK, 263
  of ECK, 2, 8
  effects of our, 87, 176, 223
  of God, 82, 83
  holy, 12, 86
  of the Light and Sound, 23
  message comes through writ-
    ten, 206
  and mind, 274
  negative, 87
  putting ideas into, 1, 15, 192
  secret, 52, 234, 255
  using, people understand, 159
  watching your, 49
Work(ing). *See also* Job(s)
  cycles of, 18–19

330

doing a lot of, 64, 213
hard, 27
husband and wife both, 177
against ourselves, 113
with people, 81, 148, 151, 163
World(s)
of dichotomies, 125
of duality, 38
of God, 23, 39, 75, 112, 132,
242, 248, 280, 288
of golden light, 38–39
higher, 69, 70, 95, 137, 274
how well our, runs, 192
inner, 1, 19, 86, 97, 153, 155,
166, 241, 277, 279
of Light, 67
lower, 16, 36, 66, 69, 70, 105,
106, 120, 125, 130, 160, 165,
268
negative, 176, 193
of our creation, 176

physical, 106, 203
spiritual, 38, 66, 71, 84, 125,
137, 170, 234, 247
of time and space, 38, 66, 68,
70
visiting other, 273
Worry, 120, 174, 279, 293
Write, writer(s), writing. *See*
also Editing, editors
articles, 193–94, 216
and creative process, 192
deadlines. *See* Deadline(s):
writing
ECK, 72
experiences of, 20, 113
as poetry. *See* Poetry
process of, 1, 9, 15

Youth, 254

Z, 279. *See also* Wah Z

How to Learn More about ECKANKAR

People want to know the secrets of life and death. In response to this need Sri Harold Klemp, today's spiritual leader of ECKANKAR, and Paul Twitchell, its modern-day founder, have written special monthly discourses which reveal the Spiritual Exercises of ECK—to lead Soul in a direct way to God.

Those who wish to study ECKANKAR can receive these special monthly discourses which give clear, simple instructions for the spiritual exercises. The first annual series of discourses is *The ECK Dream 1 Discourses.* Mailed each month, the discourses will offer insight into your dreams and what they mean to you.

The techniques in these discourses, when practiced twenty minutes a day, are likely to prove survival beyond death. Many have used them as a direct route to Self-Realization, where one learns his mission in life. The next stage, God Consciousness, is the joyful state wherein Soul becomes the spiritual traveler, an agent for God. The underlying principle one learns is this: Soul exists because God loves It.

Membership in ECKANKAR includes:

1. Twelve monthly lessons of *The ECK Dream 1 Discourses,* with such titles as: "Dreams—The Bridge to Heaven," "The Dream Master," "How to Interpret Your Dreams," and "Dream Travel to Soul Travel." You may study them alone at home or in a class with others.
2. The *Mystic World,* a quarterly newsletter with a Wisdom Note and articles by the Living ECK Master. In it are also letters and articles from students of ECKANKAR around the world.
3. Special mailings to keep you informed of upcoming ECKANKAR seminars and activities worldwide, new study materials available from ECKANKAR, and more.
4. The opportunity to attend ECK Satsang classes and book discussions with others in your community.
5. Initiation eligibility.
6. Attendance at certain chela meetings at ECK seminars.

How to Find out More

To request membership in ECKANKAR using your credit card (or for a free booklet on membership) call (612) 544-0066 between 8 a.m. and 5 p.m., central time.

Introductory Books on ECKANKAR

How to Find God, Mahanta Transcripts, Book 2
Harold Klemp

Learn how to recognize and interpret the guidance each of us is *already receiving* from Divine Spirit in day-to-day events—for inner freedom, love, and guidance from God. The author gives spiritual exercises to uplift physical, emotional, mental, and spiritual health as well as a transforming sound called *HU*, which can be sung for inner upliftment.

The Secret Teachings, Mahanta Transcripts, Book 3
Harold Klemp

If you're interested in the secret, yet practical knowledge of the Vairagi ECK Masters, this book will fascinate and inspire you. Discover how to apply the unique Spiritual Exercises of ECK—dream exercises, visualizations, and Soul Travel methods—to unlock your natural abilities as Soul. Learn how to hear the little-known sounds of God and follow Its Light for practical daily guidance.

ECKANKAR—The Key to Secret Worlds
Paul Twitchell

This introduction to Soul Travel features simple, half-hour spiritual exercises to help you become more aware of yourself as Soul—divine, immortal, and free. You'll learn step-by-step how to unravel the secrets of life from a Soul point of view: your unique destiny or purpose in this life; how to make personal contact with the God Force, Spirit; and the hidden causes at work in your everyday life—all using the ancient art of Soul Travel.

The Tiger's Fang, Paul Twitchell

Paul Twitchell's teacher, Rebazar Tarzs, takes him on a journey through vast worlds of Light and Sound, to sit at the feet of the spiritual Masters. Their conversations bring out the secret of how to draw closer to God—and awaken Soul to Its spiritual destiny. Many have used this book, with its vivid descriptions of heavenly worlds and citizens, to begin their own spiritual adventures.

For fastest service, phone (612) 544-0066 weekdays between 8 a.m. and 5 p.m., central time, to request books using your credit card, or look under **ECKANKAR** in your phone book for an ECKANKAR Center near you. Or write: **ECKANKAR, Att: Information, P.O. Box 27300, Minneapolis, MN 55427 U.S.A.**

There May Be an
ECKANKAR Study Group near You

ECKANKAR offers a variety of local and international activities for the spiritual seeker. With hundreds of study groups worldwide, ECKANKAR is near you! Many areas have ECKANKAR Centers where you can browse through the books in a quiet, unpressured environment, talk with others who share an interest in this ancient teaching, and attend beginning discussion classes on how to gain the attributes of Soul: wisdom, power, love, and freedom.

Around the world, ECKANKAR study groups offer special one-day or weekend seminars on the basic teachings of ECKANKAR. Check your phone book under **ECKANKAR**, or call **(612) 544-0066** for membership information and the location of the ECKANKAR Center or study group nearest you. Or write **ECKANKAR, Att: Information, P.O. Box 27300, Minneapolis, MN 55427 U.S.A.**

☐ Please send me information on the nearest ECKANKAR discussion or study group in my area.

☐ Please send me more information about membership in ECKANKAR, which includes a twelve-month spiritual study of dreams.

Please type or print clearly   941

Name

Street   Apt. #

City   State/Prov.

Zip/Postal Code   Country

(Our policy: Your name and address are held in strict confidence. We do not rent or sell our mailing lists. Nor will anyone call on you. Our purpose is only to show people the ECK way home to God.)